COMPLETING *Your* *Endowment*

THE TEMPLE ENDOWMENT SERIES

Preparing For Your Endowment

Understanding Your Endowment

Completing Your Endowment

Cory B. Jensen

Lone Peak Publishing

Lone Peak Publishing
1411 East 840 North
Orem, UT 84097
www.templeendowment.com

Completing Your Endowment/ Cory B. Jensen. -- 1st ed.
ISBN 13:978-0-9995670-0-5

Cover design by Kinsey Beckett.

For those seeking to know our Lord.
—John 17:3

CONTENTS

PREFACE

I will manifest myself to my people in mercy in this house.
—D&C 110:7

ONE NIGHT I DREAMT about the temple. In the dream, I was attending an endowment session seated near the back of the company. As the session progressed, I noticed a small door in the wall on the side of the room. It wasn't the main entrance or exit to the room. In fact, it didn't appear to have a purpose and was almost concealed, it blended into the wall so well. As I watched, a few people approached and went through the door, but most of the company was unaware of it or ignored it. Eventually, my curiosity got the best of me. I left my seat and walked over to the door, opened it, and stooped to enter.

Passing through, I closed the door behind me and found myself in what appeared to be an attic room of the temple. In contrast to the bright, clean, almost sterile whiteness of the room I had just left, this place had a more homey atmosphere. I had to round a corner and climb a few steps to enter the main part of the room. I was alone and unsure where the others who had passed through the door before me had gone. Warm wood floors and aged, exposed beams in the vaulted ceiling gave a comfortable, inviting feeling. A large stained-glass window filled the opposite wall and soft sunlight streamed through it, diffusing the room with subdued, yet beautiful hues. The room appeared unused. I was aware that it was dusty from lack of use, but it was not dirty—just old.

As I climbed the steps into the main part of the room, forgetting about the company I had left behind, I found a large table spread with a sumptuous feast. The food was fresh, warm, and very appealing despite the room appearing to have been forgotten in time. I then woke from the dream.

As I pondered on its significance over the next few days, I came to believe that the Lord was inviting me to return to the roots of the Restoration, to the foundation of our temple ordinances, and to focus my study there. Some of that study became the basis for this book. The Lord has a feast waiting for all who will come and partake. It is my hope that this book will serve as an invitation to you to receive what the Lord has specifically prepared for you.

Joseph Smith taught that knowledge is the power of salvation.[1] He affirmed that a man or woman is saved no faster than he or she gains knowledge.[2] With this in mind, we might wonder: what was the Lord's (and Joseph Smith's) purpose in introducing temple ordinances to the Church? Are they simply arcane rituals we must memorize? Do they have some inherent magic necessary for redemption? Or are they rather intended to help the Saints gain knowledge, particularly knowledge which saves? And if imparting knowledge is their purpose, then what is the Lord trying to teach us?

This book is an attempt to help you begin to answer these and other questions for yourself. It is written in the hope that it will enable you to perhaps approach the temple with new eyes. It is the third and concluding volume in a series, beginning with *Preparing for Your Endowment* and continuing in *Understanding Your Endowment.* The background provided in those two books is essential to the discussion contained in this volume, which is intended for active, believing, endowed members of the Church of Jesus Christ of Latter-day Saints. This book will be most helpful to those who have attended the temple long enough to be very familiar with the ceremonies and ordinances.

Many of the topics discussed in this book are broad enough to be the subject of an entire book. Here we will just introduce them, like the preview of a motion picture. All of us need further study and to go to the Lord for the full movie. The temple can be a great aid in that process. It is my belief that we are not going to be given more from the Lord until we first receive in gratitude, patience, and faith that which has already been given. That requires time spent in the temple and work outside of the temple learning to live our covenants.

After years of that process, another problem potentially arises. We may reach a point where we become comfortable and think we know enough. However, when it comes to the temple, we should remain as curious as a little child. I hope that this book raises as many questions for you as it answers, for it is in the quest for answers that we often grow closer to God. President Uchtdorf once asked: "How often has the Holy Spirit tried to tell us something we needed to know but couldn't get past the massive iron gate of what we thought we already knew?"[3] I would humbly ask that if you encounter things in this book that may be different from what you already know, that you would at least ponder upon the ideas presented here. And then, if appropriate, make it a matter of prayer and inquiry with the Lord.

Elder John A. Widstoe taught: "The endowment is so richly symbolic that only a fool would attempt to describe it."[4] Because the ritualistic nature of the endowment is so different from anything else we experience in the Church, I am just foolish enough to believe that we all need some help in getting started or in establishing a foundation from which to begin. To that end, I am hopeful that this volume and the other two books I have written on the topic will be useful. But I am not so foolish as to believe that they are comprehensive by any means and the only possible interpretations for the temple's symbols. Nor do they contain all that I understand or that the Lord has taught me.

I am grateful that the Church has never attempted to publish a doctrinal exposition of the temple or to attach an official interpretation to the ceremony. The temple symbols are too vast and too fluid for such categorization. I would never want anyone to take this book or my other books on the temple as attempting to provide such an interpretation or to outline the only meaning of the temple ordinances. Please accept anything herein that seems helpful to you and reject anything that does not.

I approach the topic of the temple with deep reverence and humility and do not feel qualified to be a teacher. I am still learning and growing. Much of that learning comes line upon line, here a little and there a little. New insights have come even during the writing of this book. There is more contained in the temple than I would have ever dreamed of 30 years ago when I was first endowed. There are glimpses and hints of things that I am scarcely beginning to understand even now.

Elder Widstoe continued, "[the endowment] is so packed full of revelations to those who exercise their strength to seek and see, that no human words can explain or make clear the possibilities that reside in the temple service. The endowment which was given by revelation can best be understood by revelation; and to those who seek most vigorously, with pure hearts, will the revelation be greatest."[5] We all need to go to the Lord and let him fill in the gaps for us. Part of the genius and beauty of the temple ceremony is that the Lord can personalize it for us if we permit him to.

I recognize that there are those whose beliefs and views will differ from mine. Your understanding may be different as well. And that is completely fine. I simply wish to share some of the things about the temple that are beautiful to me. I have tried to be very prayerful about what should and should not be included. Writing about this sensitive and sacred topic is always a difficult balance. It is my hope and prayer that this work will be helpful to those seeking to truly understand and live their temple endowment. In the end, however, this book is simply one person's perspective and does not represent official doctrine of The Church of Jesus Christ of Latter-day Saints. I alone am responsible for its contents.

Some may view portions of this book as somewhat of a departure from my prior two. That is not the case. The content herein was known to me prior to writing either of the previous volumes. This concluding volume deals with some doctrine and questions that were not appropriate for the earlier books. Because of this, if you are new to the temple, you may want to consider whether this book is appropriate for you. It is intended for those who are seasoned and mature in the gospel and the temple. For that audience, in some ways, it may be the most important of the three. In any case, my testimony of the temple's crucial value remains the same. It has profoundly blessed my life in many ways and can do the same for all who take it seriously.

Because the topics addressed in this volume are deeper than those raised in my prior books,some may wonder why we don't just stick to the basics. And, in terms of living the gospel day by day, I try to do exactly that. It is enough of a challenge for me to really try to live the first and second great commandments, to follow the Spirit's directions for me, to love and serve my family, and to more fully live my covenants. But in addition to doing all of these things, we are expected to learn and to gain knowledge. If the basics were enough, the scriptures could be reduced to a couple of pages and there would be no need for the temple endowment. The Lord wants us to learn and improve upon our time.

Joseph Smith counseled: "I advise all to go on to perfection, and search deeper and deeper into the mysteries of Godliness."[6] On another occasion he observed: "Thy mind, O man! If thou wilt lead a soul unto salvation, must stretch as high as the utmost heavens, and search into and contemplate the darkest abyss, and the broad expanse of eternity—thou must commune with God."[7]

The temple is given to help us in that quest.

CHAPTER 1

KIRTLAND

Organize yourselves; prepare every needful thing; and establish a house, even a house of prayer, a house of fasting, a house of faith, a house of learning, a house of glory, a house of order, a house of God.
—D&C 88:119

IN 1832, THE LORD COMMANDED the Saints to build a temple at Kirtland, Ohio. This direction came just two years after the establishment of the fledgling Church. It was a time when members were few, resources scarce, and fulfilling such an obligation would not be easy. We might ask what was the Lord's purpose in doing so at such an early point in the Restoration?

Along with the command to build a house of God, the same revelation contains a remarkable promise: "Sanctify yourselves that your minds be single to God, and the days will come that you shall see him; for he will unveil his face unto you" (D&C 88:68). Christ promised to visit His saints. These were no idle words. He meant exactly what He said and reiterated for emphasis: "Remember the great and last promise which I have made unto you" (D&C 88:69).

A few verses later the admonition is repeated: "Sanctify yourselves; yea, purify your hearts, and cleanse your hands and your feet before me, that I may make you clean; that I may testify unto your Father, and your God, and my God, that you are clean from the blood of this wicked generation" (D&C 88:74–75). The reason for these instructions is also explained: "That I may fulfill this promise, this great and last promise [to unveil my face], which I have made unto you, when I will" (D&C 88:75).

Again, a third time, immediately following the command to build a temple, essentially the same instructions and promises are repeated. This time the required sanctification is further expounded to give more detail. The Saints are to cease from lustful desires, pride and light-mindedness, idleness, fault finding, covetousness, and from all wickedness. They are to love and minister to one another and to clothe themselves in charity (see D&C 88:121–125). Following these instructions, the Lord's promise to appear to His saints is again emphasized: "Pray always, that ye may not faint, until I come. Behold, and lo, I will come quickly, and receive you unto myself. Amen" (D&C 88:126).

It is noteworthy that in the very revelation concerning the first temple built in this dispensation, the Lord outlines three times His desire for His saints—for them to sanctify themselves so that He might then appear and minister to them. Clearly, the Kirtland Temple was meant to assist in both objectives.

Two weeks later, Joseph Smith sent a copy of this revelation to William W. Phelps in Missouri along with an introductory letter that reveals some of the Prophet's feelings at the time. He wrote: "You will see that the Lord commanded us, in Kirtland, to build a house of God, and establish a school for the Prophets, this is the word of the Lord to us, and we must, yea, the Lord helping us, we will obey: as on conditions of our obedience He has promised us great things; yea, even a visit from the heavens to honor us with His own presence. We greatly fear before the Lord lest we should fail of this great honor, which our Master proposes to confer on us; we are seeking for humility and great faith lest we be ashamed in His presence."[8] Joseph understood the Lord's promise.

Not Just Ordinances

Six months later, in June of 1833, the Lord chastened the Saints for not being more diligent in building the temple and for allowing contentions to arise in their midst. He reminded them again of the purpose for the new temple: "I gave unto you a commandment that you should build a house, in the which house *I design to endow those whom I have chosen with power from on high*" (D&C 95:8, emphasis added).

Joseph clarified the nature of this promised endowment: "You need a fountain of wisdom, knowledge and intelligence such as you never had. . . . The world cannot receive the things of God. He can endow you without worldly pomp or great parade. *He can give you that wisdom, that intelligence, and that power, which characterized the ancient saints, and now characterizes the inhabitants of the upper world.*"[9] It was not merely additional ordinances. The promised endowment was to be one of wisdom, intelligence, and power. Christ would not only appear but would teach and minister to them. This was necessary to prepare the Saints, in turn, to minister to others.

A subsequent revelation, received a few months later, reiterated once again the purpose and the required sanctification: "And inasmuch as my people build a house unto me in the name of the Lord, and do not suffer any unclean thing to come into it, that it be not defiled, my glory shall rest upon it; yea, and my presence shall be there, for *I will come into it, and all the pure in heart that shall come into it shall see God*" (D&C 97:15–16; emphasis added). The Lord's purpose for the temple was made very clear, namely to sanctify His people and prepare them to enter His presence.

The Role of the Book of Mormon

Juxtaposed against these great promised blessings came a sobering warning. In the same year the Lord commanded that a temple be built and promised to appear therein, He also placed the Church under condemnation with this explanation: "And your minds in times past have been darkened because of unbelief, and because you have treated lightly the things you have received—Which vanity and unbelief have brought the whole Church under condemnation . . . even all" (D&C

84:54–56). The problem was not limited to the Saints in Missouri—it applied equally to Kirtland as well. "And they shall remain under this condemnation until they repent and remember the new covenant, even the Book of Mormon and the former commandments which I have given them, not only to say, but to do according to that which I have written. That they may bring forth fruit meet for their Father's kingdom; otherwise there remaineth a scourge and judgment to be poured out upon the children of Zion" (D&C 84:57–58).

The Lord warned of unbelief (which includes not believing His promises to us), not taking seriously the things already given, and for neglecting the Book of Mormon and the covenant it contains. We might pause here and ask parenthetically if this applies to us as individuals. It certainly has at various times in my life. In 1832, the result was that the entire Church fell under condemnation.

Why send such a strong rebuke alongside the promise of such incredible blessings? These early Saints had grown up with the Holy Bible and were familiar and comfortable with it.[10] Sidney Rigdon, for example, knew it so well that he was sometimes referred to as a walking Bible. Even Joseph Smith's discourses primarily quoted from the Bible. Many saw the coming forth of the Book of Mormon as important evidence that the Lord was again working among men but nothing more. They nicknamed it the Golden Bible and went right on preaching and studying from their beloved Holy Bibles. This neglect of the new scripture prompted the Lord's ire.

The Lord's condemnation and warning occurred in the same time frame and in the same revelations commanding that temples be built in Missouri and Ohio.[11] Obviously, the Book of Mormon was to play an important role in sanctifying and preparing the Saints for the promised blessings. Indeed, Joseph Smith testified that we can get nearer to God by living its teachings than those of any other book.[12] It is something we need to take seriously.[13] Beyond this, however, there may be another critical role of the Book of Mormon in fulfilling these promises, one we will discuss later.

The Kirtland Ordinances

Following the Lord's chastening in June 1833, the Saints resumed construction on the temple with greater dispatch. As the structure slowly took shape, Joseph Smith worked to prepare the people for their promised endowment. The School of the Prophets was instituted among the brethren, and the *Lectures on Faith* provided as a textbook to help them develop the necessary faith.

In the final months preceding the dedication, quorums assembled in reconciliation meetings to work out past differences. Members were admonished to forgive one another their sins and trespasses, to eliminate contention, and to develop charity towards one another. This was required in order to be forgiven for their own sins (see 3 Nephi 12:23–24). It was also during this time frame that Joseph began to introduce new ordinances to the members.

The Lord's command was that no unclean thing be allowed in his house (see D&C 97:15). How was this to be done? It was not through a temple recommend interview. They didn't have such a thing. Rather, it was accomplished through ceremonial cleansing via the sacrament and new washing ordinances. Even before the temple was completed, Joseph began to administer these additional ordinances, often outside of the temple.

If no unclean (unwashed) thing was to enter the holy house, then the people needed to be washed and forgiven beforehand. After partaking of the sacrament, they washed their bodies (generally hands, feet, and faces) using water or sometimes whiskey mixed with cinnamon. The recently revealed Word of Wisdom taught that strong drinks were for the washing of their bodies (an antiseptic; see D&C 89:7) and the Saints made use of it for this purpose. Following this washing, they were anointed with oil, blessed, and then the blessing was sealed. No set wording was given for these ordinances; rather they were accompanied by contemporaneous blessings as directed by the Spirit. This was then sometimes followed by the washing of the feet as directed in Doctrine and Covenants 88:139–141.

On January 21, 1836, Joseph's journal records that he administered these ordinances to the First Presidency and others beginning in the loft of the printing office and concluding in the west room of the still unfinished temple.[14] Following these ordinances a vision of the celestial kingdom unfolded: "the heavens were opened upon us, and I beheld the celestial kingdom of God, and the glory thereof" (D&C 137:1). This vision was a foretaste of the endowment of power promised at the dedication of the temple.

These basic ordinances (washing, anointing, and the sacrament) were repeated in the following weeks and months. Quorum leaders were given them and then asked to provide them for their quorums and others. From January to March 1836, each quorum of the priesthood met together to receive their washings and anointings. Again, this was to fulfill the Lord's command that no unclean (unwashed) thing be permitted in His house. They participated in these ordinances to receive forgiveness and cleansing before entering the temple.

Perhaps there is a lesson for us here as well. It can help us recognize where our spiritual cleanliness comes from—ultimately it is from Christ. Our own "righteousness" and best efforts are described by Isaiah as "filthy rags" (see Isaiah 64:6). It is not our "righteousness" of being able to successfully pass a recommend interview that grants us entrance to His holy house. Rather, it is His grace extended to us as His guests. That is not to say our efforts are not important. We should not partake of the sacrament unworthily (see 3 Nephi 18:28–29). Nor should we come to the temple unworthily. However, our "worthiness" may have more to do with our intent and desire to follow Christ and our reliance upon His Atonement than on how perfectly we are living every commandment at the moment (see Luke 18:9–14).

An Endowment of Power

Aware of the Lord's promises, the Saints flocked to the dedicatory services expecting a Pentecostal type of experience. They understood that the ordinances were not the endowment—the Pentecostal experience was to be the endowment. The Lord further described the nature of this endowment of power in the dedicatory prayer of the temple: "that thy servants may go forth from this house armed with thy power, and that thy name may be upon them, and thy glory be round about them, and thine angels have charge over them" (D&C 109:22).

The dedicatory services extended over a week, beginning on Sunday, March 27, 1836. At the conclusion, the Savior indicated that an endowment from heaven had indeed been given: "Yea, the hearts of thousands and tens of thousands shall greatly rejoice in consequence of the blessings which shall be poured out, and the *endowment with which my servants have been endowed in this house*" (D&C 110:9, emphasis added).

What did this endowment look like in the lives of the members? In the days and weeks surrounding the dedication, some saw angels, a few saw the Savior, and others experienced a Pentecostal outpouring of the Spirit. Oliver Cowdery wrote: "The Spirit poured out—I saw the glory of God, like a great cloud, come down and rest upon the house, and fill the same like a mighty rushing wind. I also saw cloven tongues, like as of fire rest upon many (for there were 316 present) while they spake with other tongues and prophesied."[15] These kinds of spiritual experiences occurred both before, during, and after the dedicatory services. Many attested to receiving such blessings.[16] From the surviving accounts, it would seem the participants were endowed to the extent they were spiritually prepared. Perhaps there were also some who were disappointed.[17]

Regardless, the key point is that the promised endowment was not just the additional physical ordinances. The ordinances were part of it, but they were a preparation for the spiritual experiences that followed. These spiritual experiences provided the promised power. That is not to diminish the value of the ordinances. Both are necessary, but one without the other is incomplete.

This truth is evident in the ordinances of baptism and of the sacrament. The physical ordinance of baptism is mandatory but must be accompanied by the baptism of fire and the Holy Ghost to be complete. Likewise, the emblems of the sacrament are physical but we are to be filled by the Spirit while partaking. If we are only receiving the physical portion of the ordinance and not experiencing the spiritual portion then we are not gaining the promised "power of godliness" (see D&C 84:20).

If you have been endowed in the temple, pause to think about your own endowment: not in terms of the physical ordinances but rather your spiritual experiences with God. How great is the endowment you have received? Is your endowment complete if you have only received the physical ordinances without also experiencing their spiritual counterparts? What could you do in your life to prepare for a greater spiritual endowment from God?

Just as in Kirtland, one of the primary purposes of our own temple endowment is to likewise invite, testify, and prepare us to behold our Savior's face in mortality (see D&C 93:1). As a group, Latter-day Saints tend to resist that idea. We may feel it is a privilege reserved for special prophets and leaders or that it is utterly beyond our reach. Perhaps the early Saints of this dispensation felt these things as well.

The promise of seeing the Lord is not something we should pass over lightly. Indeed, the Lord taught Alma: "Marvel not that all mankind, yea, men and women, all nations, kindreds, tongues, and people, must be born again; yea, born of God, changed from their carnal and fallen state, to a state of righteousness, *being redeemed of God*, becoming his sons and daughters" (Mosiah 27:25 emphasis added). We miss what this scripture is trying to teach unless we recognize what the phrase being "redeemed of God" means. Our Redeemer defined *redemption* as being brought back into His presence (see Ether 3:13). To be redeemed is to meet our Redeemer!

Homework

1. Study Doctrine and Covenants 84 and Doctrine and Covenants 88. In particular, study them as temple texts. Those sections provide profound insights into our temple worship.

CHAPTER 2

NAUVOO

To prepare the way for a greater revelation of God.
—Joseph Smith

A FEW DAYS FOLLOWING the initial dedicatory service of the Kirtland temple, Joseph recorded: "I had now completed the organization of the Church, and *we had passed through all the necessary ceremonies.*"[18] In spite of that declaration, six years later, in May 1842, Joseph introduced a greatly expanded set of ordinances in Nauvoo. Two distinct possibilities for this addition emerge: either Joseph was mistaken about having given all the necessary ordinances; or he was correct, and the expanded ordinances given in Nauvoo served another purpose. We will consider both possibilities, along with the idea that the truth may be a combination of the two.

RESTORATION OF KEYS

Despite being tutored by heaven, Joseph still learned incrementally. Scripture records some of the angels who ministered to him, and that from them, he was given "line upon line, precept upon precept; here a little, and there a little" (D&C 128:20–21). Joseph's understanding and knowledge clearly expanded throughout his life.

For example, just four days after declaring that everything was complete, Joseph and Oliver were visited by Jehovah, Moses, Elias and Elijah in the new temple on April 3, 1836 (see D&C 110).[19] The keys transmitted in this experience seem to form the basis of the expanded endowment ordinances given in Nauvoo. It is possible that as a result of these visits, Joseph realized that the ceremonies were not complete, but in fact more remained to be done. In that case, his earlier statement was incorrect.

However, a second possibility as to why Joseph expanded the ordinances emerges if we assume that everything necessary was in fact given in Kirtland, at least as pertaining to the living.[20] A comparison of the Kirtland ordinances and their subsequently expanded versions follows:[21]

KIRTLAND	NAUVOO
Washing of the Body	Washing and Sealing
Anointing, Blessing and Sealing	Anointing, Blessing and Sealing
	Clothing
	Aaronic Portion of the Endowment
	Melchizedek Portion of the Endowment
	Marriage Sealing
Washing of the Feet	Second Anointings[22]

The purpose of the final ordinance of washing of the feet in Kirtland was to seal the recipient up unto eternal life as instructed in Doctrine and Covenants 88:139–141. It was clearly reminiscent of the Savior's act of washing his disciples' feet at the Last Supper (see John 13:4–17). The significance of this ritual was not understood by the apostles until later: "Jesus answered and said unto him [Peter], What I do thou knowest not now, but thou shalt know hereafter" (John 13:7). After performing this same ordinance for several Elders, Joseph pronounced them "clean from the blood of this generation" by the power of the Holy Ghost and "sealed up unto eternal life."[23]

It may be that what Joseph meant by stating that the Church in Kirtland had passed through "all the necessary ceremonies" was simply that this final seal (washing of the feet) needs to be put into place for each individual meriting it.[24] If that is the case, then the later Nauvoo ordinances may have served primarily to instruct and prepare the Saints to receive this final seal.

Moses, Elias, and Elijah

The modern endowment ceremony opens with the dawn of creation. Following a recital of the creative periods, the endowment then proceeds with Adam and Eve in the Garden of Eden, their subsequent fall, their journey through mortality, and eventual redemption by Jehovah. Participants in the endowment company are told to consider themselves as if they were Adam and Eve or, in other words, to assume their roles in the drama as it unfolds. The story presented is the universal story of humankind. The purpose of life is explained utilizing the symbolism of two trees: the tree of knowledge of good and evil and the tree of life.

At first glance, however, the temple ordinances seem to be given out of order. For example, following their expulsion from the garden, Adam and Eve were subsequently baptized (see Moses 6:64). Yet, the endowment company does not break at that point for the participants to go and perform baptisms for the deceased, and then return to continue the drama. Is this solely for convenience in administering the ordinances, or is there another reason?

Obviously, it would be impractical to administer the endowment drama in a way that mirrors the sequence in which Adam and Eve received the gospel ordinances. But we can recognize where the gospel ordinances would fit in the ceremony. Beyond logistics, however, there may be an important reason for the order of the temple ordinances. The keys delivered to Joseph in the Kirtland Temple help provide an answer (see D&C 110). They form a framework for understanding the expanded ordinances given in Nauvoo as summarized in the table below:

Messenger	Keys	Related Ordinances
Moses	Gathering of Israel	Baptism & Initiatory
Elias	Gospel of Abraham	Endowment & Temple Sealing
Elijah	Sealing	Second Anointing

These topics—the gathering of Israel, the gospel of Abraham, and the sealing power—are broad gospel subjects and cannot be fully covered here. We will simply consider these keys as a structure for our modern temple ordinances.

Each of us must pass through three phases in the path back to God as represented by these keys: 1) first, we are "called" or gathered out of the world and invited into the kingdom of God. This is the *Moses* phase. 2) Next, comes a period of growth, development, and testing. We learn more about our Lord. We grow in our ability to communicate with Him and to follow His spirit. We gradually become fully consecrated to Him. This is our *Elias* phase. We are promised the blessings of the Gospel of Abraham conditionally during this phase. 3) Eventually, we can reach a point where these promised blessings are secured. This requires a final seal or capstone to be put in place. This is the *Elijah* phase. There are ordinances associated with each phase.

Moses—The Gathering of Israel

Moses delivered the keys of the gathering of Israel (see D&C 110:11). Gathering implies combining together into a group. It also implies a sorting process between those who are gathered and those who are not. The scattering and gathering of Israel are part physical and part spiritual. For our purposes, we will primarily focus on the spiritual gathering, though in the past the two were often tied together.

Christ lamented during His mortal ministry, "O Jerusalem, Jerusalem, which killest the prophets, and stonest them that are sent unto thee; how often would I have gathered thy children together, as a hen doth gather her brood under her wings and ye would not!" (Luke 13:34). Those in Jerusalem were already gathered physically, so what Christ mourned was the spiritual condition of the people. They would not receive the things He wanted to give them. And he foretold the result, "behold, your house is left unto you desolate" (Luke 13:35).

This can be understood in at least two ways. If *house* refers to the temple in Jerusalem, then Christ's lament is that it had become desolate or void of saving power, the irony being that the temple was His house and the ordinances therein testified of Him. If the Jews rejected the very Christ of whom their ceremonies testified, then their ceremonies and their temple were indeed desolate and of no value (see Mosiah 3:15).

On the other hand, *house* could also refer to their place in God's family or kingdom. Christ testified that in His Father's house are many mansions (John 14:2). The religious Jews who rejected Christ would have no place there. For them the house was again desolate. Joseph Smith added his own witness to this truth: "Jesus did everything to gather the people, and they would not be gathered, and He therefore poured out curses upon them."[25]

The topic of the gathering of Israel can be confusing, in part because of various definitions for Israel. A brief review here may be helpful. Jacob received the new name of Israel from God at the time they wrestled (embraced) through the veil (see Genesis 32:28 and 35:10). His new name, Israel, means "one who prevails with God." This new name was given as part of the covenant Jacob received accepting him as a son of God and as part of God's family or household.[26] Jacob was thus saved. He was bound to Christ by a covenant, having been spiritually begotten by Him as His son (see Mosiah 5:7).

Because of the covenant given to Abraham and then renewed with Isaac and Jacob, all who would be saved thereafter as part of God's family were to be accounted Abraham, Isaac, and Jacob's seed (see Abraham 2:10). Or in other words, all who will be saved thereafter become part of the house of Israel or the family of Christ. Those who receive the same priesthood held by these ancient patriarchs become their seed (see D&C 84:34). This is more than appears on the surface and is intimately connected to the temple as we will discuss later in this volume.

It is important to recognize that the seed of Jacob, or Israel, can refer to the literal descendants of his body or to the spiritual heirs to the same blessings he inherited. The two groups overlap but are not necessarily the same. To keep this straight, I prefer to think of the physical descendants as the house of Jacob and the spiritual heirs as the house of Israel. Jacob's physical descendants have blessings and promises extended to them, but ultimately to become of the house of Israel they must qualify for these spiritual blessings in the same way that their father Jacob obtained them or as any other person may obtain them.

Admittedly, the scriptures generally do not distinguish between the house of Jacob and the house of Israel in the manner we are describing

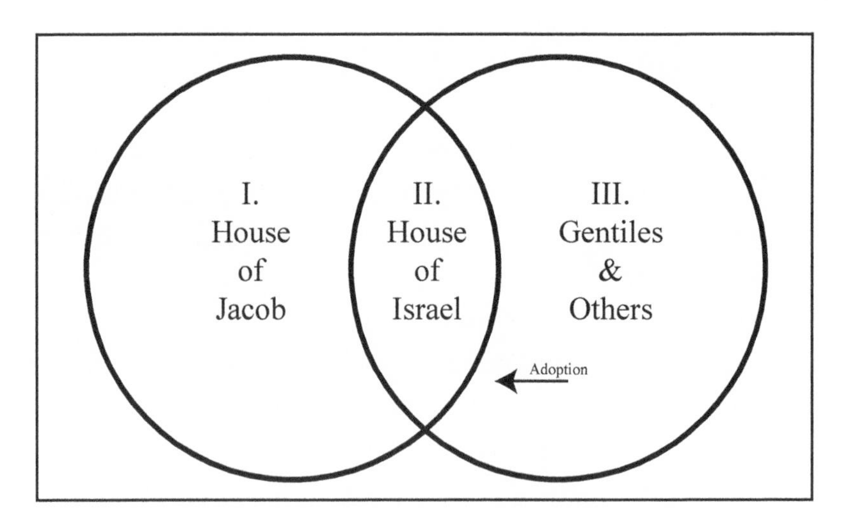

I. The House of Jacob refers to the physical descendants of the patriarch Jacob. This group includes the Jews as well as the Lamanites.

II. The House of Israel refers to the spiritual descendants of Jacob or those who become accepted by covenant as part of God's eternal family. These two groups overlap but are not necessarily the same. For example, using this definition, Nephi would be included as part of the House of Israel while Laman and Lemuel would not, despite having the same parents and the same lineage through the patriarch Jacob.

III. The Gentiles are a third group that includes physical descendants from other families, even though these people may also have trace amounts of the blood of Jacob in their genealogy. These must be adopted into the House of Israel.

here. So, it is important to recognize and understand to which group a particular scripture is referring when Israel is mentioned.

Because covenants anciently extended to the posterity of the original parties, the Jews often misunderstood their status. Many believed themselves to be God's chosen people and automatic heirs to Israel's spiritual blessings. John the Baptist refuted this notion stating, "Bring forth therefore fruits worthy of repentance, and begin not to say within yourselves, We have Abraham to our father; for I say unto you, that God is able of these stones to raise up children unto Abraham" (Luke 3:8). The ancient Jews needed to qualify to become Israel through repentance and doing the works of Abraham. And the same is required of any and all who become part of Israel.

Those who are not among the literal seed of Jacob are brought into the house of Israel through adoption. Joseph Smith taught, "It is one thing to see the kingdom of God, and another thing to enter into it. We must have a change of heart to see the kingdom of God, and subscribe to the articles of adoption to enter therein."[27] How does this adoption occur? The initial steps are an authorized baptism and then receiving the Holy Ghost. Joseph further declared, "The effect of the Holy Ghost upon a Gentile, is to purge out the old blood, and make him [or her] actually of the seed of Abraham."[28] Baptism and the reception of the Holy Ghost are the beginning points of the spiritual gathering of Israel.

With this background in mind, why is the physical gathering of Israel also important? Joseph Smith answered:

> What was the object of gathering the Jews, or the people of God in any age of the world? . . . The main object was to build unto the Lord a house whereby He could reveal unto His people the ordinances of His house and the glories of His kingdom, and teach the people the way of salvation; for there are certain ordinances and principles that, when they are taught and practiced, must be done in a place or house built for that purpose. It was the design of the councils of heaven before the world was, that the principles and laws

> of the priesthood should be predicated upon the gathering of the people in every age of the world.[29]

The physical and the spiritual gatherings of Israel are both about salvation. Joseph Smith continued,

> It is for the same purpose that God gathers together His people in the last days, to build unto the Lord a house to prepare them for the ordinances and endowments, washings and anointings, etc. One of the ordinances of the house of the Lord is baptism for the dead. God decreed before the foundation of the world that the ordinances should be administered in a font prepared for the purpose in the house of the Lord.[30]

The keys of the gathering of Israel restored by Moses in the Kirtland Temple preceded the work of baptism for the dead that commenced in Nauvoo.

Anciently, Solomon's temple had a font (or a "sea") for baptisms (or "washings of the priests"). The font sat upon the backs of twelve oxen: three faced north, three faced south, three faced east, and three faced west (see 1 Kings 7:23–25). Though perhaps largely unrecognized at the time, these oxen foreshadowed the scattering of Israel to the four corners of the earth. This scattering began at the death of King Solomon, when the kingdom of Israel divided along the north and south.

The northern kingdom, containing ten of the tribes, was carried away around 725 B.C. by Assyria. They were subsequently lost to history as they scattered northward. The southern kingdom comprising the remaining two tribes stayed together a little longer but eventually was also carried away captive by Babylon around 600 B.C. (shortly after the time of Lehi leaving Jerusalem). The Babylonians destroyed Solomon's temple, at which point all of Israel was effectively scattered. The physical kingdom was no more.

Some 70 years later, a remnant of these Babylonian Jews returned to Jerusalem, under the direction of Zerubbabel and Joshua the high priest, with the purpose of reclaiming the land and rebuilding the temple (see Haggai 1). They constructed a second temple, which was later renovated and expanded by King Herod and was sometimes referred to as Herod's temple. It is this temple that stood during the Lord's mortal ministry. Following their rejection of the Messiah, these Jews were again scattered and their temple destroyed, this time at the hands of the Romans around 70 A.D.

Today, just as in Solomon's temple, the fonts in many of our temples sit upon the backs of twelve oxen. These oxen are likewise divided into groups of three and face the four cardinal directions. However, rather than symbolizing the scattering of Israel, the oxen now represent the gathering, back from the four corners of the earth.

The scattering of Israel occurred as the result of apostasy, rebellion, and wickedness. The gathering is intended to reverse this condition bringing about restoration and righteousness. It is interesting to note that scattering and gathering are also images of planting and harvesting. The Lord has purpose in both, namely to produce fruit worthy of preserving. The allegory of Zenos explains the scattering and gathering of Israel and the Lord's purposes for it (see Jacob 5).

This is an extensive topic and one we usually think of as it applies to groups of people. But what about the gathering of Israel on an individual basis, specifically as it relates to you and me? Here, the Book of Mormon speaks to us plainly, though to understand the message we need to clarify the audience. As members of the LDS Church, we like to think of ourselves as part of the house of Israel. Our patriarchal blessings identify the tribe we belong to within that house. Be that as it may, in the vernacular of the Book of Mormon most members of the Church are referred to as Gentiles. The title page to the Book of Mormon identifies three groups as its intended audience: the Lamanites, the Jews, and the Gentiles. Most members of the Church with European ancestry are certainly not Lamanites or Jews—and are therefore considered Gentiles. It is important to recognize this or we risk missing many of the Book of Mormon's messages and warnings to us, thinking they apply to others. The fact that most LDS Church members are considered Gentiles is confirmed in the Doctrine and Covenants as well (see D&C 109:60).

With the idea that we are part of the Gentiles, the Book of Mormon plainly gives us the key to being gathered and adopted into the house of Israel: "Turn, all ye Gentiles, from your wicked ways; and repent of your evil doings, of your lyings and deceivings, and of your whoredoms, and of your secret abominations, and your idolatries, and of your murders, and your priestcrafts, and your envyings, and your strifes, and from all your wickedness and abominations, and come unto me, and be baptized in my name, that ye may receive a remission of your sins, and be filled with the Holy Ghost, that ye may be numbered with my people who are of the house of Israel" (3 Nephi 30:2).

Repentance followed by the ordinances of baptism and receiving the Holy Ghost begins the process of gathering. We must receive these for ourselves and provide them for our dead. These ordinances initiate the spiritual gathering of Israel. In essence, they provide an invitation or a calling to come and join the family of God.

Elias—The Gospel of Abraham

Following Moses, Elias then "appeared, and committed the dispensation of the gospel of Abraham, saying that in us and in our seed all generations after us should be blessed" (see D&C 110:12). This verse raises several questions. First, what is the "gospel of Abraham [and of Sarah]"? From the scriptures it is clear that Abraham and Sarah possessed more as part of their "gospel" than may be generally appreciated (see Abraham 1:2–4; 2:9–12). Since this dispensation was restored at Kirtland, perhaps the temple will teach us something about how to obtain it for ourselves.

Secondly, a question arises as to Elias. The identity of Elias here is unknown, but the function or purpose of Elias can be known. Joseph

Smith taught, "the spirit of Elias is to prepare the way for a greater revelation of God."[31] This statement provides a crucial insight into the purpose of our temple endowment. Once we have been gathered through baptism and the initiatory ordinances, we are then invited through the endowment to receive a greater revelation of God. The endowment does this in at least three important ways: First, it teaches us more about what the Gods do and their purposes. Second, it outlines and invites us to begin following the same path. And third, the ceremony provides an blueprint or prototype for returning to God's presence.

Once admitted into the celestial realm of the temple, we can then be sealed together as couples and as families for time and eternity.[32] In that sacred setting, we are taught more concerning the gospel of Abraham and Sarah. In the sealing ordinance, a husband and wife are jointly promised all of the blessings of Abraham, Isaac, and Jacob conditioned upon their subsequent faithfulness. Our temple sealing provides an authorized invitation to claim these blessings for ourselves. It is up to each individual member who is thus endowed to subsequently rise up and eventually receive the actual blessings that are promised. Notice that Abraham received these blessings from Jehovah upon entering His presence (see Abraham 2:8–12). That is ultimately how they are to be obtained. Part of the endowment is about our personal redemption from the Fall and our claiming all of the blessings of Abraham and Sarah. This doesn't happen overnight. It is a process that requires time and unfolds line upon line, precept upon precept.

Our temple endowment and sealing ordinances provide a map. They give us hope by previewing the blessings awaiting us at the end of the path. They give us faith and confidence that we are authorized and invited to take the journey for ourselves. And, if we know and recognize the road marks, God can use the endowment ceremony to let us know our position on the path.[33] They provide comfort, reassurance, and strength along the way. Finally, they provide a beautiful opportunity for service as we return to perform these ordinances for our deceased ancestors. For all of these reasons, the endowment and sealing ordinances are critical for us. However, we must also recognize that these rites, as currently administered, are utterly insufficient to save. More is required. This is plainly stated in the endowment itself where we are reminded that the realization of all of these promised blessings depends upon our faithfulness.

Because the blessings in our temple sealing ordinances are part of the gospel of Abraham and because they are given conditionally, I choose to group the endowment and sealing ordinances together as the "Elias" portion of the temple. They provide us with an opportunity over time to come to know the Lord more fully. The Elias phase is a time to work these things out and prepare "for a greater revelation of God."

Elijah—A Final Seal

Following Moses and Elias, Elijah appeared in the Kirtland Temple (see D&C 110:13–16).[34] This series of heavenly messengers and related keys suggests a progression of calling or gathering; learning, growth, and testing; and then a final sealing, which is reflected in our temple ordinances. In Kirtland, the final seal was put into place through the ordinance of washing of the feet.[35] By the Nauvoo period, this crowning ordinance was expanded into what became the ordinances of the second endowment or second anointings, but the intent remained the same—namely to make one's calling and election sure and seal the recipient up unto eternal life.[36]

During the initiatory ordinances we are anointed that *we may become* a king and a priest or a queen and a priestess unto God. The anointing hints at a future event. Joseph Smith confirmed that at some point in our journey we could be accepted by the Lord and the conditional aspect of our blessings removed.

These capstone ordinances were administered frequently in the early part of the Church's history until being dramatically curtailed by President Heber J. Grant in 1926.[37] It is my understanding that these second anointings are still performed on a very limited basis at present, though there appears to be some question among general authorities today as to whether they are essential.[38] Those who receive them are given the charge to not speak of them, and I would hasten to clarify that I have not received any such ordinances from the Church.[39]

In the world-wide organization today, some very practical obstacles exist with respect to these final ordinances. One challenge is the simple fact that the majority of everyday members do not have access to anyone authorized to administer these blessings. Most members will never have the opportunity to receive these additional ordinances, even if merited, simply because of their own obscurity within the Church. There is also the practical problem of determining who would qualify for such a blessing. Surely the Lord alone is capable of making such a judgment. These obstacles were less prevalent in Joseph's day, when he rubbed shoulders with many of the Saints in Kirtland and Nauvoo and the Spirit could easily direct his actions. Fortunately, the scriptures indicate there is another way to obtain these blessings—one available to all regardless of where they live. We will discuss it in the next chapter.

Conclusion

In conclusion, the failure at Kirtland to bring the body of the Saints into Christ's presence combined with the keys delivered by Moses, Elias, and Elijah seem to have contributed to the expanded ordinances given in Nauvoo. It may be that Joseph recognized there was too large a gap between the initial "gathering" ordinances and the final "sealing" ordinances as administered in Kirtland. Time was needed for additional growth and preparation and spiritual maturation—an *Elias* period preparing for a greater revelation of God. The expanded Nauvoo endowment provided for such a need.

HOMEWORK

1. Many of the topics in this book are covered only in a brief, introductory overview or summary. If there are topics you would like to understand better or even perhaps some ideas you may initially disagree with, please make them a matter of prayer and further study. The endnotes in this book contain references and additional information that may be a helpful starting point. Ask the Lord to teach you and give you further light and understanding. He can direct you to the answers that you need. For example, I recently wanted to understand a topic better and took my question to the Lord. In response, He directed me to re-read the Book of Mormon but in a way that I had never before considered. Sure enough, the answers to my questions where there although I had never seen them previously.

CHAPTER 3

YOUR CALLING AND ELECTION MADE SURE

Wherefore the rather, brethren, give diligence to make your calling and election sure: for if ye do these things, ye shall never fall.
—2 Peter 1:10

In an online forum discussing LDS doctrine someone posed the question: "At what point do you have confidence you are going to be exalted?" All kinds of speculative answers were posted in response and served as a great example of the confusion that exists among Church members on this topic. It is an important question. What is your standing before God? How can you know?

Joseph Smith left important instructions on this point along with a very simple way to know. He summarized the entire process:

> After a person has faith in Christ, repents of his sins, and is baptized for the remission of his sins and receives the Holy Ghost, (by the laying on of hands), which is the first Comforter, then let him continue to humble himself before God, hungering and thirsting after righteousness, and living by every word of God, and the Lord will soon say unto him, Son [or Daughter], thou shalt be exalted. When the Lord has thoroughly proved him, and finds that the man is determined to serve Him at all hazards, then the man [or woman] will find his calling and his election made sure, then it will be his privilege to receive the other Comforter.[40]

In response to the forum's question, you can have confidence when you receive a promise of exaltation by covenant from the Lord. In its simplest form that is what it means to have your calling and election made sure. There is more to calling and election, but we are going to focus on this part of it—receiving the promise of exaltation from the Lord.

Peter describes this as a "more sure word of prophecy" or a "light that shineth in a dark place" (2 Peter 1:19). Latter-day revelation clarifies that this "more sure word of prophecy" means knowing you are sealed up unto eternal life (see D&C 131:5). Joseph Smith's statement is worth parsing through in greater detail because it outlines how one might secure this blessing and comfort for oneself.

The Path Back to God

I. "Hungering and thirsting after righteousness."

The process Joseph Smith outlined begins with the Doctrine of Christ—faith, repentance, baptism and receiving the Holy Ghost. This doctrine is explored in chapters 3–6 of *Preparing for Your Endowment*. We won't repeat that material here, except to reiterate that these principles of faith, repentance, baptism, and following the Holy Ghost comprise the foundational path we all must take. And we never outgrow these core principles. Learning to recognize and heed the voice of the Lord through the Holy Ghost is essential to making any progress. Humility is also vital. We must have a broken heart and contrite spirit or we cannot be acceptable before God (see Moroni 7:44). Part of hungering and thirsting after righteousness is recognizing our lack and turning to God who can fill us.

II. "Living by every word of God."

This involves striving to keep the commandments. But it is also something more personal and individual—following God's direction in our lives. Joseph continued:

> The Spirit of Revelation is in connection with these blessings. A person may profit by noticing the first intimation of the spirit of revelation; for instance, when you feel pure intelligence flowing into you, it may give you sudden strokes of ideas, so that by noticing it, you may find it fulfilled the same day or soon; (i.e.,) those things that were presented unto your minds by the Spirit of God, will come to pass; and thus by learning the Spirit of God and understanding it, you may grow into the principle of revelation, until you become perfect in Christ Jesus."[41]

If you want to follow the path outlined and receive the blessings indicated, you have to learn how to communicate with God and receive revelation for yourself.

Notice that Joseph is not just speaking of this first Comforter as a feeling we have—it is pure intelligence or strokes of ideas or insight. The Holy Ghost communicates information and helps you to understand things that you previously did not know. If you have not learned to hear the voice of the Spirit, you need to do so. You won't make much progress in this process until you do. Ask the Lord to help you learn how He speaks to you. Pray for ears to hear and eyes to see.

Nephi taught: "if ye will enter in by the way, and receive the Holy Ghost, *it will show unto you all things what ye should do*" (2 Nephi 32:5; emphasis added). We need the Holy Ghost in our lives to the greatest extent possible. One blessing of regular temple worship is the opportunity to be in a place free from distractions where we can be immersed in the Spirit.

One of the most helpful things in my personal journey has been the practice of going to the Lord in prayer and asking Him to tell me one thing that I still lack or what the next step is for me. I listen for His answer to that question. Usually the answer comes as a very quiet suggestion. Sometimes it is very clear, but other times I am not completely sure that the thought is from the Lord rather than something I am thinking on my own. But I act on these ideas in faith. As I accomplish the task, I return to the Lord in prayer and report back.

Inevitably, I either learn something through doing what the Lord required or am taught more as I return in prayer. I record these things in a separate spiritual journal. Over time, my ability to receive revelation has increased and I find myself on a path back to Him. A similar practice may be helpful in your own search to know the Lord.

III. "The Lord will soon say unto him, Son [or daughter], thou shalt be exalted."

This step may not always be an actual event, but in my case, it was. I first became aware of and desired to eventually receive these blessings while serving as a young missionary. Some years later, while attending the temple, I picked up a copy of the scriptures. The page fell open to 2 Nephi 32. I began in the middle of verse three, which reads:

> Wherefore, I said unto you, feast upon the words of Christ; for behold, the words of Christ will tell you all things what ye should do.
>
> Wherefore, now after I have spoken these words, if ye cannot understand them it will be because ye ask not, neither do ye knock; wherefore, ye are not brought into the light, but must perish in the dark.
>
> For behold, again, I say unto you that if ye will enter in by the way, and receive the Holy Ghost, it will show unto you all things what ye should do.
>
> Behold, this is the doctrine of Christ, and there will be no more doctrine given until after he shall manifest himself unto you in the flesh. And when he shall manifest himself unto you in the flesh, the things which he shall say unto you shall ye observe to do. (2 Nephi 32:3–6)

This scripture came to me very powerfully. It seemed that the Lord was giving these words directly to me. And the Spirit enlightened my understanding so that for the first time I recognized that the words, "he shall manifest himself unto you" refer to a personal manifestation of Christ unto us in this life (in the flesh). I had always thought it referred to Christ's visit to the Nephites after his resurrection. (And, in truth, it may mean both.)

A few days later, as I continued to ponder over this message, the Spirit enlightened me further and I was given to understand that this experience was the Lord's way of saying to me, "Son, thou shalt be [or at least can be] exalted," just as Joseph Smith outlined in his statement. Again, this surprised me. I had not expected it to be an actual event or a step in the process. And it may not be for others. But the Spirit taught me that this experience was this point in the journey for me.

That moment served as a trail sign along the path. It let me know where I stood in the process and the scripture taught what I needed to do to continue moving forward. I also knew that the Lord was helping me on the path and that the path Joseph outlined was real. The whole experience was very sacred to me. I share it here only to testify that the process that Joseph Smith outlined in his teaching is real and is meant for each of us.

In the years following this experience, I thought often on 2 Nephi 32 and tried to heed the direction I had been given by the Lord. I wish I had been more diligent in doing so. But in the busyness of finishing graduate school, starting a career, and raising four children there were seasons when my personal scripture study and prayer slipped, and I neglected my relationship with the Lord. My wife and I always remained active in the Church and served faithfully in whatever callings we received. We held family home evening diligently each week along with daily family prayer and scripture study. Despite this there were times in my life where I found myself living much like the Zoramites with their stupid Rameumpton—attending Church every Sunday, feeling blessed and chosen of God, but then being so caught up in things during the week that I scarcely thought of Him until the next Sunday.

Other years I did better at keeping personal, daily prayer and scripture study a priority. These times tended to be seasons where I had much more of the Spirit in my life and where I grew spiritually and felt closer to the Lord. Keeping this focus a priority and not allowing other things to crowd it out is always a challenge. Overall, I wish that I had been more consistently diligent in this aspect of my life. It is in these personal daily practices of devotion that our relationship with the Lord is developed and where spiritual growth truly occurs. When we neglect these practices, we hurt ourselves.

Isaiah penned a beautiful phrase that seems appropriate here. He lamented, "O that thou hadst hearkened to my commandments—then had thy peace been as a river, and thy righteousness as the waves of the sea" (1 Nephi 20:18). I love his phrase—righteousness as the waves of the sea. I pondered this scripture one day while vacationing at the beach. Two thoughts came to me. One is that there is a constant ebb and flow to the ocean's waves. Perhaps some ebb and flow is natural in our own spiritual progression as well. We may have seasons where we are filled with the Spirit and other times where we struggle to connect at all. There is always opposition in everything we do. Our growth and progression is usually not a straight line. We all make mistakes and our paths are more of a jagged line with peaks and valleys. The important thing is where the trend is heading over time. Are we trending upward or downward? The other thing about waves is that they are relentless. No matter how many times they recede into the ocean, they always come pounding back once again. I think that is a good message for us as well.

Some six or seven years after my experience in the temple, the Lord sent several experiences and a dream that got me back on a track of diligently seeking further spiritual growth in my own life. At that time, I had started to study and understand the Atonement better and to appreciate more all that the Lord had done for me. As a result, I desired to do something for Him and felt that I should begin attending the temple weekly. We live about five miles from a temple, so this was very possible. It just meant getting up extra early one morning a week to attend the first session of the day before going to work.

I soon found this practice blessed my life in ways I hadn't expected. Although I intended it to be about giving back, I gained far more from it than I could give. In time, I recognized that I needed to attend the temple to learn and then I needed to go back out into the world to try to live the principles during the ensuing week. I would then return again to the temple the following week to evaluate how I had done. This weekly attendance, together with striving to repent more completely and really live the temple covenants, changed me and made me a better person. It blessed and strengthened my marriage and family as a result. It helped me have a much greater measure of the Spirit in my life. And it provided strength and refuge through some of the most difficult years of my life. In addition, the doctrines of the temple began to slowly distil upon my soul. My understanding and comprehension grew a little at a time.

Some people claim they learn something new every time they attend the temple. It certainly hasn't been that way for me. Sometimes I have found myself distracted or even bored. But as I have persisted in regular attendance and study, over time, insights have come. The temple has been an indispensable part of my spiritual growth and development. I will be eternally grateful to the Lord and to Joseph Smith for providing these ordinances and for the blessing they have been in my life. I hope your experience has been similar.

Despite all of this, by 2009, I found myself once again on a spiritual plateau—this time feeling like I had gained and received enough from the Lord and just needed to "endure to the end" as I was. I had great peace and felt content. Fortunately, the Lord knew how much I still needed to learn and brought some things to my attention that began a whole new level of learning, growth, and development. One of the key things that the endowment teaches us is the need to constantly seek after further light and knowledge. We should ask and watch for messengers sent from God. Wait for and receive messages from God in whatever form they take. God knows what you need and how to best supply the answers.

In my case, one of the messages came in the form of a book. It answered some questions and led to a renewed desire to press forward and receive for myself the blessings Joseph described and not to be content to wait to receive them in the next life or in my old age. My search to know the Lord resumed once again in earnest. Like Amulek, who was called many times but did not hear because of the cares of the world, the Lord has had to wake me up spiritually at several points in my life (see Alma 10:6). It is so easy for the cares of this world to take over our lives. Fortunately, the Lord in His mercy continues to work with us and give us additional chances. We need time to grow and develop.

An Abrahamic Test

IV. "When the Lord has thoroughly proved him, and finds that the man [or woman] is determined to serve Him at all hazards, then the man will find his calling and his election made sure."

In order to know our Lord, each of us must pass through some form of our own personal Gethsemane. Not in the sense of atoning like our Savior did, but in the sense of experiencing trials and burdens so great they may cause us to want to shrink at times. Part of these experiences occurred during the most difficult years of my life. There were a series of difficult trials that culminated in a test.

Our spiritual development inevitably involves sacrifice as we seek to know the Lord and to do His will in our lives. It is only through obedience and sacrifice that we obtain real faith. One part of the gospel of Abraham is that an Abrahamic type test will eventually be required of all who complete the path. Joseph Smith taught this truth in the *Lectures on Faith*:

> A religion that does not require the sacrifice of all things, never has power sufficient to produce the faith necessary unto life and salvation; for from the first existence of man, the faith necessary unto the enjoyment of life and salvation never could be obtained without the sacrifice of all earthly things. *It was through this sacrifice, and this only, that God*

> *has ordained that men should enjoy eternal life*; and it is through the medium of the sacrifice of all earthly things, that men do actually know that they are doing the things that are well pleasing in the sight of God.
>
> When a man has offered in sacrifice all that he has for the truth's sake, not even withholding his life, and believing before God that he has been called to make this sacrifice, because he seeks to do his will, he does know most assuredly that God does and will accept his sacrifice and offering, and that he has not nor will not seek his face in vain. Under these circumstances then, he can obtain the faith necessary for him to lay hold on eternal life. (Lecture 6:7; emphasis added.)

If you seek the blessings of the gospel of Abraham, at some point in your progression, the Lord will require a sacrifice of you, one which will be very personal and uniquely customized for you.

This is not something you can invent or offer up on your own. Nor will it be the same as is required for another person. What may be a great sacrifice for me might be easy for you and vice-a-versa. It will be something the Lord Himself requires you to lay upon the altar as you seek to do His will in your life. The sacrifice will be both a test and a blessing to you. The Lord will supply the test through the individual circumstances of your life as soon as you are ready. You may not even recognize it for what it is until after it is over. There is no other, easier way. Joseph continued:

> It is in vain for persons to fancy to themselves that they are heirs with those, or can be heirs with them, who have offered their all in sacrifice, and by this means obtained faith in God and favor with him so as to obtain eternal life, unless they in like manner offer unto him the same sacrifice, and through that offering obtain the knowledge that they are accepted of him. (Lecture 6:8)

The faith required for eternal life can only be obtained in this manner. You cannot obtain eternal life without this sacrifice! To drive the point home even further, he explained:

> Those who have not made this sacrifice to God, do not know that the course which they pursue is well pleasing in his sight; for whatever may be their belief or their opinion, it is a matter of doubt and uncertainty in their minds; and where doubt and uncertainty are, there faith is not, nor can it be. For doubt and faith do not exist in the same person at the same time. (Lecture 6:12)

Doubt and faith cannot exist together at the same time. You cannot have full confidence of receiving eternal life until you have made this sacrifice. Until then you must press forward, working out your salvation with fear and trembling before the Lord.

To be honest, this truth troubled me for a long time. I first read the *Lectures on Faith* while serving as a missionary. I wondered about this sacrifice and what would be required. I felt that I had sacrificed all things in leaving to serve a mission. I had given up my educational plans, car, job, girlfriend, family, and possessions. In a very real sense I had given up everything at that point in my life to serve the Lord. I wondered if that was all that was required or if there would be more in the future. I was afraid of what the Lord might ask and that I would not pass the test. You may have similar feelings upon learning this gospel requirement.

This sacrifice is a very personal matter between each individual and their Lord. It will likely be different for every person who seeks Christ. So it may be different for you than it was for me, but in my case, more was still required. The sacrifice that began on my mission eventually culminated in an Abrahamic type of test for me at the age of 48. My sacrifice was not in the magnitude of what Abraham experienced in offering up Isaac, but it was still extremely difficult for me. It came through the everyday circumstances of my life as I sought to come to the Lord and to do His will first and foremost. In truth, I didn't recognize the sacrifice for what it was until it was over. It manifested as part of the trials I went through at the time.

In hindsight, this sacrifice is not something that I should have feared. Though difficult, the Lord strengthens us. To reiterate, it is not just a test, but also a great blessing. There are things you learn from the experience that you cannot gain in any other way. That is why it is necessary. The Lord knows when you are ready and will provide it at the right time. It is not something you can invent or offer up on your own. It will be an experience customized by the Lord just for you. If such a test has not been given you, then it is because the Lord knows you are not yet prepared to face it. As soon as you are prepared, you will encounter it.

Calling and Election Made Sure

V. *"Then the man will find his calling and his election made sure".*

Following the offering of this sacrifice, the Lord accepts you and seals you his (see Mosiah 5:15). This seal is part of the intent of the second anointing or second endowment ordinances of the Church. However, as we discussed in the previous chapter, most members will never have access to these ordinances from the Church in their lifetimes. Fortunately, the scriptures make it clear that there is another way to receive this seal and that is directly from our Savior who is the keeper of the gate (see 2 Nephi 9:41).

A beautiful example of this in the scriptures concerns Alma the Elder. As a young man, Alma was the wicked apostate priest of King Noah. And yet he reached a point later in his life where the Lord said to him, "Thou art my servant; and I covenant with thee that thou shalt have eternal life" (Mosiah 26:20). This blessing didn't come to Alma because he held a high leadership position. It didn't come to him because he lived a life free of mistakes and regrets. And he wasn't perfect at the time he received this promise. It came because he had faith in the word of the Lord delivered by Abinadi. That testimony led Alma to repent and serve the Lord. Alma began seeking to do the Lord's will. Eventually he received this promise and blessing directly from the Lord. And it came very quietly as Alma went about his service.

The intent of this promise is to give a firm hope. Like faith, hope may start as a small seed but it can grow into something more concrete. In the fullest scriptural sense of the word, hope is not a flimsy wishy-washy thing like purchasing a lottery ticket and hoping the odds are in your favor. Faith and hope grow together. Both start as a small seed and reinforce one another along the path. Initially, both come by hearing and then acting upon the word of God. Hope sustains you during the period between receiving a promise from the Lord of a blessing and its eventual fulfillment.

A firmness of hope is obtained when God makes a promise directly to you by covenant. Because the Lord cannot lie and because He can see the end from the beginning, He can give us this "more sure word of prophecy" or a covenantal promise of eternal life. Though you may still have much left to learn and accomplish, the Lord gives you an assurance of the eventual outcome. The result of your mature faith is a secure, mature hope. In this way, these two principles are tied together.

Joseph Smith was outlining the path each must follow to obtain salvation. In the LDS faith, we sometimes make this concept of calling and election into something unattainable. We may believe it is reserved for apostles or upper Church leaders and not available to ordinary members. We may feel that it requires such perfection that virtually no one obtains it. We can come up with a million reasons why it does not apply to us individually. And yet Joseph includes it as a step on the path back.

Joseph admonished all of the Saints in his day to obtain it. His word still applies: "I would exhort you to go on and continue to call upon God until you make your calling and election sure for yourselves, by obtaining this more sure word of prophecy, and wait patiently for the promise until you obtain it."[42] In this quote it seems that Joseph anticipates the promise coming from God. Our Savior holds these keys and can make this promise and covenant to whom He wills, regardless of their access or lack of access to the second anointing or endowment ordinances administered in the temple. The scriptures testify that Christ alone is the keeper of the gate and that He employeth no servant there (see 2 Nephi 9:41). So, either way, at some point, Christ must be directly involved.

I share all of this with you as prelude to my testimony of the truth of the process that Joseph outlined and that we have been discussing. The path is real and available to even the least of the Saints, if we will give heed unto it. The result of the personal journey I have been describing in this chapter is that on April 30, 2013, the Lord gave me a promise of eternal life by covenant just as Joseph described and as Alma testified happened to him. It also happened in my life. I am not anyone important like Joseph or Alma, nor do I want to be. There is nothing significant about me or about my life. In fact, I have made a lot of mistakes and gotten many things wrong. I have never held a significant leadership position in the Church. I am just like many other ordinary members. But I believed and tried to follow the path that Joseph Smith outlined and can now add my own testimony that it is true and works.

I share this testimony very reluctantly. I would prefer to keep it to myself. By nature, I am a very private person so this is very uncomfortable for me. But even more, I am reluctant because I fear that some will misunderstand my intentions. The only reasons for including my experience is to, I hope, clear up some common misunderstandings concerning receiving your calling and election and that my story may help you in your own journey to receiving these same blessings. I am NOT trying to set myself up as an absolute authority, nor do I wish to attract any attention to myself. I do not matter here, but you do. I share this witness only by way of invitation for you to press forward until you receive the same blessing for yourself, if you have not already. My sincere hope and desire is that my testimony helps you in your own individual journey to Christ. If it does not, then please disregard it. In any case, do not misunderstand me. I am nothing but weak and prone to error.

In fact, when the Lord made this promise it came about in the ordinary course of a prayer and I had a hard time believing or accepting it at first, precisely because I know my own weakness. I was not perfect at the time and am not perfect today—not even close! There were things in my life I was and am still trying to work on and refine. After all of Nephi's great spiritual experiences, he still exclaimed, "O wretched man that I am" and sorrowed for his imperfections (2 Nephi 4:17). That is not false modesty on Nephi's part. I think he knew and understood how imperfect he still was even after everything he had experienced. It is that moment of Nephi's life that I relate to more than any other.

I have had far too much pride in my life. Some of that has come as a result of being a Mormon and really trying to live the gospel standards. When we feel self-righteous and better than others who are struggling, we are missing the heart of the gospel. I look back and cringe at many things in my life. I am grateful for the Lord's patience and mercy. So many times, I have been off course in subtle ways, despite my best efforts. Sometimes my progress seems so slow. I still get up every day and try to be a better person than I am. We owe the Lord the best we can give Him in our struggle to live the gospel. There is purpose in the growth, struggle, learning, and weakness we experience here. In the end, however, it is through Christ's grace and His merits that we are accepted. Our salvation is a gift. It is not something we earn but it is something we have to qualify ourselves to be able to receive.

If we had to be perfect before receiving our calling and election, no one would ever receive it. This idea is probably one of the most common misperceptions on this subject. Many believe you either have to be perfect or really, really darn close. We can even pull out a few quotes that seem to reinforce that idea. I thought the same thing for a long time. But perfection (or close to perfection) is not what is required. What is required is that we put the Lord first in our lives and that our faith be developed to the point that the Lord accepts us as His. We still continue to press forward on the journey even after receiving such a promise, but thereafter with the hope provided by the Lord that we will in fact finish the course. Look back at Joseph Smith's teaching of what is required: we have to be determined to serve God at all cost. When you do this, putting God first in your life, you are on a path that will eventually culminate in this blessing.

Because of my weakness, at first I refused to believe the Lord's words to me. I had a hard time accepting this blessing because I did not feel worthy of it yet. (The idea of near perfection is so ingrained that I doubted God's word and promise even when it came.) Furthermore, I felt that I had not yet passed a final Abrahamic test. When I raised this objection, the Lord simply told me that I would pass it when it came. He then asked me a question: "Is it not as easy to tell thee now as at some future time? Why do you doubt?" I didn't have a good answer for that.

This brings up another point we should discuss briefly. Joseph outlined certain steps on the path back to God. Each step is important, but the steps do not always occur in precisely the same order. For example, Lehi saw the Father and the Son in vision before sacrificing everything in leaving Jerusalem. In Lehi's case, the blessing came before the required sacrifice. Likewise, Joseph Smith returned to the presence of the Father and the Son in the First Vision, many years before his calling and election was made sure. So the required steps do not always manifest in the same sequence in each life.

I also want to clarify something else here. For me (others may be different) this was not an extraordinary, spectacular kind of spiritual experience. There were no angels or an audible voice or anything unusual. It came very quietly through the voice of the Spirit as I was praying one morning. It was very much like the experience that Alma records. As you will recall, Alma was praying about how to handle a situation that had come up with certain members in the Church.

Along with the answer to that problem came the promise of eternal life from the Lord (see Mosiah 26:13–20).

As I chose to believe the Lord's word, peace and joy filled my soul, though it was still a little hard for me to fully accept. In the months following this experience, there was nothing that magically changed in me. I was still the same person. There were and are no major sins in my life, but I still struggled with some of the same small things that had troubled me for years. In my heart, I had reached a point where I no longer desired to sin but I am still weak and prone to mistakes. You will still rely upon the Atonement, even after having your calling and election made sure by the Lord. You are not magically transformed by the experience. You will still learn and grow and stumble and make mistakes along the way. You will still have a lot to learn.

With this covenantal promise as reassurance, I continued to press forward, seeking our Lord. About a year and a half later, I passed through my Abrahamic test. The specifics of that trial are not important. It came about as part of the experiences I was going through at the time as I sought to put the Lord's will first in my life. Again, it is not that we need to prove ourselves to the Lord. He already knows what we will do and knows the end from the beginning. The trial is given to help us learn. It is, in fact, a great blessing.

It was not until nearly a month after the test that one evening, with the help of the Spirit, I recognized it for what it was and realized with joy that I had passed. At that moment, the Lord reiterated that my calling and election was made sure and reminded me that He had previously told me I would pass. When I later asked, He gave me discretion as to when and where I share these experiences. I have been very reluctant to share them at all. I record them here only by way of testimony that it is possible for an ordinary member of the Church to receive these blessings.

Please do not question your personal salvation all of your life. Seek Christ until you, too, find Him and receive this promise for yourself. The endowment teachings show the path we must walk. Work on living the covenants more fully in your life. Doing so gradually helps to transform our character. Seek to have the Holy Ghost always. Consider how the temple endowment relates to Joseph's statement about the path back to God. You must not only come to understand but also to live your endowment. Ask the Lord to show you what you still lack. Ask Him for true messengers to guide you in your path. Press forward until you obtain the promise from Him. This is the seal that you still need upon your temple ordinances. It is the Holy Spirit of Promise. It is a tender mercy from the Lord and flows from His grace.

The Second Comforter

VI. "Then it will be his privilege to receive the other Comforter."

We can have the privilege / blessing / tender mercy of receiving Christ. This blessing, like our salvation, comes from Christ's grace—not from our merits. Our calling and election is not the end of the path. To complete our endowment, we must also receive the Second Comforter. Joseph clarified exactly what he meant by this statement.

> Now what is this other Comforter? It is no more nor less than the Lord Jesus Christ Himself; and this is the sum and substance of the whole matter; that when any man [or woman] obtains this last Comforter, he will have the personage of Jesus Christ to attend him, or appear unto him from time to time, and even He will manifest the Father unto him, and they will take up their abode with him, and the visions of the heavens will be opened unto him, and the Lord will teach him face to face, and he may have a perfect knowledge of the mysteries of the Kingdom of God.[43]

This appearance has several purposes, according to Joseph's explanation:

"Jesus Christ will attend to him, or appear unto him from time to time." The Lord has a ministry to perform that He reserves to Himself. Part of that is to teach us and give us further instructions (see 2 Nephi

32:6). The temple endowment reinforces this idea. At the conclusion of the ceremony, we are presented at the veil in order to learn something from the Lord. In the scriptural record, those who entered the Lord's presence, e.g. Joseph Smith, Nephi, and the brother of Jared, to name a few, also sought answers from Him.

"He will manifest the Father unto him." Christ will manifest the Father. A beautiful order is set out. If we will receive and hearken to the Holy Ghost, it will bring us back into the presence of Christ. Christ will then prepare us to return to the Father. There is a gospel progression by which we are put back into contact with each member of the Godhead in our journey home (see also D&C 84:47–50). "And he that receiveth me receiveth my Father; and he that receiveth my Father receiveth my Father's kingdom; therefore all that my Father hath shall be given unto him" (D&C 84:37–38).

"And they will take up their abode with him." An abode is a house or home. In part, this is referring to becoming a part of God's family. The "Father teacheth him of the covenant" (D&C 84:48). We become sons and daughters of God by receiving a covenant from the Father (see Moses 6:68). This is why Christ must introduce us back to the Father. The sealings performed in the temple are done in the celestial realm following the endowment ordinances because they foreshadow or testify of this greater reality.

"And the visions of the heavens will be opened unto him." The Book of Mormon alludes to these blessings: "Therefore, I would that ye should be steadfast and immovable, always abounding in good works, that Christ, the Lord God Omnipotent, may seal you his, *that you may be brought to heaven*, that you may have everlasting salvation and eternal life" (Mosiah 5:15, emphasis added). The Doctrine and Covenants spells them out even more clearly, speaking of those who will be heirs of celestial glory: "These are they *who have come* unto Mount Zion, and unto the city of the living God, the heavenly place, the holiest of all. These are *they who have come* to an innumerable company of angels, to the general assembly and Church of Enoch, and of the Firstborn. These are they whose names are written in heaven." (D&C 76:66–68; emphasis added. This scripture is referring to those who have been taken to heaven during their mortal existence.)

"The Lord will teach him face to face." Such persons know things that are unlawful to be uttered (see D&C 76:115). Joseph Smith once stated that if we could gaze into heaven for five minutes we would know more than we would by reading everything written on the subject.[44] He also stated, "the only way to obtain truth and wisdom, is not to ask it from books, but to go to God in prayer, and obtain divine teaching."[45] There are some things that we can learn in no other way.

"He [or she] may have a perfect knowledge of the mysteries of the Kingdom of God." The end result of all of this is to help us gain a perfect knowledge of God and His kingdom. This is the endowment of wisdom, intelligence, and power that the ancient Saints possessed and that Joseph wanted all to receive. The only way to acquire such knowledge is directly from God. Those who gain it are prevented from sharing the full extent of what they know but rather seek to invite others to come and obtain the same. "Neither is man capable to make them known, for they are only to be seen and understood by the power of the Holy Spirit, which God bestows on those who love him, and purify themselves before him; to whom he grants this privilege of seeing and knowing for themselves" (D&C 76:116–117).

In all of this, please recognize that the timing of these blessings is largely up to the Lord. We seek to qualify ourselves, but the blessings come "in his own time, and in his own way, and according to his own will" (D&C 88:68).

Conclusion

We are each invited to receive the blessings discussed in this chapter for ourselves. The temple endowment is intended to prepare us. Despite all of this, we still sometimes hear cautions voiced in the Church against the mysteries. As well intended as this advice may be, it is anti-scriptural and anti-prophetic.

Joseph counseled, "The Savior has the words of eternal life. Nothing else can profit us. . . . I advise all to go on to perfection, and search deeper and deeper into the mysteries of Godliness."[46] The Book of Mormon echoes his advice: "He that will not harden his heart, to him is given the greater portion of the word, until it is given unto him to know the mysteries of God until he know them in full" (Alma 12:10). The converse is also true. "And they that will harden their hearts, to them is given the lesser portion of the word, until they know nothing concerning his mysteries; and then they are taken captive by the devil, and led by his will down to destruction" (Alma 12:11).

When Joseph taught that we cannot be saved in ignorance, the kind of knowledge he was referring to are the things we have discussed in this chapter. When we believe that the basics are enough, we are selling ourselves short of what God is willing to give us, and we will eventually come to regret it. Joseph further testified: "It is the first principle of the Gospel to know for a certainty the Character of God, and to know that we may converse with him as one man converses with another."[47] The scriptures echo these truths. "And this is life eternal, that they might know thee the only true God, and Jesus Christ, whom thou hast sent" (John 17:3).

Despite how plainly this is taught, we have a hard time believing that it applies to us as individuals. That is part of our "veil of unbelief" which we must rend (see Ether 4:15, also verse 13). Joseph Smith explained the process as clearly and plainly as he could in the statement we have parsed in this chapter. Nephi outlined the same process at the end of his record (2 Nephi 32). The temple endowment likewise testifies of and prepares us to receive these things.

We have been given multiple witnesses of these truths through three primary sources: in the Book of Mormon from those who received these blessings, from Joseph Smith and Sidney Rigdon's testimony of these things as modern-day witnesses (see D&C 76:22), and through the ordinances of the temple endowment (see D&C 84:19–22). We reject or disbelieve these witnesses at our own peril. We should be seeking after these blessings instead of fearing them.

In the previous chapter, we discussed the endowment ceremony as the Elias portion of our ordinances or that portion preparing us for a greater revelation of God. The blessings we have discussed in this chapter are those greater revelations. The Elias portion is associated with the blessings of the gospel of Abraham. We sometimes think that is what we possess as a people, but Abraham had a far greater knowledge of the gospel than we do. The gospel that Abraham received was given to him when he was redeemed and brought into Jehovah's presence (see Abraham 2:6–12). It included a greater knowledge of the priesthood, of the beginning of creation, and the planets and the stars (see Abraham 1:31), along with a detailed knowledge of the premortal life and Abraham's role there (see Abraham 3). The temple endowment gives us glimpses of these things, as though through a glass darkly (see 1 Corinthians 1:12), but then also invites us to pass through the veil to receive the full, unobstructed view for ourselves.

Homework

1. Obtain and study the *Lectures on Faith.* Faith is a critical key to our progression along the path discussed in this chapter.

2. Work at learning to better recognize and listen to the voice of the Spirit in your daily life. I experience the Holy Ghost in several different ways and it is probably the same for you, but the most frequent and common is as a "still, small voice" or quiet thoughts that enter my mind. Sometimes I recognize those thoughts as being distinctly not my own. At other times, they are so subtle that I have to pause to pay attention or to ask for a confirmation. Learning to hear and heed the voice of the Spirit is crucial in our spiritual progression. It is one of the things the Lord says separates the righteous from the wicked (see D&C 84:52–53). How often we hear the Lord's voice is perhaps a good spiritual thermometer

for each of us. You may wish to keep a separate spiritual journal of personal revelations and how you followed them. That practice can be a helpful tool in learning to better communicate with God.

CHAPTER 4

THE FULNESS OF THE PRIESTHOOD

And there were many, exceedingly great many, who were made pure and entered into the rest of the Lord their God.
—Alma 13:12

IN THE FIRST TWO CHAPTERS we discussed the keys delivered by Moses and Elias as a framework for understanding the expanded temple ordinances given in Nauvoo. To review and summarize quickly: We are gathered out of Babylon and invited to join Israel through baptism and the initiatory ordinances. These rites are associated with our spiritual re-birth and constitute the Moses portion.

Next, we are given the Aaronic and Melchizedek parts of the endowment. These, together with the temple marriage sealing, form the Elias portion of our ordinances and are given to prepare us for a greater revelation of God. They prove and test us and outline the path and the covenants we must follow in our search to know Christ. We receive instructions and blessings, both to assist us in our journey and for the future. These ordinances are associated with our spiritual growth and maturation. Everything we receive up to this point is given conditionally, hinging upon our faithfulness.

We are promised that at some point the Lord will accept us and make our calling and election sure. This is sometimes referred to as the Holy Spirit of Promise (see D&C 88:3–4). We are invited in the endowment, to come and converse with the Lord through the veil.

And we are given information in the endowment ceremony that points to some of the blessings we may receive from Him.

Eventually, we must actually make the journey through the veil. We are invited to do this in mortality. Elder Bruce R. McConkie testified plainly, "The purpose of the endowment in the house of the Lord is to prepare and sanctify his saints so they will be able to see his face, *here and now*, as well as to bear the glory of his presence in the eternal worlds."[48] This is consistent with Joseph Smith's teaching that "the spirit of Elias is to prepare the way for a greater revelation of God."[49]

Joseph Smith also taught: "No man can be the minister of Jesus Christ, except he has the testimony of Jesus & this is the Spirit of Prophecy. Whenever Salvation has been administered it has been by Testimony."[50] He further clarified that the "testimony of Jesus" means that we are sealed by the Holy Spirit of Promise or, in other words, our calling and election has been made sure.[51] The testimony of Jesus is not simply our testimony of Him. It is also receiving Jesus' testimony to us that we are His. That testimony is the Holy Spirit of Promise.

We then reviewed some of the things Joseph said we could expect once our calling and election has been made sure and we pierce the veil. These last things pertain to the Elijah portion of our endowment and prepare us to more fully minister to others. The Elijah portion involves receiving a fulness of the priesthood and necessarily requires Christ. In this chapter, we will explore these concepts further. The purpose here is not to fully explain or develop them, but merely to introduce the ideas, and to help point out that there is more here than we may realize.

Perhaps some may feel that these things are unnecessary. And for a time in my life, I felt content with what I had received and was not aware of how much I still lacked and how much more the Lord was willing to give. When it comes to these topics, it would be best to approach the Lord as little children, seeking to be taught rather than assuming that we already understand and know enough. I am very much still learning and growing and seeking further light and knowledge from the Lord.

In some ways, I would have preferred to leave these subjects alone, but it was important to include a few thoughts here in the hopes that they will be useful in making others aware of how much more is available to us, if we will seek for it. Through the remainder of this chapter, it will be helpful for you to keep in mind the ceremony at the temple veil and the information you are given there.

The Elijah Portion of our Endowment

A few months prior to his death, Joseph Smith gave further instructions related to this topic that are worth careful consideration: "The spirit, power and calling of Elijah is that ye [you] have power to hold the keys of the revelations, ordinances, oracles, powers and endowments *of the fulness of the Melchizedek Priesthood* and of the Kingdom of God on the earth and to receive, obtain and perform all the ordinances belonging to the Kingdom of God even unto the sealing of the hearts of the fathers unto the children and the hearts of the children unto the fathers even those who are in heaven."[52]

When you were anointed to become a priest or a priestess in the temple, what does that really mean? Have you ever stopped to think about it? Is that similar to a priest in the Aaronic Priesthood or a high priest in the Melchizedek Priesthood or is it something altogether different? Are the temple ordinances pointing us to something greater? When might such an ordination occur? And how would it happen? How would you prepare for it? Is that ordination reserved for the next life or is it to be received here?

The second anointing or second endowment was sometimes referred to as receiving a fulness of the priesthood. In part those ordinances were intended to confer such an ordination.[53] Given that, why were they administered frequently in the early part of the Church's history but rarely today?[54] How could one obtain a fulness of the priesthood today? What is the temple trying to teach us about priesthood?

And how does this tie into the gospel of Abraham that we discussed in the last chapter? These questions are worthy of our careful consideration, study, and inquiring for answers from the Lord. This chapter will give you some background and some things to ponder as you search.

Joseph Smith first introduced the endowment ceremony in the room over his red brick store in May of 1842, about two years prior to his death. Church history records that he spent the day in company with several others,

> Instructing them *in the principles and order of the Priesthood*, attending to washings, anointings, endowments and the *communication of keys* pertaining to the Aaronic Priesthood, and so on to the highest order of the Melchizedek Priesthood, setting forth the order pertaining to the Ancient of Days, and all those plans and principles by which any one is enabled to secure the fulness of those blessings which have been prepared for the Church of the Firstborn, and come up and abide in the presence of the Eloheim in the eternal worlds. In this council was instituted the ancient order of things for the first time in these last days.[55]

Pause here for a moment to consider carefully this description of the endowment's purpose. It is different from Brigham Young's description about passing angelic sentinels quoted at the onset of the endowment ceremony today. This statement provides us with some important clues to Joseph's purpose and makes it clear that one was to teach us more about the priesthood.

Before digging further into what the temple is trying to communicate, let's step back and consider the topics of priesthood and priesthood keys in a simple way that may give us a fresh look at them.

Priesthood

What exactly is priesthood? If you study the scriptures, the endowment, and the teachings of Joseph Smith, it becomes apparent that priesthood involves more than the simplified explanations we often give. Perhaps one way to better understand this topic is to break the word priesthood down. The word *priesthood* is a combination of two separate words: priest and hood.

In considering the first part—priest—we confront the question: what is a priest in the temple sense of that word? The Church offices of deacon, teacher, priest, elder, seventy, high priest, and apostle are offices within the Church. They are not separate priesthoods. Please do not confuse a priest in the Aaronic priesthood or even a high priest in the Church with the anointing to become a priest or priestess in the temple. The temple is talking about eventually receiving a fulness of the priesthood, which is a very different thing.

One basic scriptural definition of a priest is found in John the Baptist's words when he restored the Aaronic Priesthood. He stated: "Upon you my fellow-servants" (D&C 13:1). A priest or a priestess is therefore a servant, or one who serves God. Let's use that definition as the basis for our understanding of priesthood. If you are anointed a priest or a priestess, you are called to serve. "He that is ordained of God and sent forth, the same is appointed to be the greatest, notwithstanding *he is the least and the servant of all*" (D&C 50:26; emphasis added). The anointing we receive to become such in the temple is probationary. It is an invitation to practice, prepare, grow, and to become worthy of something potentially much greater.

The priesthood is not given as a means to control others. "No power or influence can or ought to be maintained by virtue of the priesthood" (D&C 121:41). None. The priesthood is not given to maintain power or influence. As soon as that occurs, priesthood becomes priestcraft. You can only wield influence by persuasion, long-suffering, gentleness and meekness, and genuine love (see D&C 121:41). "When we undertake to . . . exercise control or dominion or compulsion upon the souls of the children of men, in any degree of unrighteousness, behold, the heavens withdraw themselves; the Spirit of the Lord is grieved; and when it is withdrawn, Amen to the priesthood or the authority of that man" (D&C 121:37). The Lord could not be any clearer on this point. Despite the warnings, almost all men will fail (see D&C 121:39–40).

With this definition of a priest or priestess as a servant in mind, we then turn to the second part: what is a *hood*? There are several dictionary definitions of the word. A *hood* can be a modifier to indicate a condition or a group. For example, mother*hood* denotes women who share the common trait of being a mother. Neighbor*hood* likewise indicates a group; we see the same with fatherhood, brotherhood, or sisterhood. So, by combining this sense of the word hood with the word priest, we find that the word *priesthood* indicates a fellowship.

But a hood can also be an article of clothing—something that covers our head and neck. Like a mantle of charity, this definition also fits. My current ward calling is with the teacher's quorum. When I teach the young men a lesson on priesthood, I try to help them see that priesthood should be a way of life. It should cover everything else and all other aspects of life. It is so much more than just showing up once a week on Sunday and performing a few duties. We should be living as servants of God, in joint fellowship with other fellow servants.

Obviously, priesthood is a more complex topic than we have described here and is well worth studying further in the scriptures and in the teachings of Joseph Smith. It has more depth than we generally discuss in the Church. For example, in the book of Abraham, we learn that a knowledge of the beginning of creation and also of the stars was part of the original priesthood held by the ancient patriarchs (see Abraham 1:31). Why would that specific knowledge pertain to priesthood? And note that this question is but one example of the many facets of priesthood we could discuss.

Despite the fact that priesthood is a vast topic, at its heart is service and fellowship. That is why we have defined it simply here. Notice too that this basic definition can also fit and accommodate Satan's priesthoods. Those involved therein, serve their master and also form a sort of fellowship. Here we are focused solely on God's priesthood.

Three Levels of Priesthood

In Nauvoo, Joseph taught that "all priesthood is Melchizedek but there are different portions or degrees of it."[56] In the beginning the priesthood was unified and called the "Holy Priesthood, after the Order of the Son of God" (D&C 107:3). This original priesthood was later named Melchizedek Priesthood (see D&C 107:4). When Joseph stated that all priesthood is Melchizedek, he was referring to the fact that all priesthood is part of this greater whole. Later this unified, singular priesthood was divided into portions or degrees.

Today there are, in fact, three levels of priesthood or "three grand orders of priesthood."[57] Joseph labeled these three levels of priesthood as Aaronic, Melchizedek, and patriarchal. We are familiar with Aaronic and Melchizedek Priesthoods but less so with what is meant by patriarchal priesthood. These labels have created some confusion among LDS scholars and even among General Authorities as to exactly what patriarchal priesthood entails. There lingers today disagreement over how to resolve the topic.

In my view, it is best to forget the labels and simply recognize that there are three levels of priesthood, and that all three divisions are part of a greater unified whole. In the mainstream Church we see the first two levels, the Aaronic and Melchizedek Priesthoods, functioning (see D&C 107:1). In the temple we find hints and clues as to the highest or third level of priesthood. This is the fulness of the priesthood. Joseph instructed, "Go to and finish the temple, and God will fill it with power, and you will then receive more knowledge concerning this priesthood."[58] This was another clear indication that this highest priesthood is tied to God and to the temple.

When we are anointed to become a priest and a priestess unto God, we are anointed to eventually receive this highest level or fulness of priesthood. Joseph's discourse confirms this, stating: "Those holding the fulness of the Melchizedek Priesthood are kings and priests [or queens and priestesses] of the Most High God, holding the keys of power and blessings."[59]

So how does one obtain a fulness of the priesthood? Joseph answers that question as well: "If a man gets a fulness of the priesthood of God he has to get it in the same way that Jesus Christ obtained it, and that was by keeping all the commandments and obeying all the ordinances of the house of the Lord."[60] That tells us what must be done in order to qualify, but how would one receive such an ordination? We find a plain answer in the Book of Mormon.

Priesthood in the Book of Mormon

The Book of Mormon has some very interesting things to teach about priesthood. For example, in the early chapters we find Lehi acting in the role of a priest in building an altar and offering sacrifices (see 1 Nephi 2:7, 5:7, 7:22, etc.). This is very curious as the priesthood at that time was restricted, not just to males, but specifically to the Levites, and Lehi was a descendant of Manasseh (see Alma 10:3). He, therefore, was from the wrong tribe and could not have received a priesthood ordination while in Jerusalem.

Lehi is also an interesting example because he entered into the presence of the Father and the Son in the first chapter of the Book of Mormon. We learn from modern revelation that for a man to enter the Father's presence requires Melchizedek Priesthood (see D&C 84:21–22). How did Lehi return to the Father's presence without priesthood when Latter-day revelation indicates that is not possible? We also find examples of Lehi, Nephi, Moroni, and others in the Book of Mormon using the sealing power (see, for example, 2 Nephi 33:15; Ether 3:22, 4:5; Moroni 10:2; 2 Nephi 4:5–7). It is clear from these and other scriptures that priesthood is a more complex topic than we sometimes recognize.

Fortunately, Joseph Smith provided us with some help. As for how Lehi obtained the priesthood, Joseph Smith taught, "all the prophets had the Melchizedek priesthood and were ordained by God himself."[61] This is a very interesting statement considering that in Jerusalem during the time of Lehi and many of the other Old Testament prophets, the Aaronic Priesthood was all that functioned under the direction of the Levites. Moses and the Melchizedek Priesthood had been taken from Israel centuries earlier (see D&C 84:25). Despite this obvious limitation to the group, the fulness of the priesthood was still available to individuals who rose up to receive it directly from God. Lehi is one example of these. Our Savior would obviously have been another. He was from the tribe of Judah and therefore also not eligible for the priesthood under the existing hierarchy. It is one of the reasons that the rulers and leaders of his day continually questioned his authority and where he had obtained it.

Alma confirms these teachings of Joseph Smith. He gave the single greatest discourse on priesthood in the Book of Mormon (see Alma 13). He delivered it to a wicked, apostate group who would ultimately reject his words and be destroyed. Alma began by teaching the same thing Joseph Smith did, namely that the Father Himself ordained these priests in the past. "And I would that ye should remember that the Lord God [the Father] ordained priests, after his holy order, which was after the order of his Son, to teach these things unto the people" (Alma 13:1).

A priest after the holy order of God after the order of His Son is what we are anointed to *become* in the temple. It is not what we are given there, but we are pointed to it. Alma 13 is discussing a fulness of the priesthood. It is not the same thing as a priest in the Aaronic Priesthood or a high priest today. Those are offices in the Church.

This can be confusing because of the term high priest. From Moses to Christ, there was only one high priest in Israel and he was the head of the Aaronic or Levitical Priesthood. Today, we associate the office of high priest with the Melchizedek Priesthood and we have many high priests in the Church. But that is not what Alma is referring to in his discourse. Alma is teaching about the fulness of the priesthood or a priest in the temple sense of the word. And he tells us how the fulness is obtained. The Lord God (Alma meant the Father) ordained these priests (see Alma 13:1). That is an incredible revelation!

Those called to this Holy Order of God are called because of their exceeding faith and repentance and their righteousness before God (see Alma 13:10). "Therefore they were called after this holy order, and were sanctified and their garments were washed white through the blood of the Lamb. Now they, after being sanctified by the Holy Ghost, having their garments made white, being pure and spotless before God, could not look upon sin save it were with abhorrence; and there were many, exceedingly great many, who were made pure and entered into the rest of the Lord their God" (Alma 13:11–12). Now if you understand the phrase entering "the rest of the Lord," you know what Alma is teaching these people.

Moreover, the whole point of Alma's discourse is to invite his audience to receive the same blessings for themselves. "And now, my brethren, I would that ye should humble yourselves before God, and bring forth fruit meet for repentance, *that ye may also enter into that rest*" (Alma 13:13, emphasis added). This is astonishing doctrine, particularly when we remember that Alma is teaching a wicked group of apostates. It is, therefore, not a topic that is too holy or off limits, but rather something that we should understand.

How did Alma know this? Where did he get his understanding of this priesthood? Remember this is Alma the Younger who was a wicked young man prior to being called to repentance by an angel. By the time of Alma 13, he is much older and has dedicated himself to serving the Lord. He was ordained and consecrated as a high priest over the Church by his father (see Alma 5:3). That was his original ordination. But then later, here in chapter 13, he gives a discourse on the fulness of the priesthood or the Holy Order after the Son of God, and of entering into the rest of the Lord, and receiving an ordination directly from the Father. How did Alma obtain this knowledge? The answer is in verse 9. Alma simply declares, "And thus it is. Amen." (Alma 13:9). Here Alma subtly reveals something about himself. He understands this doctrine because he has lived it. He is one of these priests after the Holy Order of God. Alma received his original ordination and calling from his father, but then went on to eventually receive "power in his priesthood" or a fulness of priesthood by also obtaining this final ordination and covenant directly from the Father. Alma is a high priest in our temple sense of that word.

We learn more about these priests and about a fulness of the priesthood from the Joseph Smith Translation of Genesis which gives us more detail about Melchizedek:

> 26. Now Melchizedek was a man of faith, who wrought righteousness; and when a child he feared God, and stopped the mouths of lions, and quenched the violence of fire.
>
> 27. And thus, having been approved of God, *[Melchizedek was approved because of his exceeding faith just as Alma taught; notice too that he manifested faith prior to his ordination]* he was ordained an high priest after the order of the covenant which God made with Enoch, *[see Moses 6:26–39, for the example of Enoch]*
>
> 28. It being after the order of the Son of God; which order came, not by man, nor the will of man *[this fulness of priesthood does not come because of an ordination by another mortal]*; neither by father nor mother *[it does not come by lineage or based upon heritage]*; neither by beginning of days nor end of years *[once obtained, such a calling is meant to be eternal]*; but of God *[it can only be obtained directly from God as the next verse indicates]*;
>
> 29. And it was delivered unto men by the calling of his own voice, according to his own will, unto as many as believed on his name. *[This is how this fulness is obtained—by God's own voice. It is thus a very private matter between an individual and the Lord.]*
>
> 30. For God having sworn unto Enoch and unto his seed with an oath by himself; that every one being ordained after his order and calling should have power, by faith, to break mountains, to divide the seas, to dry up waters, to turn them out of their course;

> 31. To put at defiance the armies of nations, to divide the earth, to break every band, to stand in the presence of God; to do all things according to his will, according to his command *[those holding this power only use it at God's command and in accordance with His will]* (JST Genesis 14:26–31).

These last two verses show us how we can know who holds this priesthood. Those who hold it are meek and humble. They often do not say that they possess it. But the fact that they do gets demonstrated in their lives through these types of miracles. If you want to know who held this fulness of the priesthood in the past, then look for these types of events in the scriptural record of their lives.

We can know Alma held this type of power, not just from his inference in chapter 13, but because we see it exercised in his life. Only those who submit their own will to God's are fit to hold such power. We see an example of this when, as a result of their preaching, Alma and Amulek are forced to watch the martyrdom of their believers by fire. In the face of that awful scene, Amulek wanted to use the power to save them (see Alma 14:10). But Alma refused: "The Spirit constraineth me that I must not stretch forth my hand; for behold the Lord receiveth them up unto himself in glory" (Alma 14:11). Alma would not use the power the Lord had given him when it was not His will to do so.

We see the same principle in Nephi's life when he broke the bands which would have bound him to his death (1 Nephi 7:17), but then later was subject to the bands which tied him to the mast (1 Nephi 18:12). In one instance, he was permitted to use the power he had been given and in the other he was not. He suffered patiently when it was in accordance with the Lord's plan and purposes.

Alma and Amulek likewise suffered for their testimony (see Alma 14:14–26). Some suffering is generally required of those who receive this calling and fulness of priesthood because of the wickedness of the world. In the end, however, Alma and Amulek were permitted to exercise their power and their bands were broken, the prison tumbled to the earth, and they walked free (see Alma 14:26–29). Breaking these bands was one of the signs listed and is therefore evidence of Alma's calling to this fulness of priesthood (see JST Genesis 14:31). We see further evidence when he cursed Korihor (see Alma 30:49–50), and again when Alma was translated (see Alma 45:19). Translation was another sign of this priesthood (see JST Genesis 14:32).

Nephi, the son of Helaman, is another great example from the Book of Mormon (see Helaman 10). He served the Lord diligently with great faithfulness, seeking first and foremost the Lord's will above all else. As a result of this, the Lord declared to him:

> Behold, thou art Nephi, and I am God. Behold, I declare it unto thee in the presence of mine angels, that ye shall have power over this people, and shall smite the earth with famine, and with pestilence, and destruction, according to the wickedness of this people. Behold, I give unto you power, that whatsoever ye shall seal on earth shall be sealed in heaven; and whatsoever ye shall loose on earth shall be loosed in heaven; and thus shall ye have power among this people. And thus, if ye shall say unto this temple it shall be rent in twain, it shall be done. And if ye shall say unto this mountain. Be thou cast down and become smooth, it shall be done (Helaman 10:6–9).

Nephi is given this power and at the same time told the purpose for which he shall use it. We see him later persuade the Lord to replace the war with a famine to give the people time to repent (Helaman 11:4). Nephi sought the welfare of their souls. He interceded on their behalf to perhaps save some few. Such priests ordained to this order, like the Son of God, seek to bless and intercede on behalf of others.

The Temple's Invitation to Prepare

Returning to Alma's discourse, we learn that these priests were "called with a holy calling, and ordained with a holy ordinance" (Alma 13:8). This basic description is further expanded by Alma later in the same chapter: "Now these ordinances were given after this manner, that thereby the people might look forward on the Son of God, it being a type of his order, or it being his order, and this that they might look forward to him for a remission of their sins, that they might enter into the rest of the Lord" (Alma 13:16).

This verse provides us with an excellent description of our temple ordinances and their purpose. From it, we can determine that our endowment ceremony will, first, teach us more about the Son of God and, second, will either contain His order or a type of His order (see Alma 13:16). A type is a reflection, shadow, model, or representation of something greater. It is not the actual thing but teaches you about the real thing. Alma teaches that there are ordinances that are the actual induction into the Holy Order after the Son of God and there are ordinances that are only a type of that order but are not the actual order. A type would be given as instruction and preparation for the real thing, which could potentially follow. This is what we are being given in the temple. The ordinances thereof are a type designed to prepare us to one day receive actual power and a fulness of priesthood from the Lord. The conclusion of the endowment ceremony at the veil plainly teaches us that receiving the real thing will involve the Lord directly. It truly comes not by man, nor will of man, nor by father or mother, but of God (see JST Genesis 14:28).

Joseph Smith knew and understood this doctrine of the priesthood. Like the ancient prophets we have discussed, Joseph also held it and had obtained it from God. Like Alma, Joseph also wanted to invite and prepare others to receive the same. This is amply testified to in his sermons.[62] But it can be summarized simply by his statement: "If a man gets the fulness of God he has to get [it] in the same way that Jesus Christ obtained it & that was by keeping all the ordinances of the house of the Lord."[63]

Now, consider how this process is tied together in both the temple and in the oath and covenant of the priesthood, described in section

84 of the Doctrine and Covenants. It is quoted below along with a possible temple interpretation:

> 33. For whoso is faithful unto the obtaining these two priesthoods of which I have spoken, and the magnifying their calling *[think of the "calling" and invitation you receive in the temple initiatory. Magnifying that calling eventually involves receiving the fulness of the priesthood]*, are sanctified by the Spirit unto the renewing of their bodies *[how does that occur? Is it here and now, or in the resurrection? Does this also tie to the fulfillment of the initiatory blessings?]*
>
> 34. They become the sons of Moses and of Aaron *[both Moses and Aaron were the "sons of Levi" and are here associated with the Aaronic or Levitical priesthood]* and the seed of Abraham *[who is the father of the righteous and is associated with the spirit of Elias or preparation for a greater revelation of God]*, and the church and kingdom, and the elect of God *[Church and kingdom in the fullest sense refers to the Church of the Firstborn—those who are kings and priests and queens and priestesses. Here we see the Elijah portion (see D&C 76:54–56).]*
>
> 35. And also all they who receive this priesthood receive me, saith the Lord *[We must seek Christ until we receive Him. This is why Joseph teaches that once our calling and election is made sure we can expect the Lord to attend to us from time to time. One purpose of this priesthood is to allow men to stand in the presence of God (see JST Genesis 14:31);]*
>
> 36. For he that receiveth my servants receiveth me; *[Receiving God's servants is taught in the endowment as a necessary step which Adam and Eve took.]*
>
> 37. And he that receiveth me receiveth my Father *[This is part of Christ's ministry once He has brought you through the veil as Joseph testified: "and even He will manifest the Father";]*
>
> 38. And he that receiveth my Father receiveth my Father's kingdom; therefore all that my Father hath shall be given unto him *[Therefore receiving a fulness of the priesthood*

> *necessarily involves the Father. "And the Father teacheth him of the covenant" (D&C 84:48). The fulness is obtained from the Father just as Alma testified (see Alma 13:1).]*
>
> 39. And this is according to the oath and covenant which belongeth to the priesthood. *[A type or testimony of this ordination is given in the endowment, but actually obtaining it involves receiving, first, the servants or angelic ministers and, then, the ministry of the Son. All of these scriptures, Joseph's teachings, and the temple ceremony tie together and reinforce one another.]*
>
> 40. Therefore, all those who receive the priesthood *[meaning the fulness, becoming a priest as we are anointed to become in the temple]*, receive this oath and covenant of my Father which he cannot break, neither can it be moved. But whoso breaketh this covenant after he hath received it, and altogether turneth therefrom, shall not have forgiveness of sins in this world nor in the world to come *[to do so is the sin against the Holy Ghost because they have come to know the Godhead. If they reject this, once it is received, they become sons of Perdition by their willful rebellion.]*
>
> 41. And wo unto all those who come not unto this priesthood *[because we have been invited and called through the temple to receive it, but we have failed to rise up and do so. We have wasted a precious opportunity in mortality]* (D&C 84:33–41).

Joseph learned through the vision of the degrees of glory more about those who receive a fulness of the priesthood: "They are they who are the Church of the Firstborn. They are they into whose hands the Father has given all things—They are they who are priests and kings, who have received of his fulness, and of his glory; And are priests of the Most High, after the order of Melchizedek, which was after the order of Enoch, which was after the order of the Only Begotten Son" (D&C 76:54–57).

We may receive an ordination to the priesthood in the Church. It should be clear from these scriptures, however, that our ordination as an elder or a high priest in the Church is not the same as the fulness of the priesthood or becoming a priest after the Holy Order of the Son. We receive an invitation to the fulness of the priesthood, or to become a priest after the order of the Son of God, in the temple. But as Joseph, and the temple testify, actually receiving priesthood power and blessings can only come directly from the Lord. Despite such glorious blessings being offered, we are warned that "many are called but few are chosen" (D&C 121:40). Most will fail to receive what the Lord offers.

Why We Fail to Receive the Fulness

Men, like Melchizedek, Enoch, or Moses, who hold a fulness of the priesthood are relatively rare in this world. They are those whom God can trust not to abuse or misuse His power and authority. They, like their Master, are meek and lowly in heart (see Numbers 12:3). Most do not even proclaim the power and authority they have been given. Indeed, you often have to look in the scriptural record for the fruits of this priesthood to be manifest in their lives to even know that they possess it.

Such individuals are the opposite of those who come among us foolishly proclaiming their own greatness and wanting others to follow them. Anyone going around boasting about possessing this type of priesthood most assuredly does not have it. They are engaged in priestcraft—which is the polar opposite of priesthood. Priestcraft seeks for recognition, acclaim, honor, and monetary gain and often does so by preaching a message that is popular with and flattering to the listeners (see 2 Nephi 26:29). Priesthood does not. Priestcraft is seeking to elevate oneself. Priesthood is humbling oneself to lift and elevate others. Priestcraft seeks pleasure and power. Priesthood holders are required to sacrifice and often suffer in order to bless others.

The order of Nehor is given in the Book of Mormon as a stark contrast to the Order of the Son of God. It eventually led to destruction for its founder and for those who later upheld it. Nehor sought popularity and recognition by preaching vain and flattering doctrines, which were the opposite of repentance (see Alma 1:4). He taught people that the Lord had created and redeemed all men and that in the end all would have eternal life. Many believed his words because they were easy and appealed to the "natural man" or our carnal nature. He taught that the people should support their priests and teachers so they didn't have to labor with their own hands. Nehor gained much worldly success and was lifted up in pride (see Alma 1:6).

This is exactly the opposite of how Christ and His true servants minister. They teach and minister at a cost to themselves. They preach repentance even when it seems harsh and does not flatter their hearers. They often suffer for their testimonies and on behalf of those whom they serve. They neither ask for nor receive any monetary gain for their preaching. They preach truth even when their message is unpopular and causes them to be despised and rejected. They humble themselves and seek the Lord's will first. This is difficult, which is partly why it is so rarely seen among men.

In fact, we are given in the Book of Mormon a key to discernment. Nephi gives four signs of those practicing priestcraft: they seek 1) to get gain; 2) to gain power over others; 3) to become popular; or 4) the lusts of the flesh and the things of the world (see 1 Nephi 22:23). These are the hallmarks of the order of Nehor. When any individual or institution claiming priesthood authority is seeking after one or more of these four things—we can surely know they do not possess priesthood from God. They are instead engaged in priestcraft. We must avoid that error and repent speedily to the extent our heart is in the wrong place. Nephi testifies that the end of all such is to share in the fate of Nehor—they will be brought down into the dust and consumed (see 1 Nephi 22:23).

The order of Nehor is part of Satan's priesthoods—those who serve or follow him to some degree. It is interesting that the Book of Mormon primarily describes the order of Nehor in terms of its basic tenets, beliefs, and objectives—not in terms of its organizational structure or any other aspect. Which raises an interesting question: what are the tenets of the Holy Order after the Son of God? We ought to know them. They are outlined in the endowment and in the Sermon on the Mount. To become a better servant of God or a better priesthood holder we should be seeking those things in our lives—even the more difficult ones, like learning to love our enemies.

Joseph Smith summarized the reason for our collective failure. It is because our hearts are set too much on the things of this world and the honors thereof (see D&C 121:35). The allure is so great that when we are not focused on the Lord's plan for us, we can spend much of our lives seeking after things that in the end amount to nothing. In our pride and competitiveness, we seek to excel over others rather than to humble ourselves and serve (see D&C 58:41). We cover up our sins, follow after our own vain ambitions, seek to control others, and exercise unrighteous dominion. In doing so we grieve the heavens, causing them to withdraw, thereby forfeiting our priesthood power and authority (see D&C 121:37). "Hence, many are called, but few are chosen" (D&C 121:40). Failure is the rule. Success the exception.

When we leave the temple feeling superior to others who have not been endowed, we are already started in the wrong direction. Such an idea is like the Zoramites, with their stupid Rameumpton, declaring how they were favored and chosen of God while others were not. Instead of falling into that trap, we should recognize our endowment as a calling to render greater love and service to God and to our fellowmen.

Conclusion

Our discussion of priesthood in this chapter has been primarily from a male perspective. We have not specifically addressed the topic of women and the priesthood. However, many of the principles we have discussed certainly apply equally to the sisters.

What we have in the temple is a type of God's holy order—and, ultimately, it involves male and female together in the image of God.

The temple is the house of God, but is also teaching us about the *house of God* or the family or household of God. In that household, God's sons and daughters are unified as part of a greater whole. Much like the Book of Mormon, the temple is given as a starting point to prove us (see 3 Nephi 26:9–11). If we will give heed to it, then eventually the Lord will provide us with more concerning the priesthood.

In the meantime, recall Joseph Smith taught that the Holy Ghost is God's messenger in all these priesthoods.[64] Therefore, whether male or female, let's focus our daily effort there—on receiving the Holy Ghost to a greater degree and following its direction more closely in our own lives to better serve Him. Let's recognize the endowment covenants as the basis for God's holy order and seek to live them more fully.

Brethren, if we want to advance in priesthood, let's really live the Sermon on the Mount. And then leave it up to God himself to provide power in our priesthood as He sees fit. It is in actually living our temple covenants that the transformation and blessings we seek can be obtained from God. Until we have individually received power in our priesthood as described in JST Genesis 14, we have not arrived.

Men receive an ordination to the priesthood in the Church. Men and women both receive an additional ordination in the temple. We should value that ordination, but should also recognize it is not complete without power from the Lord. There is a large difference between being ordained and receiving power. They are two different matters. Ordination is an invitation. Receiving actual power involves heaven, as we learn at the temple veil (see also D&C 121:36). We are warned that most will fail. Rather than feeling proud, we should leave the temple in great humility: "He that is ordained of God and sent forth, the same is appointed to be the greatest, notwithstanding he is the least and the servant of all" (D&C 50:26).

Homework

1. Study Joseph Smith's teachings on the priesthood. This is a little challenging because he never gave a consolidated discourse on the topic, but rather gave snippets here and there. You have to piece these fragments together to better understand and view the overall topic of priesthood. One very helpful resource is *The Words of Joseph Smith* compiled and edited by Andrew F. Ehat and Lyndon W. Cook. We owe them a debt of gratitude for their work in assembling and preserving these teachings of Joseph Smith. It is well worth studying the entire volume.

2. Research the topic of priesthood in the scriptures. You may wish to use as a starting point some of the key scriptures cited in this chapter (Alma 13, JST Genesis 14, D&C 84 and 121). There is much more to this topic than we have discussed here.

CHAPTER 5

PRIESTHOOD AND TEMPLE KEYS

Now the great and grand secret of the whole matter, and the summum bonum of the whole subject that is lying before us, consists in obtaining the powers of the Holy Priesthood. For him to whom these keys are given there is no difficulty in obtaining a knowledge of facts in relation to the salvation of the children of men, both as well for the dead as for the living.
—*Doctrine and Covenants 128:11*

WHAT EXACTLY are priesthood keys? We hear about priesthood keys regularly in the Church, yet oftentimes the keys being referring to are not clearly defined by the one speaking of them. And some things we hear taught may be incomplete or incorrect; for example, the notion that in a ward only the bishop and the quorum presidents (elders, teachers, and deacons) hold keys. That idea may possibly be true in a very narrow definition of keys, but it is certainly not true in a more general sense.

In the scriptures, the word *keys* seems to be used with a couple of different meanings, but is often associated with an assignment or stewardship or with specific knowledge (see, for example, Revelation 1:18, D&C 6:28, D&C 7:7, D&C 128:14, 21). The temple can further add to our understanding of priesthood keys. Recall Joseph Smith's description of the endowment as communicating the keys of the Aaronic up through the highest order of Melchizedek Priesthood.[65] Therefore, the endowment is revealing or at least concerned with priesthood keys. How are we to understand those keys?

Furthermore, a few days before introducing the endowment, Joseph Smith promised the Relief Society sisters that they would receive the "keys of the kingdom" in conjunction with the elders in the temple, indicating that these keys are administered equally to women and men.[66] To begin to understand these statements and this topic, we need to have a broader view of priesthood keys.

Just as we did with the term *priesthood*, let's take a step back and look at the word *key*. There are several ways to define a key. A key can open something that is locked or hidden, for example the key to a treasure chest. A key can also be an essential piece of knowledge for understanding something, for example the key to a map. Or a key can give access to something that is otherwise unusable, for example the key to a car. What if instead of viewing priesthood keys as authority, or as defining a hierarchy of command, we instead saw these keys more in terms of the definitions above. Then some scriptural references and Joseph Smith's statements begin to make more sense.

Two Types of Keys

It may be helpful to separate in our minds two different types of priesthood keys. For simplicity, we will refer to them as administrative and ministerial keys. Administrative keys will refer to the way keys are traditionally defined in the Church. The *Encyclopedia of Mormonism* defines priesthood keys as: "The keys of the priesthood refer to the right to exercise power in the name of Jesus Christ or to preside over a priesthood function, quorum, or organizational division of the Church. Keys are necessary to maintain order and to see that the functions of the Church are performed in the proper time, place, and manner. They are given by the laying on of hands in an ordination or setting apart by a person who presides and who holds the appropriate keys at a higher level."[67]

These administrative keys provide order and structure within the Church. However, we still need to better understand what is meant by these keys. If we say that an elders quorum president holds keys but a ward Relief Society president does not, what do we really mean? In the active function of their roles in the ward, both administer home and visiting teaching assignments; both minister to the needs of their members; both are entitled to receive inspiration or revelation; both are obligated to teach doctrine; and both help to oversee the ward family. In a practical day-to-day sense what really is the difference in their roles? (Apart from one ministering primarily to the men and the other to the women.) You could say that the elders president also has the responsibility to administer to the sick and to give priesthood blessings, but then so do all of the elders in his quorum.[68] Those functions are not unique to a president, and so the question remains: what really are the keys that an elders quorum president holds?

In my view, these administrative keys amount to a stewardship. Once a person is called of God through revelation, sustained by a vote of the members, and set apart, he or she then holds the keys or stewardship to that office and is authorized to perform a certain function within the Church. I do not have the keys or authority to direct my stake or my ward or anything else unless I am called to that position by revelation and sustained by a vote of the members of the ward or stake. This provides for order within the Church organization. However, the Relief Society president is also called and sustained in the same manner. So, in the end, it is not readily apparent what, if anything, these keys entail other than a stewardship or an assignment or a responsibility. And, in fact, a stewardship or assignment is frequently the meaning of the word keys in scriptures.

Regardless of how you define them, these administrative keys are not our primary concern. We've discussed them only to draw a distinction in your mind between them and the "ministerial" keys we will discuss next. The ministerial keys are integral to the priesthood. What are those keys? They are defined in the scriptures. The Aaronic Priesthood holds the keys of the gospel of repentance, baptism by immersion and the ministering of angels (see D&C 13:1). The Melchizedek or greater priesthood holds the keys of the mysteries of the kingdom and the key of the knowledge of God (see D&C 84:19, 107:19). Modern Church leaders have confirmed that these priesthood keys are potentially held by all Aaronic and Melchizedek Priesthood holders regardless of their Church callings.[69] It is, therefore, incorrect to say that only the bishop and a few others hold priesthood keys in a ward. Every priesthood holder in the ward can hold these keys. And, according to Joseph Smith, the sisters should too. And these are the keys that are really important! So how are we to understand these priesthood keys?

If we view priesthood as a calling to serve God, then how do we accomplish that? How are we to be useful servants? We certainly cannot serve Him in the way He desires, if we are not able to communicate with Him and receive instructions from Him. And, so, the first *keys* to unlock our priesthood service are repentance and baptism by immersion. They are a key to our service to God because they place us in a position to receive the Holy Ghost and to receive further light, instructions and knowledge from the Lord. We have to follow or receive these keys before we can progress further. These are the first two keys of the Aaronic Priesthood. In this sense, these keys are guideposts in our service. We cannot serve the Lord without them.

These priesthood keys show us what we must first obtain for ourselves, e.g. repentance and baptism. But then they also show how we are to thereafter serve God. In that sense, the keys can help to define our callings or authority within the priesthood as well. For example, once we have truly repented and received baptism ourselves, we are to preach repentance and invite others to baptism for Him. We then "hold these keys" because we have lived the principles, received these blessings in our own lives, and now understand how to bring them to others.

These are the first two keys of the Aaronic Priesthood. The other one is the key to the ministering of angels. This key raises a whole set of additional questions. What is really meant by this key? Is it inherent in the priesthood or is it received in the Aaronic portion of the endowment? Is this key another guidepost along our path? Should we be seeking for angelic messengers from our Father to teach us as the endowment implies?

Why does Nephi teach about angels as part of the doctrine of Christ (see 2 Nephi 32:3)? And why does Mormon list their ministry as one of the signs that faith is present and warn that faith has ceased when angels cease to minister (see Moroni 7:36–37)? Why did Paul teach, "be not forgetful to entertain strangers: for thereby some have entertained angels unawares" if such does not occur (Hebrews 13:2)? If it happened in Paul's day, does it still happen today? Why do LDS people generally believe these things are possible but reserved for others and not themselves? What does that say about our faith?

Does a young man ordained to the Aaronic Priesthood automatically hold the keys to the ministering of angels? Or does he need to be endowed in order to receive them? If he possesses the keys, does that guarantee he will entertain angels? What about a woman who receives an angel, such as Mary (see Luke 1:26–27)? Who actually holds this key: Mary or a priest in the Aaronic priesthood who has never received an angel? Can the keys thus be separated from the priesthood? And if so, might keys perhaps be very different from how we typically view them? Are they not, in many cases, related to acquiring knowledge or experience? And, finally, how is all of this related to the spiritual gift of the ministering of angels (see Moroni 10:14)?

We are not going to attempt to address these questions here. I raise them simply to point out that we often pass by things superficially with too little curiosity about important matters. I hope that you will start to view keys as a much broader subject than the way we typically define them. I also hope that you will inquire into this topic further, first, through the scriptures and the temple, and then through prayer and asking God for added light and knowledge.

The Aaronic Priesthood keys we have discussed come first and help prepare us for the Melchizedek keys, which are defined in the scriptures as the keys of the mysteries of the kingdom and the key of the knowledge of God (see D&C 84:19). Knowing God is the very definition of eternal life (see John 17:3). When we have the attitude that we should stick to the basics and leave the mysteries alone, then our very unbelief cuts us off from the blessings and keys of the Melchizedek Priesthood.

Returning to the temple and in light of our discussion, if we are given these priesthood keys in the endowment, what does that mean? How do we use them? If the keys to my car just sit in my pocket, they are no good to me or anyone else. I have to use them to start the car before they have any value. Likewise, the keys outlined in the scriptures and in the temple may be inherent in the priesthood, but they do us no good, if we do not learn to use them. Recognize too that these blessings are available equally to women and men.

Keys in the Book of Mormon

Curiously, other than the keys to Laban's treasury, the Book of Mormon makes no specific mention of keys at all. For a time, this puzzled me, especially since the Book of Mormon contains the teachings and doctrine essential to our salvation. If keys are a critical topic, we should expect the Book of Mormon to address it in some way.

One day it dawned on me that these priesthood keys are found throughout the Book of Mormon, but instead of listing them as such, we are given example after example of individuals who used or acquired them. Their stories are shared to invite us to do the same. How many stories are there in the Book of Mormon about repentance, baptism, receiving the ministry of angels, being taught the mysteries of the kingdom, and even being redeemed into the Lord's presence? We are shown the keys in action, and examples are found from beginning to end in the Book of Mormon. It invites us, over and over, to go and do likewise. These principles are expounded and clarified in great detail; the Book of Mormon just never calls them keys, so you have to look for them. The Book of Mormon is actually a very powerful witness of these keys in our path back to God.

The Book of Mormon continually affirms that it is our unbelief (either lack of belief or belief in false teachings) that is the problem (see, for example, Ether 4:13–15, Mormon 9:20, Moroni 7:37, Moroni 10:19). The view of priesthood keys as being restrictive (for example, only the President of the Church or other senior leaders are authorized to exercise the keys of the mysteries or of the knowledge of God) is anti-scriptural and makes God a respecter of persons (i.e., he will listen to one person who holds keys but not to another who does not). This idea may be part of our collective unbelief, but it counters the teachings of Joseph Smith, and even modern-day Church leaders, that these keys are available to all. Rather than seeing the keys as authority, we should perhaps view them as knowledge which helps us shed our unbelief. In that sense, the keys do grant access to the mysteries and to God.

Temple Keys

With this background in mind, let's return to the temple. During the endowment presentation, we pass through four levels or degrees in the ceremony: two are associated with the Aaronic Priesthood and two with the Melchizedek Priesthood. In each of these four phases we are presented with a covenant, name, sign, and token. For a long time, I wondered about these seemingly disparate elements. Are they four separate things or is there a common thread that binds them together? One day, the realization dawned that these elements form a key. That is the thread that binds them together into one and gives them cohesion.

It would seem to follow that if a portion of the endowment gives us two keys associated with the Aaronic Priesthood, then those keys must be related to the keys inherent in that priesthood—namely repentance, baptism, and the ministry of angels. And that is exactly what we find. Similarly, we would expect the keys given in the Melchizedek portion of the endowment to be related to the keys of that priesthood—or the mysteries of godliness and the knowledge of God.

When Joseph Smith spoke of delivering the "keys of the kingdom" to the elders and to the sisters, he was talking about keys in a very different sense than we generally use the word today. Three days before introducing the endowment, Joseph Smith gave another lecture in which he further defined the keys of the kingdom as "certain signs and words by which false spirits and personages may be detected from true, which cannot be revealed to the Elders [and sisters] till the Temple is completed."[70] Accordingly, what we receive in the temple are the keys of the kingdom, and are received by both women and men. And, at least in part, those keys provide a way to discern true messengers from false ones.

This idea is worth considering further. Why would the general membership of the Church need to possess such keys unless Joseph expected that we would be experiencing the ministry of angels? Furthermore, are these keys limited to angels or are they applicable to any messenger or message we might receive from any source? For example, how might they apply to a dream or vision or other communication from God? Why are such keys necessary, if we are to know the truth of all things by the power of the Holy Ghost? Are these keys one way we are to distinguish truth from "the philosophies of men mingled with scripture"? And if so, are these keys something more than a handshake?[71] Why would they also include a covenant, name, sign, token, and penalty?

In addition, discerning between true and false messengers may not be the only purpose for these temple keys. On the 28th of April 1842, six days before introducing the endowment, Joseph addressed the Relief Society and apparently indicated that the temple's keys allow one to go to God and obtain answers to one's questions: "He spoke of delivering the keys of the Priesthood to the Church, and said that the faithful members of the Relief Society should receive them with their husbands, that the Saints whose integrity has been tried and proved faithful, might know how to ask the Lord and receive an answer; for according to his prayers, God had appointed him elsewhere."[72]

On another occasion, Joseph observed, "thus we behold the Keys of this priesthood consisted in obtaining the voice of Jehovah that he talked with him in a familiar and friendly manner."[73] This gives an indication that receiving the keys involves more than simply a way to obtain God's word—it is actually obtaining "the voice of Jehovah".

From these statements, I take it that the keys given in the endowment are something we should consider carefully and thoughtfully and not pass over lightly. How the endowment elements form a key, what those keys can then open or access, how they are to be used, are all questions you should probably seek further enlightenment on from the Spirit. There is more to all of that than we can or should cover here. You are going to have to get this knowledge on your own. What follows are simply some thoughts to get you started. Recognize that much of what is given us in the temple is symbolic, not literal, and is meant to teach us. It also invites us to further inquire of the Lord to find what it is He would have us learn.

The Endowment Symbols as Keys

To get started, what if we viewed the endowment's keys as guideposts or milestones, markers on our journey to know God? I suggested this approach briefly in *Understanding Your Endowment* and want to return to it now to develop the idea more fully. In doing so, I wish to emphasize again that this is certainly not the only way to interpret or understand the endowment's symbols, but for me it has been a helpful starting point. Please take what seems right to you from what follows and discard anything that does not.

A clue to this potential interpretation comes from Joseph Smith in a discourse he gave on the 20th of March 1842—a little over a month prior to inaugurating the temple endowment. He stated:

> I do contend that baptism is a *sign* ordained of God for the believer in Christ to take upon himself in order to enter into the Kingdom of God . . . [and] those who seek to enter in any other way will seek in vain *for God will not receive them neither will the angels acknowledge their works*

> *as accepted, for they have not taken upon themselves those ordinances & signs which God ordained* for man[kind] to receive in order to receive a celestial glory . . . & we should not obtain the blessing by pursuing any other course except the way which God has marked out.
>
> What if we should attempt to get the Holy Ghost through any other means except the *sign* or way which God hath appointed[;] should we obtain it[?] certainly not all other means would fail The Lord says do so & so & I will bless so & so *their is certain key words & signs belonging to the priesthood which must be observed in order to obtain the blessings* The sign of Peter was to repent & be baptized for the remission of sins, with the promise of the gift of the Holy Ghost & in no other way is the gift of the Holy Ghost obtained.[74]

In this sermon, Joseph equates the signs of the priesthood with ordinances. That is an important clue. He also mentions key words and Peter. Notice too that we will not pass by angelic sentinels (or have them accept our works) unless we have taken upon ourselves the ordinances and signs God has ordained. This is consistent with Brigham Young's explanation of the endowment. Therefore, one way to interpret the signs given us in the temple is as representing gospel ordinances, those we must receive on the path back to God.

It seems obvious that ordinances, such as baptism and the sacrament, are a sign to the heavens and before the world that we are accepting a covenant with God. So, if ordinances are signs, then it makes sense that the "signs of the priesthood" symbolically point us back to the ordinances thereof.

Recall that many gospel ordinances have two parts, a physical and a spiritual component. We accept the covenant through the physical portion of the ordinance and must then live up to the terms of the covenant. God acknowledges our effort by providing the spiritual portion. For example, following our sincere repentance and baptism of water, He promises to provide a baptism of fire and of the Holy

Ghost. Receiving the full ordinance requires both the baptism of water and the baptism of fire and the Holy Ghost. The sacrament, likewise, involves the physical action of partaking of bread and water by which we witness that we have complied with the requirements of the covenant. If that is the case, the Lord promises to fill us with His Spirit, the spiritual component of the ordinance (see Moroni 4:3).

In the temple, we receive covenants along with a corresponding name, sign, and token. These elements form a key and point to gospel ordinances. The signs represent the physical portion of the ordinance and its associated covenant. We take the covenant upon ourselves when we make the sign. The token is sent back to us from God. It represents the accompanying spiritual blessing of the ordinance and is evidence of His acceptance of our covenant.

In the endowment ceremony, the token and sign are given together. In our daily lives, there is often a period of testing, learning and growth in between the making of the sign (a gospel ordinance) and receiving the token (God's acceptance of or seal on that ordinance). In the temple, we also receive a name with each token. The name marks a transition in our status or in our relationship with God.[75] There is also a corresponding priesthood mark that memorializes or witnesses the covenant. All of this is in perfect accordance with ancient covenant formulas.

So, to briefly recap before continuing: each sign represents a physical ordinance (or a stage in our progression). It is accompanied by a token (symbolizing a spiritual component which comes from God) showing His acceptance and blessing. Each ordinance embodies a covenant from God. There is also a name that is related to the corresponding blessing or which indicates a change in our status. These names are important and can teach us something about what is being received. Finally, there is a mark associated with each as well. These marks serve as a reminder or witness of the covenant. We will discuss these marks later. Please keep this framework in mind as we proceed.

Aaronic Priesthood Keys

Let's now examine the first two keys of the Aaronic Priesthood more specifically to illustrate these meanings. The first sign of the endowment represents the first ordinance of mortality—birth. Though we may not generally think of birth as an ordinance, it is, especially when it occurs within the new and everlasting covenant of marriage as God intends.[76] The associated covenants are to obey God and to offer sacrifice. This ordinance is performed through the sacrifice of the woman as part of her role as priestess. She brings forth life. Her blood is shed in giving birth as a new covenant is formed with her child. The sacrifice then continues as both parents work to raise and provide for the child. These covenants of obedience and sacrifice are not only required of the parents, but also apply to the new child. They help to explain much of our life's purpose here in mortality. We probably made similar covenants with God before descending into mortality. In this life it is possible to truly sacrifice and learn obedience, often through the things we suffer (see D&C 105:6).

The first token (what we receive from God as part of the ordinance of being born into this world) is the light of Christ. It is given as we grow into accountability as a guide to help us in our journey back to Him. In the endowment ceremony, Adam and Eve receive this sign, token, and covenant in the Garden of Eden, but for us this garden period is symbolic of our birth and early childhood. We often refer to the light of Christ as our conscience, but this light is much greater than that very limited definition (see D&C 88:7–13).[77] It originates from God and connects us to Him. So, the token is also a connection. Despite being separated by a veil in a fallen condition, mankind is still connected to God by the light of Christ. In fact, we find a progressively greater connection to God symbolized in the remaining tokens.

This token is not only a blessing and a connection to God, but also a key to our progression. Mormon teaches us that the light of Christ is given to every person so that he or she may know good from evil (see Moroni 7:16). He then pleads with us to "*search diligently in the light of Christ* that ye may know good from evil, and if ye will lay hold upon every good thing, and condemn it not, *ye certainly will be a child of Christ*" (Moroni 7:19, emphasis added). Our careful attention to this guide will be needed throughout our life. And it will help prepare us to receive the second sign and token.

The second sign of the Aaronic priesthood represents the next required ordinance of mortality—baptism, or being born again. Baptism of water is the physical portion of our spiritual rebirth. It is ideally performed by the man in his role as a priest. The covenant associated with this ordinance is the Law of the Gospel. We agree to live this law at our baptism for the remainder of our lives. The token (what we receive back from God) represents the baptism of fire and the Holy Ghost. This increases our connection with God beyond the first token which was the light of Christ. We are now put in more direct contact with the Godhead through the Holy Ghost.

Now, visualize how this second sign is formed. It can teach us something about this process. A cupped hand is associated with two things: one is an offering and the other is the symbol of a beggar, one who is asking to receive something. In this case, the sign is both an offering we make to God and a petition for the Holy Ghost. The offering is our broken heart and contrite spirit. That is the prerequisite to receiving the baptism of fire (see 3 Nephi 9:20). Our hearts and desires are to be given to him.

The baptism of fire is more than we sometimes think it is. It is not the same thing as laying on of hands and being told to receive the Holy Ghost. It is an actual event where we are literally baptized by spiritual fire and made a new creature in Christ. Our baptism or spiritual re-birth is not complete until we receive both the baptism of water AND the baptism of fire and the Holy Ghost. The baptism of fire is the spiritual portion of our spiritual re-birth. It is God's witness or token back to us that He accepts our repentance and baptism of water.

In both the physical birth and spiritual births, God is an active partner along with the man as priest and the woman as priestess.

Our complete birth into God's kingdom requires the work and participation of all three parties. No one is less or more, rather each is required.[78]

As we enter mortality, our spirits are veiled in flesh. Like Adam and Eve, we become subject to the conditions of the Fall and forget everything. Our spirits once participated in and witnessed the Grand Council in Heaven where some were chosen for assignments here (see Abraham 3:22–28). Our memory of that and all that went before is blocked by the "veil of the flesh" that now covers our spirits (see Hebrews 10:20). Somewhere within us the knowledge of what occurred before, or "the record of heaven," is still locked away (see Moses 6:61).

Our spiritual rebirth of water and the Spirit marks the beginning of a reversal of this fall. The physical veil begins to thin as our spirits actually receive the Holy Ghost, and as we learn to subject our bodies to our spirits. Our spirits re-connect with God in a greater degree as the initial connection through the light of Christ is strengthened and increased by receiving the Holy Ghost, or first Comforter. The name of this token is a critical key to understanding all of this. Your body receives your spirit, which in turn is to become holy as it "hearkens" unto the Father.

You were anointed from head to toe in the initiatory ordinances with olive oil, which is a symbol of the Holy Ghost. In part, the purpose of this anointing is to make your ghost or your spirit holy. This is what Joseph Smith was referring to when he made statements such as "the Holy Ghost is now in a state of probation" or "the Holy Ghost . . . is a personage of Spirit. Were it not so, the Holy Ghost could not dwell in us" (D&C 130:22). What is it that dwells within you? The temple anointing is teaching us something about the process involved, but the ordinance alone is not enough; we must actually receive the Holy Ghost. We must become a holy vessel. "What? Know ye not that *your body is the temple of the Holy Ghost which is in you*, which ye have of God, and ye are not your own?" (1 Cor. 6: 19; emphasis added).

Book of Abraham Facsimile 2 Figure 7.

Pay attention to the imagery found in Facsimile 2 from the Book of Abraham, Figure 7, and in particular note the seated figure. The description of this image is that it represents "God sitting upon his throne, revealing through the heavens the grand Key-words of the Priesthood; *as, also the sign of the Holy Ghost* unto Abraham, in the form of a dove" (Facsimile 2, Pearl of Great Price; emphasis added). It should therefore be apparent that one of these grand "key-words" is the sign of the Holy Ghost.

There is much more to the topic of the Holy Ghost than we typically teach or that many even understand in the Church. For example, the Lord taught Adam that the Holy Ghost which can abide in us is "the record of heaven; the Comforter; the peaceable things of immortal glory; the truth of all things; that which quickeneth all things, which maketh alive all things; that which knoweth all things, and hath all power according to wisdom, mercy, truth, justice and judgment" (Moses 6:61). We are not going to fully delve into the topic here, but it is something you should seek further revelation and knowledge on.

In the endowment's first two signs and tokens, we find symbols representing our descent into mortality and then our entering the gate to begin our return home through spiritual rebirth into God's kingdom. These symbols are tied to the *keys* of the Aaronic Priesthood, namely the gospel of repentance, baptism by immersion and the ministry of angels. These all occur in the telestial realm and are given to help prepare us to enter the terrestrial. The second group of signs and tokens (the Melchizedek ones) relate to our continuing spiritual growth and maturity. There is a marked shift between the Aaronic and Melchizedek portions of the endowment.

Melchizedek Priesthood Keys

The first covenant of the Melchizedek portion of the endowment is the law of chastity. This may seem surprising at first glance. We have previously covenanted to live the law of the gospel. Isn't chastity just a subset of that law along with obedience and sacrifice? In a sense, we have already agreed to it, so why is it mentioned again, specifically and separately? I used to think that this law was singled out because it tends to be a challenge for many to live today. But there may be more to this covenant given its introduction at this point in the ceremony.

The next sign or ordinance we encounter is tied to this law. Recall that one of the endowment's purposes is to give us a type of the fulness of the priesthood (see Alma 13:16). The first sign of the Melchizedek Priesthood represents the ordinance of the new and everlasting covenant of marriage. There can be no fulness of the priesthood outside of this order (see D&C 131:2). A fulness of priesthood necessarily involves a man and a woman joined as one in an everlasting covenant (see 1 Corinthians 11:11).

When Adam was found alone in the Garden of Eden it was not good in the sight of God (see Genesis 2:18). He was finite, limited, and incomplete. None of us possess all of the feminine and masculine attributes alone. The image of God is both male and female—together, united as one. Both are halves of a greater whole. Completeness or perfection is only found in the union of the two. Therein can be found: father and mother, begetter and bearer, knowledge and wisdom, justice and mercy, etc., all of the male and female attributes combined in one great whole. This identity was reflected anciently in the two cherubim figures atop the Ark of the Covenant. One of these figures was male and one was female—representing the two aspects of God—a father and a mother. Separately, a man and a woman are incomplete and finite, but together they can become whole, complete, and endless through their posterity.

Adam and Eve were married by God in the Garden of Eden prior to the Fall and the conditions of mortality. Marriage was meant to endure. Of everything here in this transitory world, it is marriage and family that God most wants to preserve. Its presence at this point in the endowment should tell us something of its importance. This is the next ordinance and is presented with the law of chastity as a corresponding covenant, which raises another question: do the temple covenants take on additional meaning when combined as part of the associated ordinance? For example, the law of chastity seems to have additional meaning within the context of marriage rather than simply as part of the gospel law.

In a godly marriage, two separate and unique individuals work toward becoming one—one flesh, one heart, and one mind. The power to create offspring is one of the gifts of God to mankind and ideally is intended to be used only within the new and everlasting covenant of marriage. There it encompasses the obligation for the two parents to bring forth and care for children (see 1 Timothy 5:8). The parents are to teach their children the ways of God (see D&C 68:25). In later years, the children are in turn obligated to honor and care for the parents (see Mosiah 3:20). The law of chastity therefore encompasses the entire cycle of life, providing for families and generations. It connects man, woman and God in the image of God. The law of chastity is at the heart of our own potential kingdom. It is much greater than a simple list of don'ts we are taught as youth.

The token associated with this sign represents having one's calling and election made sure. It is to be sealed up to eternal life by the Holy Spirit of Promise. This is far greater than being sealed in the temple together as a couple. The initial temple sealing on a wedding day is the beginning (the sign). Like all gospel ordinances, it is first given conditionally. The blessings are promised based upon our faithfulness.

The Holy Spirit of Promise is the Lord's later, final seal upon a union that He intends to preserve into eternity. It is the token (spiritual component) back from the Lord and comes about in the Lord's due time as a result of our faith, sacrifice, and obedience. It may require many years of working and growing together between the initial temple marriage and later receiving this final seal from Lord. Ideally, this promise will occur within a marriage union worthy of preserving into the eternities. We cannot be exalted, in the fullest sense of that word, alone. In fact, the greatest place to work on really living and implementing all of the covenants of the temple is within our own marriages and families.

In saying this, please recognize that what is symbolized in the temple and what we are discussing here is the ideal. It is a blueprint or prototype. Our personal reality doesn't always conform exactly to this ideal. You may not currently be married. Or you may be married but in a difficult situation, such as with a spouse who has lost his or her faith. These types of circumstances may be important for our individual growth or as part of the service we came down here to render. Though they may try our patience and our faith, they are not an impediment to the Lord blessing us as we merit individually.

For example, I know of two women who are divorced and single but who have received their calling and election made sure from the Lord, despite the fact that neither is currently married. If your individual circumstances at present are less than ideal, make that a matter of prayer with God. Let God comfort and instruct you concerning your state and standing. Remember, things do not always unfold exactly as we expect or in a precisely given order. About the time we figure that the Lord has to do something in a certain way, we can find exceptions in the scriptural record. These steps may unfold slightly differently in your life as well. The important point is that we will eventually be exalted as a couple—two individuals becoming one in the image of God.

Recall Brigham Young's description of the endowment: "Your endowment is to receive all those ordinances in the house of the Lord which are necessary for you . . . to enable you to walk back to the presence of the Father, *passing the angels who stand as sentinels*, being enabled to give them the key words, the signs, and the tokens pertaining to the holy priesthood and gain your eternal exaltation."[79] Now compare that language with section 132 of the Doctrine and Covenants which states: "if a man marry a wife by my word, which is my law, and by the new and everlasting covenant, and *it is sealed unto them by the Holy Spirit of Promise . . . they shall pass by the angels, and the gods, which are set there*, to their exaltation and glory in all things, which glory shall be a fulness and a continuation of the seeds forever and ever" (D&C 132:19; emphasis added).[80] It should be abundantly clear that passing by the angelic sentinels to return to the tree of life involves more than simply memorizing the tokens given in the temple.

To paraphrase Brigham Young's description of the endowment, using the symbols we have discussed here, we could understand it to mean: if we give diligent heed to the light of Christ, receive and follow the Holy Ghost, and eventually are sealed by the Holy Spirit of Promise thereby making our calling and election sure; then we will be able to pass by the angels and return to the presence of the Father (see Mormon 7:19, 2 Nephi 32:5, D&C 88:3–4). One who has received these actual tokens will eventually receive his or her exaltation.[81] The tokens given in the temple are symbols and are meant to teach us about this process. But to receive the actual blessings, we have to live the associated covenants.

Which brings us to the final sign and token of the endowment. Recall that the keys of the Melchizedek Priesthood are associated with the "mysteries of the kingdom, even the key of the knowledge of God" (D&C 84:19). Those keys are symbolized in this final token. Notice that this final key is not complete in the endowment ceremony until we are presented at the veil to converse with the Lord. Don't miss that point. It is teaching us about the reality of receiving this key. This final token is symbolic of receiving the Second Comforter and being taught by our Lord. It is being redeemed from the Fall and being brought back into the presence of God (see Ether 3:13). It is not enough to simply have your calling and election made sure. You must also press forward until you pass through the veil back into Christ's presence. Once there, He can teach and unfold the mysteries of the kingdom and prepare you to be introduced to the Father (see D&C 76:114–118).

The scriptures teach that in order to be exalted we must be valiant in the testimony of Jesus (see D&C 76:51, 79, 101). I used to believe that the testimony of Jesus was simply our testimony of Christ. One day, however, the Spirit taught me that this testimony actually has three parts: 1) The first part is our testimony of Him as witnessed to us by the Spirit. 2) The second part of the testimony of Jesus is *His testimony* back to us. It is the "testimony of Jesus". It is carefully worded in scripture because it is both our testimony of Him and Jesus' testimony back to us. What is His testimony? It is His covenant to us of eternal life. As the keeper of the gate, He testifies that He has sealed and accepted us as His. It is another term for receiving our calling and election. But it does not end there. 3) The third part of the testimony of Jesus is His testimony to the Father concerning us. We see an example of this in section 88: "sanctify yourselves; yea, purify your hearts, and cleanse your hands and your feet before me, that I may make you clean; that *I may testify unto your Father, and your God, and my God, that you are clean* from the blood of this wicked generation" (D&C 88:74–75, emphasis added). Valiance in the testimony of Jesus involves all three parts. Press forward until you receive each. Christ in his role as the Second Comforter has a ministry to prepare and re-introduce you to the Father.

The ordinance associated with this final sign is the second endowment or second anointing. In its simplest form, this ordinance is the washing of the feet. This washing is a sign of being clean from the blood of this generation (see D&C 88:138–139). Those who are thus cleansed, how beautiful upon the mountains are their feet (see Mosiah

15:13–17). This is a capstone gospel ordinance. It may be why the Prophet, after restoring this ordinance in Kirtland, made the comment that they had then passed through all the necessary ceremonies, although these ordinances were subsequently expanded in Nauvoo.[82]

In the early history of the Church, these second anointing ordinances were administered frequently.[83] Today, the opposite is true. The fact that these capstone ordinances are not commonly administered in the Church today should not discourage you. That reality is not an impediment to receiving the Second Comforter. And receiving Christ is the important part. He can provide for whatever we may lack. And those who have received the ordinances of the second anointing from the Church but who have not also received the Second Comforter have something that is either invalid or incomplete, like receiving the baptism of water without also receiving a baptism of fire and the Holy Ghost.[84] The one is incomplete without the other—and the most critical portion is the spiritual component (the Second Comforter).

Please recognize that we can return to the presence of the Son and the Father in this life. It needn't wait for the next life. The climax of the endowment ceremony testifies to this fact. You are presented at the veil, but without any mention of death. The endowment is given to prepare us to receive the Second Comforter. Joseph Smith testified repeatedly that this was the purpose of the gospel. So do the scriptures. And so does the temple endowment. We have these three witnesses and invitations for us to do likewise. The scriptures attest, "if ye shall receive me *in the world*, then shall ye know me, and shall receive your exaltation . . . This is eternal lives—to know the only wise and true God, and Jesus Christ whom he hath sent" (D&C 132:23–24; emphasis added).

Conclusion

This interpretation of the temple keys is merely an expansion of Joseph Smith's statement we covered in the previous chapter:

> After a person has faith in Christ, repents of his sins, and is baptized for the remission of his sins and receives the Holy Ghost, (by the laying on of hands), which is the first Comforter, then let him continue to humble himself before God, hungering and thirsting after righteousness, and living by every word of God, and the Lord will soon say unto him, Son, thou shalt be exalted. When the Lord has thoroughly proved him, and finds that the man (or woman) is determined to serve Him at all hazards, then the man will find his calling and his election made sure, then it will be his privilege to receive the other Comforter.[85]

I hope this statement has greater meaning for you now. I think it is an excellent way to succinctly summarize the endowment.

Given that, the question then arises: why doesn't the endowment just spell all this out more plainly? Why encode it in symbolism? One reason is because this is just a part of what we can be taught. The symbols have more to offer as we are ready. Like Lehi's dream, these elements of the endowment are plain and straightforward. However, these symbols can be interpreted simply (as Lehi did with his family and as we have done here) or in a much more thorough and complex manner (as Nephi subsequently learned and explained). This is why ultimately the Spirit has to teach us. I'm sure there are things that the temple symbols contain that I still do not understand.

With this simple interpretation, the endowment provides us with a road map home. And if you will accept it, the Lord can use that map to show you exactly where you are in your progression. You can know what you have received and what you still lack. For example, one may sincerely wonder if he or she has received the baptism of fire. Go to the temple and attend an endowment session. Ask the Lord to show you where you are and what your next step should be. If you do so in faith, He will answer and can indicate to you where you are in the process.

There is more to the topic of the endowment's keys than we have discussed here, but this is a good starting point. Recognize that we truly only "possess" a key once we have gained understanding of its meaning and know how to use it. You do not truly possess the temple's keys until you do. Ask the Lord to help you.

The temple is to give us a type (see Alma 13:16). It is to teach and prepare us. Our real endowment is to be found in our experiences with and our connection to God. Completing our endowment requires us to search diligently in the light of Christ to learn and discern truth from error. It requires us to actually receive the baptism of fire and of the Holy Ghost and to rely upon it as our guide. It requires us to receive true messengers and reject false ones. It requires us to press forward in our covenants until our calling and election is made sure and we are prepared to be received by Christ at the veil, there to be redeemed into his presence and given further instructions (see 2 Nephi 32:6). Ultimately, completing our endowment is receiving the Second Comforter and all that His ministry subsequently entails.

HOMEWORK

1. If you are unsure as to your personal standing with the Lord, make that a matter of prayer. Many members still lack the baptism of fire and the Holy Ghost. Others may be ready to receive their calling and election. You may have received these blessings already, or there may be things you still lack. The Lord can let you know where you are at individually and what steps you need to take.

2. You may want to diagram potential interpretations of the temple symbols including the one partially explored in this chapter. (This exercise is meant to help you think about these things carefully. We did not cover every element in this chapter. You will have to prayerfully consider how to fill in the gaps. Seek added revelation and insight from the Lord.)

   Consider the following diagram as a helpful mental framework:

Covenant	Name	Sign	Token	Mark

Why is each of these separate elements (covenant, name, sign, etc.) necessary? How do they combine together to form a key? How are they interrelated to one another? What can that relationship teach us about each stage in the process of returning to God? What else could these things symbolize? What could you also learn by considering them in a series (e.g., a progression of four names or four signs, etc.)?

CHAPTER 6

THE ENDOWMENT'S TESTIMONY OF CHRIST

All things are created and made to bear record of me.
—Moses 6:63

A FEW MONTHS prior to his death, Joseph Smith delivered one of his greatest sermons, the King Follet Discourse. In it, he stated:

> Here, then, is eternal life—to know the only wise and true God; and *you have got to learn how to be Gods yourselves, and to be kings and priests to God,* the same as all Gods have done before you, namely, by going from one small degree to another, and from a small capacity to a great one; from grace to grace, from exaltation to exaltation, until you attain to the resurrection of the dead, and are able to dwell in everlasting burnings, and to sit in glory, as do those who sit enthroned in everlasting power. And I want you to know that God, in the last days, while certain individuals are proclaiming his name, is not trifling with you or me.[86]

God is not messing around with us. We have to learn to be kings and priests and queens and priestesses unto God. You are anointed to become such in the initiatory ordinances. One way, therefore, to view the initiatory and endowment ceremony is as a coronation ritual. Several LDS scholars have suggested this approach to interpreting the endowment and have traced evidences of correlating symbols in ancient historical records and rites.[87] While this interpretation can be instructive for our own course in life, it primarily reveals a profound testimony of our Savior.

One of our Lord's titles is King of Kings (see Revelation 19:16). He is the great King and the prototype of all true kings. As such, the endowment contains a beautiful witness of our Savior and of the path He trod as a king. We will consider it in this chapter along with its opposite. The true principles of kingship are easily corrupted. Just as priestcraft is the opposite of priesthood, here too we find an opposing image. We will also look at what that entails, so we can avoid it.

All Things Testify of Christ

In my view, the endowment contains one of the most beautiful testimonies of our Savior in all of the restored gospel, although I needed some help to really see it.[88] This chapter will be most meaningful to those who are very familiar with the endowment. At each point in the discussion, try to visualize in your mind the portion of the ceremony being discussed. We want to connect meaning and potential interpretations with the various symbols without disclosing those symbols or addressing them in a manner that would be inappropriate. This is a delicate balance that I have approached carefully and prayerfully. It is my hope that you will be able to follow along and make the appropriate connections in your mind.

Joseph Smith, Brigham Young, and other early Church leaders administered the full temple ordinances outside of the temple when necessity required. While there is no such need today, our appropriate desire to avoid disclosing things we should not sometimes leads us to the conclusion that any discussion of the endowment outside of the temple is strictly prohibited. That this is not the case should be evidenced by the vast amount of scholarly LDS temple related work published. Much of this material has been supported by Church-backed institutions such as BYU or the Maxwell Institute (formerly FARMS, or the Foundation for Ancient Research and Mormon Studies). Most of our current temple ceremony has been discussed in these publications. Furthermore, much of the endowment dialogue is contained in scripture.

In the discussion that follows, we will discuss potential meaning for some of the endowment symbolism as it relates to Christ and our connection with Him, hopefully in a manner that you will feel is appropriate. It is my desire and intent to enlighten without offending or treating lightly the sacred. Again, please try to visualize in your mind the appropriate portions of the temple ceremony and see what connections you can make as you go through this chapter.

The Endowment as a Coronation Ceremony

In ancient Judaism, the king was considered "God's chosen, his anointed one (messiah), the man sanctified by God's spirit. The relationship between God and the king was perceived as that of father and son (see Psalm 89:27)."[89] This is an important point. The role of king or queen was divine and tied to God. In some cultures, kingship was also sacral, that is identical with the role of a priest or judge, while in others the priestly and ruling roles were separate. In the temple, they are combined. The connection is inherent in the priesthood as Melchizedek is a compound of two words which mean *king* and *priest.* In Christ, we find the fulfillment of both as he is the King and the great High Priest (see Mark 15:26, Isaiah 6:1, Hebrews 4:14–15).

In ancient, and even some modern, cultures there were various accoutrements or emblems associated with the monarch, king or queen. These often included a scepter (staff, or sometimes a rod, representing justice, authority and judgement)[90], an orb (symbolizing a connection with the spiritual realm; the oracles or enlightenment of God; or sometimes a dominion or realm)[91], a sword (connoting strength and power)[92], a robe (marking authority and identity)[93], and a crown (denoting victory, triumph, honor and glory)[94]. Since we are anointed to become kings and queens, it is not surprising to find these emblems symbolically reflected in the temple ceremony.

For example, the first sign of the Aaronic Priesthood symbolizes justice, but can also depict a scepter (see, for example, Abraham seated upon Pharaoh's throne with the scepter of justice and judgment in his hand in Figure 1 of Facsimile 3 in the Pearl of Great Price). In the second sign, we encounter the cupped hand as a receptacle for the orb. In the next sign, the first of the Melchizedek portion, we find the sword and then finally the crown in the final sign of the endowment. We will consider each of these individually in greater detail.

The Scepter or Rod

Part of a monarch's duty is to administer justice and judgment. The scepter is a symbol of his or her power and authority to do so. Christ as the King is our judge (see John 5:22). The endowment testifies of this fact.

Let's return to the first sign of the endowment. If you are familiar with it, visualize it in your mind. We discussed earlier how this sign can symbolize our birth, the ordinance of mortality which gives life. At first glance this symbol might seem an odd fit, but upon closer consideration perhaps the sign can teach us something about the nature of this ordinance and our purpose and condition here. The sign can represent the horizontal intersection of the earth with the vertical intersection of the heavens. Symbolically, birth is the intersecting point where the spirit and body join together and time and eternity meet.[95] It is therefore fitting of this symbol.

Beyond that, the symbol can also represent exactness. A draftsman might use a square in planning his creation and a carpenter may use the same square to ensure his work conforms exactly to the blueprint. As such, this symbol might also represent the plan or blueprint we came into mortality with and our desire to fulfill it. The covenants which correspond to this sign are obedience and sacrifice. It is here in this life, behind the veil and with the burdens of mortality, that true sacrifice is possible and our obedience can be proven. We seek to understand and then live by the Father's plan for our life.

A square is exact and unyielding. There is no room for error or deviation. It can therefore also symbolize justice. Part of our condition here in mortality is that we become subject to justice as we reach the age of accountability. The sign testifies to this fact. The demands of justice must be fully satisfied. Part of a king's duty is to administer it to his subjects. The scepter is included as part of a coronation ceremony because it represents his obligation and power to do so.

In the case of Christ, He not only administers justice but also completely fulfills the demands of justice Himself in order to be able to also extend mercy. Christ, as the King, is the only one who entered mortality and conformed His life perfectly to the Father's plan. He alone owes no debt to justice. In every aspect, His life meets the exactness of the square. Despite whatever goodness there may be in our lives, we do not. We are subject to justice. Christ is not indebted to it.

The Orb

The next emblem of kingship is the orb. The orb represents communication with the spiritual realm, or the king's connection to God. It can be associated with seeing or seer stones. (A crystal ball would be a perversion of this principle, but the image may be helpful to understand the orb). More than a physical device, however, the orb represents the king's ability to receive and speak God's word and instructions. The king is entitled to "hold" the oracles (or revelations) of God.

Statue of Jupiter holding the scepter and orb.

Joseph Smith taught the kingdom of God is found wherever there is a prophet, priest or righteous man to whom God gives His oracles.[96] He further added, "if we do not get revelations we do not have the oracles of God."[97]

We encounter the cupped hand as a receptacle for the orb in the second sign of the endowment. We discussed earlier how this second sign represents the ordinance of baptism as entrance into God's kingdom. In part, it symbolizes our broken hearts and contrite spirits offered up to God. But here this sign also signifies holding the orb or receiving personal revelations and knowledge from Him. It is therefore associated with the Holy Ghost and the spirit of prophecy and revelation to be obtained after baptism. It represents our increasing connection to God. We are entitled to receive revelation but are also cautioned to beware how we hold the oracles of God (see D&C 90:5). Or in other words, take care how we heed the revelations we are given. This is critical in our lives if we hope to make any real progression.[98]

In Christ's case, He held a fullness of this light. John testified that even in mortality Christ received not a measure or a degree of the spirit, but that He received it in full (see John 3:34). His connection to God the Father was such that Christ could say they were one (see John 17:21). In fact, He testified: "I am the light of the world: he that followeth me shall not walk in darkness, but shall have the light of life" (John 8:12).

The corresponding covenant is the law of the gospel, which is part of the light we must receive. This law is also symbolized by the orb. We are to receive the law of the gospel and the Holy Ghost to guide us, illuminating the path ahead and enabling us to know and then do our Father's will. Again, Christ is our perfect exemplar. So fully did Christ conform to the Father's word that he testified, "this is the gospel which I have given unto you—that I came into the world to do the will of my Father, because my Father sent me" (3 Nephi 27:13).

In related imagery, we are also to be lights unto the world: "therefore let your light so shine before this people, that they may see your good works and glorify your Father who is in heaven" (3 Nephi 12:16). Christ is the light we are to hold up: "therefore, hold up your light that it may shine unto the world. Behold, I am the light which ye shall hold up" (3 Nephi 18:24).

The Sword

The sword is another emblem of kingship. We find it represented in the third sign of the endowment ceremony in our outstretched arm. Primarily a symbol of power and might, the sword is a reminder of the king's duty to protect his people. He is to fight or lead their battles and vanquish their enemies, even laying down his own life if required. This motif was often depicted in ancient belief and rituals.[99] Coronation ceremonies frequently depicted a mock battle where the king defeated a common foe of the people.[100] In some cases, the king's life or a substitute life was required.[101]

We find real-life examples in the scriptures, such as in the case of Nephi, who slew Laban (the enemy) and returned with his sword, the brass plates (word of God), and then received the Liahona (an orb). These emblems of kingship were passed to subsequent Nephite kings (see Mosiah 1:16).[102] Moses, likewise, confronted Pharaoh with his staff and the word of God and delivered Israel. David slew Goliath and returned with his sword before becoming king (see 1 Samuel 17:51, 21:9).

However, the ultimate example again is Christ. In the story of the Fall, as Adam and Eve are driven out of God's presence, cherubim and a flaming sword are set to guard the way to the tree of life (see Genesis 3:24). They stand there as sentinels against fallen, natural man, now an enemy to God. We have become the problem. It is only through Christ that a way back is prepared. He defeated mankind's common enemies—death, sin, and hell—at the price of His own life. In this sense, the associated sign can represent our petitioning as a beggar for relief and His hand providing a covering for us through the Atonement.

As this sign is made, symbolizing the sword, the orb is now held in the opposite hand. Here the meaning changes and the orb becomes a symbol of dominion or of His kingdom. Christ holds dominion over all creation—including death and hell—having descended below all things and then ascended above all so as to be in and through all things (see D&C 88:6). Following his resurrection, He testified that all power was given unto Him in heaven and in earth (see Matthew 28:18). So closely is Christ, the King, aligned with God His Father, that the Father's own power is now appropriately called the light of Christ in modern revelation (see D&C 88:7–13).

With respect to our lives, we mentioned this sign represents the ordinance of the new and everlasting covenant of marriage. The sword is also appropriate here as a symbol of our obligation to provide for and protect our families. This is to be done in the strength of the Lord as the Book of Mormon teaches. The accompanying covenant is the law of chastity. Interestingly, the sword is also a phallic symbol. In marriage it is covered by a sheath—the etymological definition of the term vagina is sheath.[103] In this symbol, as in the others, we find a balance of both male and female attributes in the image of God and family.

In this aspect, we see a tie to Christ as well. His Church is recognized as Christ's bride. One purpose of our marriages is to bring forth seed (posterity). Likewise, Abinadi testified that the result of Christ's offering of His soul is that He will bring forth and see His seed (see Mosiah 15:10). We become His seed through His Atonement. Once again, we see that the temple symbols apply both to Christ and to us as individuals, whether male or female.

The Robe

A king or queen's robe reflects his or her identity, authority, and reign. An example of this symbolism in the Old Testament is found when the Lord rejected Saul as a king over Israel. Saul's torn robe was seen as a sign that the "Lord hath rent the kingdom of Israel from thee this day" (1 Samuel 15:27–28). David had an opportunity to slay Saul, but refused to do so and instead cut off a portion of Saul's robe (see 1 Samuel 24:4–5). He then confronted Saul with the robe in hand as proof of his good intentions towards the king (see 1 Samuel 24:11). Saul interpreted David holding the piece of his robe as evidence that the kingdom would pass into David's hand (see 1 Samuel 24:20).

A popular story regarding the king's robe circulates among some Christian groups. According to the legend, when an ancient king defeated another in battle the victor was entitled to cut off a portion of the defeated king's robe and add it to his own as a symbol of his victory. The longer the train of a king's robe, the more battles he had won and the more victorious he stood.[104]

With respect to our Heavenly King, Isaiah testified that he saw the Lord exalted, sitting upon a throne, and that the train of his robe filled the temple (see Isaiah 6:1).[105] In other words, it covered the entire floor of the temple and testified of Christ's victory and the defeat of our enemies—death, sin, and hell. Each of our failures, defeats and weaknesses can be made perfect in Him and added to the length of His robe. Of this idea, one Christian writer expressed the following:

> If we think about the temple of the [Old Testament], it was a place where the people would come to offer sacrifices because of their sin, because of their defeatedness. It was a place where they would bring their failure, their insecurity, and their inadequacy. Not much has changed over the years. For us, the new Israel, the temple of the church is still a place where we can bring our brokenness. As we attend every week, our failures, our fears, our insecurities, and our sin all follow us through the door. But then came the revelation; 'the train of His robe filled the temple.' We worship the God of Victory, the King of kings and the Lord of lords who has defeated the power of sin, and if that piece of cloth is sewn to the end of the train of His robe, and if His robe fills the temple, then everything we bring into the temple is covered, everything we bring into the temple is defeated. We are covered by the robe of the King who

> has conquered death! His Robe signifies the defeat of the enemy, His Blood seals our redemption.[106]

I have been unable to find an historical source to verify this legend of the length of a king's robe and suspect it is probably folklore, but the idea of Christ's victory, authority, majesty, and glory is certainly reflected in the robe Isaiah saw. In Christ's case, the robe not only testifies of Him but is also meant to cover His subjects. Isaiah understood this. He later testified that God had covered him with "the robe of [His] righteousness" (Isaiah 61:10). This may be more significant than simply covering our sins. In the Savior's parable of the prodigal son, the wayward son finally returns home, recognizing his failing and desiring to be nothing more than a servant. Notice the father's response. Rather than rebuking or condemning his son, he has the best robe brought forth and clothes him (see Luke 15:22). This act was not the father's acceptance of a servant, but rather his restoration of the son as part of the family. This beautiful act may be reflected in our own temple ceremony.

The Crown

Finally, the last emblem of kingship is the crown. It is a symbol of victory, honor, triumph, and glory. We find it in the final sign of the endowment. Think of how this sign is made. The gesture may be viewed as "a coronation symbol, representing the placement of a crown or halo of glory upon the initiate's head."[107] It can also symbolize Christ's descent from on high to this realm and then his subsequent resurrection and ascent. It recalls Jacob's ladder or the bridge between the worlds (see Genesis 28:12–13).

An angel showed this reality to Nephi. After seeing the tree of life, the angel asked Nephi: "Knowest thou the condescension of God?" (1 Nephi 11:16). It is almost as if the angel is asking, "Nephi, do you get it?" To which, Nephi responds: "Well, I know God loves his children" (see 1 Nephi 11:17). While that is true, Nephi doesn't yet understand the depth of Christ's love. You can almost picture the angel shaking his head and thinking: "Nephi, you don't get it!" And so Nephi is shown the Savior's birth, ministry, and death.

Nephi sees the indescribable contrast between the realm of glory, light, and love that Christ descended from and all of the blackness, evil and opposition He confronted in this world. *The bitter irony is that our God is the very King who descends to be despised and rejected by His own subjects* (see Isaiah 53:3). He bears our griefs, carries our sorrows, and suffers to reclaim us (see Isaiah 53:5–6). The condescension is so great, it is no wonder Isaiah exclaimed: who is going to believe this (see Isaiah 53:1)? Here is a King who kneels to serve, bless, and elevate his entire kingdom.

It is only after the vision of all of this that Nephi finally begins to understand the tree of life his father saw. The angel then asks him a second time: "Knowest thou the meaning of the tree which thy father saw?" (1 Nephi 11:21). Or in other words: "Now do you understand?" To which Nephi responds: "Yea, it is the love of God." It is essentially the same answer he gave before, but now, at last, Nephi sees the depths of God's love in what He suffered for us. To satisfy justice and overcome death and hell on our behalf required the life of the King. The sign is a reminder of the price Christ paid. It is a symbol of the "condescension of God."

With respect to us as participants in the drama, this final sign is also a petition to heaven for the accompanying token, which represents the ministry of the Second Comforter. It is a testimony of our clean hands and pure hearts before God, and a recognition of the three levels that separate us in the present telestial realm from Him in the celestial realm. It is a plea for Him to again condescend to minister to us individually and to raise us up.

It is worth noting here once again, that for us as individuals, the tokens accompanying these signs reflect an increasing contact with and connection to the Godhead. We can find a progression from the light of Christ (when God first takes us by the hand), to then receiving the Holy Ghost (the first Comforter), to then receiving Christ's ministry as the Second Comforter, and finally to being presented by Him to the Father, thereby completing the process of being adopted as a son or daughter and becoming one with the Godhead (see John 17:21; Moses 6:64–68). The temple is a great metaphor explaining our religion and teaching us about the Holy Order after the Son of God (see Alma 13:16).

The King's Ransom

Prior to 1990, the endowment included a penalty associated with the names, signs, and tokens. Those endowed thereafter may not be aware of them. These penalties were removed after a survey revealed that many Church members were uncomfortable with them. That discomfort may have stemmed from the way the penalties were presented, along with a general lack of understanding of what was being taught.[108] While I see why some had these feelings, by completely removing them we may have lost something important. I will not disclose what the penalties were, but we are going to discuss what they taught because they contained a beautiful testimony of Christ. In the discussion that follows, do not worry if you are not familiar with the old penalties. The important thing is to understand the principles they conveyed.

Besides testifying of Christ, an additional, but secondary, purpose for the former penalties was to serve as a warning to the initiates. The warning being that with each sign, or in other words with each step we take toward God, there is a potential blessing (represented by the token) but also a potential liability (attested by the penalty). The temple endowment showed both. We increase our individual accountability as we approach God. In fact, many of God's gifts—our bodies, our weakness, even our lives—can be a blessing or a cursing depending upon what we choose to do with them. God provides us with an opportunity, but it is then up to us to properly utilize it. The penalties helped illustrate this truth.

For example, recall that the second sign and token can represent our baptism by water and the subsequent baptism of fire and the Holy Ghost from God. This great blessing comes with an associated penalty. Christ warned that after one has received the baptism of fire and the Holy Ghost, that if the person should then deny Him, it would be better if they had not known him (see 2 Nephi 31:14). We see this principle illustrated in the Book of Mormon when people who were once illuminated by the gospel and then subsequently fell into sin and apostasy became harder and more rebellious than before their conversion.

So, in part, the penalties were to impress upon our minds the serious nature of entering into a covenant with God.[109] Our temple covenants are not to be taken lightly![110] Penalties were an important part of ancient covenant ceremonies. They represented the consequences of failing to abide by the terms of the covenant and signaled both parties acceptance of the penalty if they failed (see, for example, Alma 46:21). For a more detailed discussion of this aspect of ancient covenants, please see chapter one of *Understanding Your Endowment.*[111]

In the case of the temple endowment, the former penalties were not tied to keeping our covenants 100% perfectly, but rather to not revealing certain information received in the endowment. Mercifully, that obligation was something everyone could choose to keep perfectly. Unfortunately, because of the presentation and the wording associated with the endowment penalties, many members only saw them as severe warnings to maintain secrecy and failed to recognize them as important teaching devices with a deeper meaning.

This narrow view of the penalties, as simply an obligation to maintain confidentiality, is essentially the same function of the penalties under Free Masonry. If the only purpose of the endowment's former penalties was to maintain secrecy, as seemed evident from the way they were presented, then why were there three separate penalties? Why not just have one that covered keeping everything confidential? The fact that there were three very different symbolic penalties and three distinct points in the endowment ceremony when they were encountered gave important clues as to their real purpose. Let's consider that meaning next as they revealed a beautiful testimony of the gospel. In the following discussion, please recognize that the penalties, like the other symbols (signs, tokens, etc.), can apply both to Christ and to us as initiates.

The penalties tied to the first two Aaronic signs represented two different ways that life could be taken. The first penalty was associated with the head and the second with the heart. Keep these two associations in mind as we proceed. The first two Aaronic signs, together with the associated penalties, testified of the conditions of mortality established by the Fall and of the divine rescue provided by Christ.[112]

As we discussed earlier, the first sign represents our birth into mortality. Accordingly, the first penalty symbolized our eventual death and return to eternity.[113] The sign and penalty were connected and presented together in the endowment ceremony. Both birth, as an entrance, and death, as an exit, were instituted by the Fall of Adam and Eve for all mankind. As part of life, we become subject to death (see Romans 6:23). In a sense, at death our souls are severed when spirit and body part. Lehi taught that as a result of this, all mankind would be lost forever. "For behold, if the flesh should rise no more our spirits must become subject to that angel who fell from before the presence of the Eternal God, and became the devil, to rise no more. And our spirits must have become like unto him, and we become devils . . . shut out from the presence of our God" (2 Nephi 9:8–9). Or to paraphrase, as part of our mortality, we become subject to the *penalty* of death.

This first penalty, like the first sign of the endowment, was also symbolically associated with justice. Like Adam and Eve, we are here to learn by our own experience and choices. Sometimes that learning involves painful mistakes and hard lessons. We all fall short and offend justice and God's law. Or as Lehi testified, by the law we are cut off (see 2 Nephi 2:5). We end up indebted to justice and subject to death. Eventually that debt to justice must be paid in full (see D&C 19:17).

The penalty attested to these two conditions. Because of the Fall, we are subject to death and hell, or in other words, physical and spiritual death (see 2 Nephi 9:10). These are the penalties of mortality. They are the high cost of this gift of life we are given. With respect to our physical death, we are helpless to avoid or reverse it. We also individually owe a debt to justice, which eventually must be paid. Those who have experienced some of this payment of their own debt describe it as a lake of fire and brimstone or an "everlasting burning" (see Mosiah 27:28). Thus, the first two signs and penalties outline the conditions and dilemma of mortality. They highlight our problem.

The associated covenant (which is the law of sacrifice) provides hope. The law of sacrifice allows for a substitute to stand in place of the sinner. For example, Adam was given a commandment to build an altar and sacrifice the firstlings of his flocks to teach him this principle (see Moses 5:5). These ancient animal sacrifices were meant to testify of Christ. An angel explained to Adam: "This thing is a similitude of the sacrifice of the Only Begotten of the Father, which is full of grace and truth" (Moses 5:7). Our endowment penalties were also in similitude of Christ's sacrifice and represented the ways that animals were sacrificed anciently as proxy or substitute.

Christ provides the solution to the dilemma of mortality. He alone was not subject to death by reason of sin and transgression. His death was given voluntarily. He alone met the exacting standard of the square. Justice was offended by His death, because it was completely unmerited. The penalties did not apply to Him. Justice and death had no claim upon Him. Because of that, He alone was qualified to stand in as our substitute. Only the King could ransom his kingdom. Peter testified: "ye were not redeemed with corruptible things, as silver and gold . . . but with the precious blood of Christ, as a lamb without blemish and without spot" (1 Peter 1:18).

The Aaronic penalties testified of the price Christ paid to redeem us. Rather than revealing the precise manner in which Christ was killed, the penalties instead taught about His suffering. Recall that the first two penalties were related to the head and to the heart. Our Savior understands perfectly everything we suffer in mortality, not only in His head, but also in His heart because He experienced it fully. Or, to use other words, we could say He suffered both body and spirit (or physically and spiritually). One was incomplete without the other. The two penalties testified of this dual nature of Christ's sufferings. The garden was not complete without the cross.

The second sign marks the beginning of the reversal of the effects of the Fall. Recall that this sign symbolizes our spiritual rebirth into God's kingdom through baptism, accepting Christ's sacrifice on our behalf. What we are offered instead of justice and death is an alternative—eternal life. Paul taught, "For the wages of sin is death; but the gift of God is eternal life through Jesus Christ our Lord" (Romans 6:23). We are provided an escape from the penalties we justly deserve. "For I God have suffered these things for all that they might not suffer if they would repent" (D&C 19:16).

The second penalty not only witnessed of Christ's sacrifice, but also showed what is required of us. It also symbolized our own offering of a broken heart and contrite spirit. "Behold, he offereth himself a sacrifice for sin, to answer the ends of the law, unto all those who have a broken heart and a contrite spirit; and unto none else can the ends of the law be answered" (2 Nephi 2:7). Without our corresponding individual sacrifice of a broken heart and contrite spirit, we will be left to eventually pay the debt to justice ourselves. This required sacrifice is more than it appears on the surface, and the condition of our own hearts is worth careful scrutiny. Learning to walk with God with a broken heart in a spirit of meekness and humility is the essence of putting off the natural man or woman and becoming a saint (see Mosiah 3:19).

Thus, we can see in the first two signs, tokens, and penalties of the Aaronic Priesthood an overview of the plan of salvation. They taught and testified both of the Redeemer and of the redeemed, outlining a gospel progression that involves the active participation and full effort of both parties. Having presented these, the endowment then moves on to the Melchizedek portion. This was and is a marked transition. In a sense, we are leaving the more "Old Testament" portion of the endowment and moving on to the more "New Testament" part. [114]

There was a penalty associated with the first sign of the Melchizedek Priesthood, but surprisingly not with the second. This omission provided an important clue. At this point in the ceremony, we are moving from the demonstration of Christ's suffering (symbolized by the first two penalties) to now witnessing the results of His sacrifice. The single Melchizedek penalty attested to the sword of justice opening the bowels of mercy. It was not truly a penalty, but rather the overturning or fulfillment of the prior penalties established by the Fall of Adam and Eve.

At this point in the endowment (the first sign, token and penalty of the Melchizedek Priesthood), the robe has been switched to the right shoulder, thereby uncovering and revealing the mark of mercy (in the garment) on the left breast of the king. This mercy, or charity, circles or encompasses all of God's dealings with His creation, not by overriding justice (the other mark over the right breast which is now covered) but by completely satisfying (or covering) it.

This sign and penalty invite us to do likewise, in similitude of our King. As we are healed by Him and receive His mercy, we are to then extend it to others. There may be those against whom we rightly could wield the sword of justice. The penalty served as an invitation to us to set aside our right to justice and instead extend forgiveness and mercy. As the King knelt to bear the full burden of all mortality, we are asked as part of the gospel to likewise help bear one another's burdens (see Mosiah 18:8). As we begin to serve, lift, and bless others—turning the other cheek and going the second mile, rather than seeking an eye for an eye—we are beginning to act in a Melchizedek and not an Aaronic manner.

The final sign of the endowment did not have an accompanying penalty. This is because it represents Christ's ultimate triumph. The King has paid the ransom in full. This final sign is a symbol of His victory! It reflects Abinadi's testimony in the Book of Mormon that Christ has "ascended into heaven, having the bowels of mercy; being filled with compassion towards the children of men; standing betwixt them and justice; having broken the bands of death, taken upon himself their iniquity and their transgressions, having redeemed them, and satisfied the demands of justice" (Mosiah 15:9).[115] *The King was made to answer in full for every shortcoming and every injustice in His kingdom.* Truly He is King of kings and Lord of lords (see Revelation 17:14).

At the Veil

The endowment ceremony concludes as we are presented at the veil to symbolically meet with our Lord and King.[116] Prior to this moment, we petition Him in prayer. This prayer is an important part of the ceremony and the only part that is not pre-scripted. It is the one unique element we contribute. Although there is only one strait and narrow path—we are all individuals with unique circumstances, needs, and situations along that path. In part, the prayer is a recognition of that reality. We will discuss this prayer later, but its positioning here is important as prayer is the portal to the veil.

At the veil, we encounter the final element of the endowment, the marks of the priesthood. The current explanation of these marks was suggested by David O. McKay and added to the ceremony around 1936.[117] It is remarkably similar to Masonry's interpretation of some of these same symbols. The square and compass are widely recognized symbols of Freemasonry: "The Square is an emblem of virtue in which we must 'square our actions by the square of virtue with all mankind'. The Compasses exemplify our wisdom of conduct . . . 'the strength to circumscribe our desires and keep our passions within due bounds.'"[118]

Though these ideas are certainly appropriate, there may be another meaning to these marks that is more personal and relates directly to our connection with Christ. Though this meaning is obscured in our modern world, it would not have been missed in ancient cultures where covenant ceremonies often left a permanent mark on the body as a token or witness of the covenant.[119]

In order for a covenant to be binding anciently, blood had to be shed. The mark was a reminder of this blood and a witness of the covenant formed. In some societies, the mark was simply the scar left from the wound. For example, in a covenant where two people became "blood-brothers," after making an incision in the palm or wrist, the two parties clasped hands or forearms to allow their blood to flow together. "Afterward, an abrasive substance was sometimes rubbed into the wound to leave a permanent mark or scar as a token of the covenant. Thereafter, when either party wanted to disclose their covenant status, hands and arms were raised to display these marks."[120]

In a similar fashion under the gospel, blood was also required to create a covenant. Most often this was the surrogate blood of a sacrificial animal. These sacrifices, however, were simply types and shadows of the true sacrifice of the future King. Ultimately, it was His blood and His life that was required. The scriptures declare: "For where a covenant is, there must also of necessity be the death of the testator [or victim]" (JST Hebrews 9:16). Of mankind was required the blood of the sacrificial lamb or victim (see Hebrews 9:19–20). But for the gospel covenant to be in full effect through eternity required the death of the covenant giver (testator) or the King (see Hebrews 9:17). Sacrifice was required of both parties (covenant maker and covenant receiver), but the greater portion from the one who offered the covenant.

When Christ introduced the sacrament, he testified that the wine "is my blood of the new testament [or covenant], which is shed for many" (Mark 14:24, see also Luke 22:20, 1 Corinthians 11:25). Christ bears the marks of this covenant in his body: "Behold, I have graven thee upon the palms of my hands" (Isaiah 49:16). This is according to the pattern by which ancient covenants were established and recognized.[121] The marks are left as a witness of the covenant.

In our temple ceremony, we find covenantal marks in the veil of the temple and in our individual garments. In the Nauvoo era, these marks were cut into the garment in front of the veil at the end of the endowment.[122] This practice made the connection between our individual garments and the temple veil immediate and obvious. It recalled the ancient covenant process. The garment was cut and marked only *after* the individuals had entered into the covenants of the endowment and served as a witness.

We are taught that our priesthood garments represent the coat (or garment) of skins that the Lord made anciently for Adam and Eve (see Genesis 3:21). In order for these garments to be supplied, the sacrifice of an animal was required. It was in that setting that the Lord taught Adam and Eve about the reality of sacrifice. In the priesthood marks, just as in the penalties, we again find symbolic teaching about sacrifice and the price of the covenant Christ offers.

One meaning of the temple veil is a symbol of the body of Christ (see Hebrews 10:20). In light of these covenantal ideas, the veil marks can, therefore, be seen to represent the wounds of Christ or the marks of His covenant. Clothed in our garments, we also bear the marks of Christ's crucifixion. Paul testified: "let no man trouble me: for I bear in my body the marks of the Lord Jesus" (Galatians 6:17). These marks witness of the potential bond that is created with our God and King as a result of His covenant. In a lesser measure, they also reflect the sacrifices that He requires of us as part of the gospel covenant.

With this background in mind, another interpretation of the priesthood marks could be as follows: "The right breast mark represents the square of unachievable justice and perfection— the Mosaic law. The left breast mark, the square turned into a compass, represents the love and compassion of God offered us through the gospel. The navel mark . . . represents the spiritual journey of descent into mortality and ascent back to God."[123] And the knee mark testifies of a King who knelt to serve and lift all of His creation.[124] Christ's ultimate victory is reflected in the priesthood marks as the square (representing justice) is turned (or overcome) to form the compass (mercy) through the condescension (descent and subsequent ascent) of Christ (symbolized in the navel and knee marks). Mercy can circumscribe or completely fulfill the exact demands of justice only because of Christ, the King.

With this interpretation, we can finally see and understand that the ritual embrace at the veil ascribes our sins and weakness to Christ and in turn the righteousness and strength of Christ to us.[125] Or in other words, Christ became "sin for us, who knew no sin; that we might be made the righteousness of God in him" (2 Corinthians 5:21). Christ assumes our sinful and fallen nature and offers in return healing through His holiness. This can occur because of His covenant. As we reach through the mark of justice (being subject to it) to our Lord, He in turn reaches out to us through the mark of charity or mercy (extending it to us) in an embrace that combines us as one. In this embrace, our identities merge.[126]

All of these symbols are meant to teach and instruct us. They represent spiritual realities we need to receive. The symbols point both to Christ and His covenant and in a smaller measure to us. Our need to accept our Savior's love and mercy, to be transformed by His grace, and to begin walking in His footsteps is reinforced in the veil ceremony. Older members of the Church and students of LDS history will recall the five points of fellowship which were included in the veil ceremony until 1990. These five points are another element of the endowment that appears to have been borrowed from Masonry. We will address the relationship between the endowment and Masonry later, but will briefly cover the five points before concluding here.

Masonic ritual describes the Five Points of Fellowship as: 1) foot to foot, 2) knee to knee, 3) breast to breast, 4) hand to back, and

5) mouth to ear. Under Masonry, these points served as a reminder of the duty and obligations members owed one another as part of their fellowship. The Masonic explanations of these symbols were varied but a representative sample follows:

- Foot to foot. He should go out of his way, and not permit his steps to halt in extending mercy and benevolence.
- Knee to knee. The knee should be bent in intercessory prayer for others, and in pleading for forgiveness for his own sins.
- Breast to breast. The man of honor should guard all just and lawful secrets inviolate within his breast.
- Hand to back. It is a Mason's duty to support his Brother, to lift him up, and to speak well of him before the world. This may also hold some symbolism of being "raised up" in other ways.
- Mouth to Ear. He should whisper good counsel into the ear of a brother, instruct him, and warn him of coming danger.[127]

It was only upon the keeping of these points of fellowship that the lost word (or final blessing in Masonry) was given to the initiate.

The meaning of these five points was never explained in the endowment. However, the intent we might surmise seems applicable. In the merging of our identity with Christ at the veil, we must then begin to follow in His footsteps (foot to foot); kneel as He knelt to minister to others (knee to knee); purify our hearts and treasure up light and truth within our soul (breast to breast); lift and support our brothers and sisters (hand to back); and keep our ears open and close to the Lord's mouth to receive His word (mouth to ear). It is only in walking the walk that we become eligible to receive the blessings we are promised at the veil.

In conclusion, at the veil we encounter: four marks, four being the number of the wounds of the crucifixion (head, side, hands and feet);

in an embrace covering five points (again pointing to Christ's wounds: head, back, side, hands and feet) for a total of nine points. Nine is a symbol of Christ's total and complete sacrifice: 1 head (crown of thorns), 1 back (given to smiters), 2 hands, 2 wrists, 1 side (pierced by spear), and 2 feet (for a total of nine). As you can see, there is great meaning and elegant beauty in our temple rituals.

Recognizing a True King

Many today seem to want a "bling" Jesus and a gospel of success. We want an easy path through life, and see Christ as being able to give that to us. The gospel testifies otherwise. Richard Rohr observed:

> Christians are usually sincere and well-intentioned people until you get to any real issues of ego, control, power, money, pleasure, and security. Then they tend to be pretty much like everybody else. We are often given a bogus version of the Gospel, some fast-food religion, without any deep transformation of the self; and the result has been the spiritual disaster of 'Christian' countries that tend to be as consumer-oriented, proud, warlike, racist, class conscious, and addictive as everybody else—and often more so, I'm afraid.[128]

Though not specifically addressing us, we as LDS members are not insulated from this problem. Becoming a true king or queen requires a transformation that is beyond our ability to accomplish solely on our own. We are in need of Christ's grace and help (see Ether 12:36).

Sacrificing to lift and bless others is sometimes painful and difficult. It wasn't easy for Christ. Nor will it be easy for any who stand beside Him as saviors on Mount Zion. It is a true principle that a descent is required before a subsequent greater ascent is possible. In a manner imitative of our Savior, others who were noble and great condescended to come down here on rescue missions. These would have included Adam and Eve, Abraham and Sarah, Joseph and Emma, and many others. We too, in our own limited spheres, may have come down with specific assignments or missions to fulfill. Before entering mortality, we may have agreed to help or bless a struggling sibling, spouse, or child. Down here, in the thick of the battle, facing these challenges can seem daunting and overwhelming at times. We have lost the perspective we had prior to our descent.

Society's traditional notion of a king or queen is completely wrong. The very idea of a king seems to be at odds with the rest of the gospel, which teaches us not to esteem any one person above another (see Mosiah 23:7). But herein lies the difference: a true king kneels to serve and lift those around him, raising them to be equal with himself. A false king serves himself. One voluntarily abases himself, while the other seeks self-aggrandizement. They are polar opposites. It is the difference between Moses and the pharaohs of this world.

In nearly every case in the Book of Mormon where we find a true king, the subsequent line of kings inevitably became corrupted, often leading to the captivity of the people. It is so easy to subvert or invert the model and replace a king who serves the people with a king whom the people serve. For example, Nephi was a true king, but corruption started in almost immediately among the people under his successor (see Jacob 1:9, 15). Nephi was not desirous to be a king or for his people to even have one, perhaps knowing where it would inevitably lead (see 2 Nephi 5:18). Likewise, King Zeniff, a righteous king, was followed by his son King Noah who became corrupt (see Mosiah 11:1).

The very idea of a king was grievous to the brother of Jared (see Ether 6:22–23) and each of his sons refused to be anointed king. The first Jaredite king, Orihah, walked in the true model, but his later posterity did not (see Ether 7:1; 4–5). The lone exception is the succession from King Benjamin to King Mosiah, both of whom were servant kings. But the line ended there and had to be replaced with a system of judges because each of King Mosiah's sons refused to become king in his turn (see Mosiah 29:3). Those who truly qualify generally don't seek or want the position.

These lessons from the Book of Mormon should be a sobering message to us with respect to the meaning of our temple anointing and how very much we still lack. The transformation the gospel requires from sinner to saint is a process that takes time. It does not occur in a two-hour temple session. The session is giving us a map, but it takes diligent effort over much of our lives to implement it and receive the potential blessings.

Some of the topics we have discussed in this book, such as calling and election and the Second Comforter, cause fear and anxiety among some Church members. That fear may stem from knowing of people who have "gone off the deep end." People sometimes use a little extra insight or knowledge that they supposedly have to make outlandish claims intended to attract attention or elevate themselves in the eyes of others. Of such we should be wary. They are following a false model. False spirits are happy to mislead those who are overanxious and impatient with the process. This can lead to outlandish and bizarre behavior, such as occurred at times in the early days of the Restoration. It saddens me to hear of it still happening today. Knowledge is power. And Satan may tempt those who possess a small, but insufficient, amount to misuse it. We have in the endowment and in the scriptures a true model to avoid being misled by such nonsense and by the model of Babylon we find all around us in the world.

HOMEWORK

1. Attend a temple endowment session and specifically look for the testimony of Christ throughout the temple. What more can the endowment teach us about our King and the path He trod?

2. How might the principles in this chapter relate to our own anointing to become a king or a queen? Does our "kingdom" potentially begin at the temple altar as a husband and wife are sealed together? If so, how do the covenants relate to serving within our own families?

CHAPTER 7

LESSONS FROM THE ENDOWMENT

To the angels is given power "to bring as many as will come to the Church of the Firstborn."
—Doctrine and Covenants 77:11

BEFORE CONCLUDING OUR DISCUSSION of the endowment's keys, let's return to Joseph Smith's stated purpose for these keys: namely, so that faithful saints might know how to ask the Lord and receive an answer, and, so that they might distinguish false spirits from true ones or, in other words, "detect everything false."[129] These functions are very different from the purpose we typically associate with our endowment. In this chapter, we will consider Joseph's statements in greater detail, along with several other lessons we can glean from the endowment.

SEEKING TRUE MESSENGERS

One message readily discerned from the endowment is the need for continued instructions from the Lord. This applies not only to the Church as an organization, but to us individually in our journey through mortality. After being cast out of the Garden of Eden, Adam and Eve lived faithfully to what they knew, all the while waiting for further instructions from the Lord. They were praying and watching for messengers from Him. We should do likewise. Some of the instruction we need in our individual paths cannot come through the Church institution because it is too unique to us and our circumstances. The iron rod includes the personal revelation and communication we receive from God.

At some point in our spiritual growth, like Adam and Eve, we may encounter angels (who are simply messengers). People tend to bristle a little at this idea in our modern world. Maybe angels appeared in biblical times or to Joseph Smith, but not today. Or if we are willing to believe it is possible, then we tend to put up all kinds of rules and conditions to such an encounter, like maybe it is possible, but only if the angel was a grandfather or other relative. Those kinds of traditions are not scriptural, indeed may be anti-scriptural. God has testified that He is the same yesterday, today and forever, and that if angels cease to minister among us then it is because of unbelief (see Moroni 7:37).

Joseph Smith seems to anticipate that such angelic ministrations are to be expected as part of our gospel education and development, hence the need for keys to be delivered to the entire Church respecting these things. These are his words: "I preached in the grove on the keys of the Kingdom ... *The keys are certain signs and words by which false spirits and personages may be detected from true*, which cannot be revealed to the Elders till the Temple is completed."[130] The keys to the ministering of angels are delivered in the Aaronic portion of the endowment as is demonstrated therein, combined with the instructions given in Doctrine and Covenants section 129. Why would Joseph include these keys and instructions unless he expected the ministry of angels to be a normal part of the Saints' experience?

The scriptures also seem to anticipate such ministration. For example, although all kinds of people are gathered by the gospel net into the Church, eventually *the angels* have the task of sorting out the good from the bad (see Matthew 13:47–49) and gathering them *before* the burning (see D&C 86:5–7). This gathering will involve their direct ministry. The Book of Mormon testifies that angels will not cease to minister so long as the earth stands and there remains even a single person thereon to be saved (see Moroni 7:36–37). The scriptures also testify that angels are responsible for gathering us into the Church of the Firstborn (see D&C 77:11). The missionaries may cast the broad gospel net into all the world, but the final gathering of those who are exalted is entrusted to the angels who stand as sentinels (meaning someone who is watching and waiting).

These verses raise an important question: can a person be saved without their ministry? Regardless of the answer to that question, we need to be seeking instructions from the Lord and watching for His answers, whether those are delivered through the Holy Ghost, a dream, a friend, the visit of an angel, or any other way the Lord sees fit to respond.

Discerning Truth from Error

Not only does the endowment impose upon each of us the obligation to continually seek further light, knowledge, and direction, we are also to test whatever we receive in order to discern truth from error and avoid being deceived. Taken along with the instructions in section 129, the keys given us in the endowment seem intended to apply to angelic visitations. But what about discerning the truth of messages delivered in another way, such as in a dream or other form of revelation? How are we to discern when the temple keys do not seem to directly apply? Perhaps there is a way to view these keys in a broader sense.

After being cast out, the endowment shows that Adam and Eve had to recognize and reject Satan's lies in the things being taught in the world around them before angels were sent to give them further directions from the Lord. Interestingly, the initial assignment the angels receive is to see whether Adam and Eve have been true to the token first given them. Recall that this token represents the light of Christ. It is that token we must learn to use before we will be entrusted with more. "Wherefore, I beseech of you, brethren, that ye should search diligently *in the light of Christ* that ye may know good from evil" (Moroni 7:19; emphasis added). We are true to this first token by following it and using it as it as a guide to distinguish between good and evil. Adam and Eve did this and therefore recognized that what was being taught was the "philosophies of men" mingled with scripture. It was not the message from God they were looking for and so they rejected it and waited on the Lord. Because they were true to this first token, the Lord sent them more.

This idea is consistent with what we learn about discernment in the scriptures. Korihor was deceived when Satan appeared to him in the form of an angel. Korihor could have avoided the deception by recognizing that the message delivered contradicted existing scripture and appealed to the "carnal" mind (see Alma 30:53). The content of the message was not what God would have delivered. On the other hand, the two disciples on the road to Emmaus spent an afternoon visiting with the resurrected Christ who withheld his identity so they did not recognize him (Luke 24:16). He opened the scriptures to their understanding. And they testified that their hearts burned within them (Luke 24:32). Though they did not recognize the messenger, they recognized the truth of his message by the Holy Ghost. Moses saw through Satan's attempted deception by his lack of glory which did not require Moses' transfiguration to be in his presence (see Moses 1:13–16, 18). From these scriptures it becomes clear there are various ways to discern.

One way to view and use the keys is to test any message against the light of Christ, the Holy Ghost, the scriptures, and what we are taught in the endowment covenants. If a message conflicts with those things, we should be very wary of its origin. Mormon taught that we may judge by whether it persuades us to do good and to serve God or not (see Moroni 7:16–17). "That which doth not edify is not of God, and is darkness" (D&C 50:23). True messages will invite repentance, testify of Christ, and enlighten our souls. False spirits and messages seek to flatter us, appeal to our pride or vanity, and cause us to be puffed up. They will direct attention to us and "our greatness" rather than pointing to Christ. False messages contradict the scriptures and appeal to our carnal natures. They spread confusion and darkness and encourage self-aggrandizement over service and sacrifice. These things are the opposite of what the temple teaches.

Still, discernment can sometimes be difficult. At times, revelations and directions from God cause distress and discomfort. We are in a process of growth and development that by nature requires us to continue learning and stretching. When new information comes from the Lord that contradicts what we formerly believed, it can be difficult to accept and integrate. We must let go of old beliefs that were wrong or perhaps discard a partial truth to grasp a greater understanding.

Fortunately, God is patient with us and quick to forgive when we get off track. For example, despite all his experience, Lehi still found himself in a dark and dreary waste after following a man in a white robe for many hours (see 1 Nephi 8:7). It was not until Lehi recognized he was not in a good place that he pled for mercy and the Lord responded. We must be open to new learning and ask for help if we get off track. We are here to grow, not to never make mistakes. Sometimes mistakes and failure can be our greatest teachers. We are true to our tokens as we search diligently in the scriptures, by the light of Christ and the Holy Ghost, and follow the prior guidance we have received from the Lord. When we are doing that and seeking for further light and knowledge, He will respond.

Peter, James, and John

As an aside, some wonder how an embodied Peter, James, and John could appear to Adam and Eve as presented. One reason is that when Peter, James, and John arrive on the scene the endowment has moved forward in time to the present day. This idea used to be more apparent in the ceremony. As it is shown today, Adam and Eve simply find themselves in a world where they encounter and must reject the philosophies of men mingled with scripture. Prior to 1990, an example of these teachings was delivered by a Christian minister. The introduction of this character clearly moved the setting of the endowment to the modern world.[131] The time shift is still there but more obscured today. If we recognize that the endowment is moving to our day and that Adam and Eve are symbols of us, then the dilemma is resolved.

Another resolution is to simply recognize Peter, James, and John as symbols, potentially representing any messenger or message sent from God. It might be best to not take such a literal approach here. Joseph Smith originally had the Father and Christ present everything in the endowment ceremony. The characters of Peter, James, and John were added later by Brigham Young. That fact raises the question as to whether the identities are important or not. You will have to decide that for yourself. And it may not be an either / or situation. It may be partially both.

If the identities are important, then why these three? Why not Moses or Elijah or someone else? One reason Peter, James, and John may be very appropriate is because they possess the keys of the kingdom (see D&C 128:20). And according to Joseph Smith those keys are exactly what is being passed on in the endowment. Furthermore, John desired to remain and bring souls unto Christ until He returned in glory (see D&C 7:1–3). John has a specific assignment to minister to those on the earth who will be saved (see D&C 7:6). His ministry appears to be shared with Peter and James (see D&C 7:7). If the endowment's Adam and Eve are symbols or types of us, and if we would like to be an heir of salvation, then how literally should we take the personal ministry of Peter, James, and John? Is this portion of the endowment literal or figurative?

Another question is why does the Lord send them down to test Adam and Eve when He already knows everything? This is simply a teaching device for our benefit. We need to know that testing does occur, often through the circumstances of our lives. "For he will give unto the faithful line upon line, precept upon precept; and I will try you and prove you herewith" (D&C 98:12). The Lord judged of King Benjamin's righteousness before sending an angel to minister to him (see Mosiah 3:4). We are first given lesser things as a test. If we prove faithful to those things, then greater things are entrusted to us (see 3 Nephi 26:9–11). The endowment reflects this principle.

Your Connection to God

The tokens can be seen as representing an increasing connection with God. When we are willing, He takes us by the hand and leads us along a path back to Him. This light or connection starts small but can grow over time by our heed and diligence. This direct, personal connection with God is described repeatedly in the scriptures. The progression can be summarized as the light of Christ, the Holy Ghost (which includes a scale from the initial "enticings of the Spirit" up through receiving a fulness of the Holy Ghost), angels (or other messages from God, e.g. dreams, visions, etc.) and, finally, the direct personal ministry of the Savior and the Father. The light is meant to grow from the earliest shades of dawn until we finally stand in the noonday sun.

In addition, the Lord uses mortal men and women to deliver His messages. The scriptures refer to these messengers as prophets or prophetesses. A prophet is simply someone claiming to have a message from the Lord, and so we find two interesting scriptural admonitions with respect to prophets: first, we are cautioned that there are both true and false prophets, and we can know them by their fruits; and secondly, Moses wished that "all of the Lord's people were prophets, and that the Lord would put his spirit upon them" (Numbers 11:29). True prophets don't envy their position but cry repentance and seek to bring others to know Christ.

With respect to prophets, the Lord's people anciently were warned, "when a prophet speaketh in the name of the Lord, if the thing follow not, nor come to pass, that is the thing which the Lord hath not spoken, but the prophet hath spoken it presumptuously: thou shalt not be afraid of him" (Deuteronomy 18:22). Joseph Smith also cautioned that a prophet is only a prophet when he is speaking as such. At other times, he is simply a man and entitled to an opinion just as any other man. We find an example of this with Paul in the New Testament. The Lord explained in latter-day revelation that Paul gave the Church in his day a commandment that was not from the Lord but was rather Paul's opinion (see D&C 74:5).

Prophets are primarily necessary when people neglect or ignore their personal connection with God and become lost in this world. When His children are not listening themselves, He has to send another messenger to wake them up. These true prophets come from those who will listen. And, so, we see an example in the opening chapter of the Book of Mormon when *many* prophets were sent to warn the people (see 1 Nephi 1:4). Lehi became one of these prophets, and we see how he was called and commissioned in this same chapter. Or as the Lord explained, "Hear now my words: If there be a prophet among you, I the Lord will make myself known unto him in a vision, and will speak unto him in a dream" (Numbers 12:5–6).

When the Lord sends a message, we better heed it. And we will be accountable for how we receive the Lord's prophets. But there is a delicate balance here that should be appreciated. We carry the notion of "follow the prophet" too far when we insert any man or woman between ourselves and our Savior. That is sacred space. And no one belongs there as an intermediary! True prophets always point to, testify of, and encourage others to develop a personal connection to God. Joseph Smith taught, "the day must come when no man need say to his neighbor know ye the Lord for all shall know him (who remain) from the least to the greatest."[132] In the model of a true prophet, Joseph repeatedly testified the things he had learned and experienced were available to all, if we prepare to receive them.

In all of scripture, you cannot find the phrase "follow the prophet," nor can you find a true prophet encouraging others to follow themselves—rather they all point to the Lord. We are not to follow any man or woman. There is only One whom we are to follow. He is the way, the truth and the life (John 14:16), and He invites us to follow Him.

Beside Him there is no other who can save (see Mosiah 3:17). This is why our personal connection to Him is so crucial.

The journey we must take is from unbelief to belief, then from belief to faith, and finally from faith to knowledge. Belief has to be based upon truth. The light of Christ and the Holy Ghost are guides. When we have belief grounded in the truth and then act upon it, it becomes faith. Faith is a principle of power. It leads us to receive angels whose ministry is to prepare us to receive Christ (see Moroni 7:25, Alma 32:32, etc.) Knowing Christ by being redeemed back into his presence is the knowledge that saves us (see Ether 3:19, John 17:3). These are the keys of the kingdom we see displayed in practice over and over again, in case after case, throughout the Book of Mormon. It is the same testimony and keys we find in the endowment.

As part of the Restoration, Joseph Smith established a priesthood structure in the Church to provide order (see D&C 107). Church leaders can render valuable service and help to us as individuals while we grow and develop in the gospel. My life has been blessed by the call to serve a mission and from other callings for service. There are many ways that Church leaders can bless our lives. But if we become dependent upon Church leaders for everything and neglect nurturing a personal relationship with Christ and learning to receive personal revelation, then the Church's leadership structure can become a stumbling block instead of a blessing. Joseph's stated objective was to teach correct principles and to allow the members to govern themselves, not to micro-manage everything.

Some believe that Peter, James and John in the temple endowment symbolize the First Presidency of the Church. I can see their point but fundamentally disagree. If Joseph or Brigham had wanted these roles in the endowment to be symbolic of the First Presidency, they could simply have had them portray the First Presidency. That may seem awkward in a drama with Adam and Eve, but the endowment had a Christian minister, so why not just introduce the First Presidency as a counter to the minister if that was what was intended?

Another reason I disagree is because the balance we have been discussing seems to have been on Joseph's mind at the time he introduced the endowment. The priesthood structure of the Church was established in 1835 (see D&C 107). This structure had been in operation for seven years when Joseph introduced the endowment on May 4, 1842. A few weeks later while addressing the Relief Society, in his very first public discourse after introducing the endowment, Joseph read the 14th chapter of Ezekiel. He summarized the message of that chapter by stating: "the Lord had declared by the Prophet, that the people should each one stand for himself, and depend upon no man or men in that state of corruption of the Jewish Church—that righteous persons could only deliver their own souls."[133] Joseph then "applied it to the present state of the Church of Jesus Christ of Latter-day Saints" and warned "if the people departed from the Lord, they must fall."[134] He cautioned that "they were depending upon the Prophet, hence were darkened in their minds, in consequence of neglecting the duties devolving upon themselves."[135]

The Saints needed personal revelation and guidance and not to depend upon the prophet, bishop, or other leaders for everything. The same principle is true today. If God is willing to have a direct, personal relationship with us, and we are unwilling to put forth the effort to learn to communicate with Him and walk with Him through life, then we will eventually come to deeply regret it. It will be one of the great tragedies and missed opportunities of mortality.

This was Joseph's concern at the time the endowment was introduced. It may be that he was trying through the endowment to establish a check and balance in the power and influence of the established priesthood structure, a little bit like the checks and balance of power established in the United States Constitution. That is why the endowment emphasizes Adam and Eve (as figures for each of us) going directly to God for answers and direction.

Brigham Young expressed a similar concern: "I am more afraid that this people have so much confidence in their leaders that they will not inquire for themselves of God whether they are led by him. I am fearful they settle down in a state of blind self-security, trusting their eternal destiny in the hands of their leaders with a reckless confidence that in itself would thwart the purposes of God in their salvation, and weaken that influence they could give to their leaders, did they know for themselves, by the revelations of Jesus, that they are led in the right way."[136]

In our return to the Lord both channels are needed. We need to receive God's servants, but that channel is primarily intended to help us eventually also receive the Lord (see D&C 84:36). We see this interplay even in the earliest stages of conversion. Initially, investigators respond to the teachings and testimony of God's servants, the missionaries. But they ultimately should receive baptism only after also receiving their own answer directly from God through the Holy Ghost. Both channels are involved in the process. At the beginning of our journey we may be more dependent upon God's servants for help, but as we mature spiritually and grow closer to the Lord that balance must necessarily shift to becoming more and more dependent upon direct, personal revelation and guidance from the Lord.

Truth Circumscribed

Conflicts can arise when Church leaders disagree or contradict one another. We see this in some of Brigham Young's teachings that were later denounced by the Church. One example was the Adam-God doctrine. Brigham Young, who was the Church's president, declared it to be revelation from God. Orson Pratt, an apostle at the time, disbelieved and opposed it.[137] Later this "doctrine" was denounced as false by President Spencer W. Kimball and Elder Bruce R. McConkie.[138] Ultimately, Orson Pratt's view was vindicated. But what if we had been living at the time? Who would we have supported, President Young or Apostle Pratt?

These types of disagreements were common among Church authorities in earlier times. Today, the Church's correlation department tries to avoid such doctrinal disagreements; nevertheless they still arise from time to time. How is one to resolve such conflicts? In our day, we seem to have adopted the curious tradition of discerning truth by who said it, their position at the time, and whether they were an earlier authority or a more current one, rather than evaluating what was said and then using the Holy Ghost to discern the truth as we are directed by the Lord in the scriptures (see Moroni 10:5). Who is speaking has become more important that what is said.

Furthermore, what are we to make of messages or "truths" that originate from outside the Church's hierarchy? How do we determine their truthfulness? Most of the Lord's ancient prophets (such as John the Baptist, Lehi, Abinadi, Samuel the Lamanite, etc.) came from outside the established hierarchy of their day. Even Christ came as an outsider. We all know that the Lord will do nothing without first revealing it to his servants the prophets (see Amos 3:7), but even Amos was not part of the establishment of his day. He testified that he was not a prophet or prophet's son, but a simple herdsman (see Amos 7:14–15). We also see scriptural examples of prophetesses, such as Deborah and Anna, delivering messages from the Lord (see Judges 4; Luke 2). If God is the same yesterday, today, and forever, then could He send you a needed message from an unofficial source?

Furthermore, at times these two channels may conflict with one another. One sister described this experience in her life:

> Rather than accepting everything I heard at face value, I started asking myself, 'Does this align with the God I know?' 'Does this align with the God I read about in the scriptures?'... Unwittingly, I jumped into the great paradox of having a priesthood line of authority (or teachings from Church leaders, prophets, and apostles), and a personal line of authority (teachings from personal revelation, my own experiences, and the Holy Ghost). Most of the time, these two sources agreed with each other . . . But some of the time, they didn't . . . I try to be wary of constructing God in my own image–a God who is comfortable, who does not require hard things, but while also reconciling it

> with the God I know, who is merciful, kind, and loving. It's a wrestle, but the friction has brought about a deeper relationship with God, and a firmer bedrock of things that I have examined and absolutely believe to be true.[139]

These types of conflicts sometimes lead to a crisis of faith. Members may experience such a crisis for a variety of reasons. One of the root causes is truths that are apparently contradictory. This paradox causes internal dissonance. How do we resolve it? One key may be found in the temple phrase that all truth can be circumscribed into one great whole. I used to think that simply meant all truth could be found in the person of God. God is a great whole because He possesses all truth. While that is true, there may another way to understand this phrase that is more directly applicable to us in this life.

As we learn and grow, we have parts of the truth but not always the whole picture. This is inevitable as we gain line upon line and precept upon precept. Sometimes we encounter two different truths that seem contradictory. Our thinking can become very black and white. If truth 'A' contradicts truth 'B' then one must be wrong. Sometimes that is the case, but often, the full truth 'C' encompasses parts of 'A' and 'B'. Like the two sides of a coin, we may only see the heads side and think we understand the coin. Another person may only see the tails side and may likewise think that he or she understands. We might even argue with one another over the nature of the coin. In reality, neither sees the entire picture. In our spiritual development sometimes we must face both the heads and the tails side of the coin in order to circumscribe them into one cohesive whole.

We find an example of this type of conflict in science. Newtonian physics (and the theory of relativity) conflicts with quantum physics. The laws we understand about the largest building blocks of the universe seem to contradict what we understand about the smallest elements. It makes no sense. Apparently, both cannot be true and yet scientists can observe the effects of both sets of laws in the natural world. Nature says they are both true, but mathematics says that they cannot both be true. (I am no scientist, so please pardon my very unscientific description of a complex, current issue). Scientists are searching for some greater theory that can unify both sets of laws or "truths." One potential model is string theory. That theory may or may not prove to be accurate. What we do know is that the reality of the physical universe is more complex than can be explained by either the theory of relativity or quantum physics. Neither one alone is the complete "truth."

This is an example of a similar process we might go through with respect to our testimonies and knowledge of the gospel. This can be difficult. Our continued learning may require us to discard something we have cherished but is either incomplete or partially wrong in order to gain a greater picture of the whole. Other times the conflict arises from asking calculus-type gospel questions when we only have a basic understanding of gospel algebra. The questions and answers are beyond our knowledge base. It may require years before we are adequately prepared to understand them. In these situations, Adam and Eve's example is notable. They offered sacrifices for years without having the entire picture. Gospel growth inevitably requires us to accept some things in faith for a time. Eventually, however, Adam and Eve received an explanation and gained understanding and knowledge. Part of this is by divine design in order to help us gain the faith we came here to obtain.

Until we possess the entire truth on a given topic, we will inevitably have only parts of it along the way. It often requires time and diligent effort to be able to circumscribe the entire truth into one great whole. It is unfortunate that some throw the baby out with the bath water, so to speak, either from impatience with the process or in reaction to having the head side of the coin flipped over and seeing the tail side for the first time. We should not be content with partial truth. We also should not let the part we have prevent us from accepting more truth, even if there is an apparent contradiction at first. Faith is required during the interim period. We should press forward until we eventually obtain the full truth.

Another point that should be obvious is the need for patience through this process, both with ourselves and with others. Sometimes arriving at closure on a difficult topic may require many years. We are each at different points in our development and understanding. Members can be very intolerant of others with different views. During Joseph Smith's day, a situation arose where a brother taught some false doctrine. In reaction, Joseph Smith said: "I did not like the old man being called up for erring in doctrine. It looks too much like the Methodist, and not like the Latter-day Saints. Methodists have creeds which a man must believe or be asked out of their Church. I want the liberty of thinking and believing as I please. It feels so good not to be trammeled. It does not prove that a man is not a good man because he errs in doctrine."[140] How many times in our own lives have our opinions or our understanding changed? This process is a necessary part of growth. May we be patient and tolerant of one another as we work toward greater understanding of truth and of God.

No Respecter of Persons

Another basic lesson of the temple is that all are alike unto God and that He is no respecter of persons. This simple truth is blatantly obvious on the surface, but we still struggle to really get it in our day-to-day lives. It is symbolically represented in the endowment session as we are all dressed in white. This lesson was vividly portrayed to me on a visit to the temple during President Ezra Taft Benson's tenure. To my surprise, he and his wife attended a session we were on. Though serving as the Church's president, he and his wife dressed like any of the other patrons. He did not get a special seat, but rather sat a few chairs down from me on the fourth row.

This idea is so completely counter to everything in the world around us. Instead of equality and cooperation, our entire society is based upon ranking and competition. We are constantly compared and graded. It is ingrained in our thinking. This sometimes carries over into our Church culture as well. We live in Babylon. The temple is trying to teach us something about Zion.

For starters, we must give up the notion that certain blessings are out of our reach because they are only reserved for a few chosen elite. God's blessings are available to all of his children on exactly the same conditions. We sell ourselves short when we believe some spiritual blessings are reserved for Church leaders or others but not for us. It is not our Church calling or position that limits our access to God and to personal revelation. To a great extent, we are the regulator of what we receive and what we reject. We must stop respecting or disrespecting ourselves (whichever the case may be) and simply recognize our need for and dependence upon God and accept His love for us.

In addition to changing our view of ourselves, we must change how we view others. The scriptures command us to not esteem one person above another (see Mosiah 23:7, 27:4; Jacob 2:17, 21). Like our Lord, we are not to be a respecter of persons either (see Alma 1:30, 16:14). One of the ways that God's thoughts are higher than ours is His concern and respect for the least among us—those outcasts whom we generally do not value at all. This is not pleasing to a God who testifies that the worth of each soul is great and that "one being is as precious in his sight as the other" (Jacob 2:21).

On the other end of the spectrum, there are those whom we esteem and value highly. The fawning regard that some members show to Church leaders and the coveting of Church positions is offensive to our Creator. We are to put our trust in God, not in the arm of flesh. We are to esteem our neighbors as ourselves. Truly seeing ourselves and others in this light is simple in concept but difficult in practice.

Selling the Sacred for Money

It has always seemed curious to me that Peter asks Adam if he has sold his tokens and signs for money. Who would ever offer to purchase such things, especially today when they are available for free on the internet? In practicality, this question seems irrelevant. But on closer consideration, it may be extremely relevant to each of us. Do we sell the sacred for money when we allow this world to take over our priorities and crowd out room for our spiritual growth and development? Christ cautioned us that we could ultimately only serve one of two masters, God or mammon. And the great revelation on priesthood warns that many men place more value upon riches and the honors of this world, rather than seeking to serve and honor God (see D&C 121:35). It seems that this is what the question really addresses and is, therefore, very relevant.

A related issue is the obligation to keep the sacred, sacred. Patrons covenant not to disclose the names, tokens and signs received in the temple. Some may wonder if this is still necessary since they are now available in the public record. However, as Hugh Nibley pointed out, the real question is: will I keep these things sacred? Can the Lord trust me not to disclose them, despite the fact that others have? This obligation may very well be a test to prove whether we can be trusted. We will never qualify to receive greater things, if we cannot be trusted with lesser ones.

The Great Lie

At one point in the ceremony, Satan declares that all those who do not walk up to every covenant that they make in the temple will end up in his power. Taken literally, this would doom us all. A good friend of mine calls this line "the great lie" and points out who is making the statement.

The embrace at the veil exposes this great lie. It is only by and through Christ's merits that we escape Satan's grasp. So, in that sense, Satan's declaration truly is a lie. None of us fully keeps our covenants 100% all of the time. We make mistakes and are prone to weakness and error. The Lord recognizes that there is a process of growth, learning, and development that must occur. The endowment provides a road map and places us under obligation to follow it, but we will still stumble along the way.

That being said, like many of Satan's lies this one also contains a partial truth. It is true that ultimately there are only two paths. One is straight and narrow and leads to Christ; all others will eventually put us in Satan's power (see 1 Nephi 14:10). The one and only path back is the doctrine of Christ. It is exemplified and demonstrated in the endowment.

Telestial, Terrestrial and Celestial Realms

We generally think of the telestial, terrestrial, and celestial worlds as realms of glory following the resurrection. One might wonder why we encounter them in the endowment? An easy answer is to simply view the ceremony as an overview of the plan of salvation. But the presence of the three degrees of glory does not quite fit with this idea because they are presented in a manner whereby the patrons move through each realm in an upward progression rather than being assigned to a realm at the end.

Recall that Joseph Smith stated the endowment was related to the principles and order of the priesthood. Elder James E. Talmage further added, "exaltation in the kingdom of God implies attainment to the graded orders of the Holy Priesthood, and with these the ceremonies of the endowment are directly associated."[141] Once we recognize that there are three levels or degrees to priesthood and that one of the purposes of the temple endowment is to help us receive power in our priesthood, then we can see that there is potentially a level of the priesthood associated with each of the three levels of glory and correspondingly with each member of the Godhead.

The fellowship of priesthood can involve—not just mortals, one with another—but can also extend beyond the veil. In other words, Aaronic Priesthood can include an association with angels and the Holy Ghost; Melchizedek Priesthood can be a fellowship with Christ; and receiving the fulness of the Melchizedek Priesthood, or actually becoming a king and a queen, includes returning to the Father. This same notion is present in the Oath and Covenant of the Priesthood. The keys in the endowment, or keys of the kingdom, also relate to these potential fellowships.

Having fellowship with the powers of heaven is not optional in our progression. We all begin in a telestial state. The endowment clearly shows you must receive angels to move from the telestial to the terrestrial realm. The angels teach you what you still need in order to ascend. While in the terrestrial realm, you must then encounter and receive Christ at the veil in order to move to the celestial realm. And Christ will return you to the Father in the celestial. Though it is perhaps not obvious, the officiator in the sealing ordinances symbolizes the Father. It is there in the celestial realm that the family of God is finally organized.

The Prayer Circle

Before concluding this chapter, let's return to the other purpose Joseph gave for the temple's keys, namely that faithful saints "might know how to ask the Lord and receive an answer."[142] The prayer circle is one of the most sacred highlights of the endowment. It has been described in some detail in several Church-related publications and therefore does not appear to be off limits for discussion.[143] Nevertheless, we will try to approach this topic with the reverence it deserves.

This portion of the ceremony is very significant. Do not skip over it lightly. What happens prior to the prayer is not a review. I made that mistake in my thinking for many years until the Lord opened my eyes and gave me a glimpse of what is really going on. Since that day, I have had an immensely greater respect for the sacred nature of that ordinance. I participate in the prayer every time I attend an endowment session. If members understood it better, I do not believe there would be a need to ask for participants. Instead many sessions would likely be unable to accommodate everyone who wished to participate.

I cannot share what I know about it, but simply plead with you to focus on this portion of the ceremony, to ponder on it, and to ask the Lord to teach you more.

It is my testimony that God hears this prayer and responds. It is a unique opportunity afforded us. Unfortunately, it has been my experience that too often this prayer seems to be virtually the same from one endowment session to the next—almost bordering upon vain repetition. Instead, it should reflect the unique needs of those who are participants. Ideally, the wording should be given by the spirit of revelation (see 3 Nephi 19:24).

In fairness to the brethren who serve as officiators, voicing the prayer can be an intimidating experience, especially for new temple workers. I served for a time as a temple trainer. The brothers are given strict guidelines with respect to the prayer.[144] It is difficult to get everything just right. As a patron, please be patient with the workers.

If you have the opportunity to serve as voice please approach that assignment with humility, reverence, and seeking the Lord's help. It always felt a little daunting to me. The time I felt most successful was one occasion when I asked the Lord to help me be aware of the needs of the company. As I sat watching the patrons enter, the Spirit let me know that there was a young man who had recently lost his job and was concerned about providing for his family. Another woman was having difficulty in her marriage. As part of the prayer that day, I included a plea for those who needed help finding employment and a plea to bless and strengthen all present in their marriages and homes. On other sessions, other promptings have come. Many patrons come to the temple with heavy burdens, seeking some answers or even just a brief reprieve. The Lord knows the needs of those present, on both sides of the veil, and if we will seek for inspiration and revelation the prayer can and should help address them. It may be more significant than we recognize.

Historical precedents for the prayer circle are numerous. LDS scholars have pointed out the prevalence of prayer circles or circular dances throughout early Christianity and in some ancient civilizations.[145] It is an interesting topic to look into. Before concluding our discussion of the prayer, I would point out an interesting connection we find here.

An architect's square can be used to draw the figure of a perfect square. With its four corners, the square is symbolic of physical matter and the earth. Throughout history it has been understood to symbolize the four corners of the earth (back when the earth was thought to be flat, it was supposed it had four corners); the four cardinal directions (north, south, east and west); the four seasons (winter, spring, summer, fall); the four elements (earth, air, water, fire) and four states of matter (solid, liquid, gaseous, energy), etc. It is also associated with time and the four corners of the year (vernal and autumnal equinoxes, summer and winter solstices). It is thus associated with the earthly realm, time, and the cycles of nature as well as the physical body and nature of mankind.

A compass is used to draw a circle. It is associated with the spiritual side of mankind, rather than the physical. The compass can draw the "bowl" of the heavens. The compass as a tool can be used to measure distances (even great distances such as those between heavenly bodies), to set boundaries and to circumscribe things. But at the same time the circle can also represent the infinite and eternal or that which has no bounds. The circle was therefore associated with heavenly realms and with the spirit of mankind.

When these two basic geometric shapes are combined, we find another common temple symbol, the circle inside the square, or alternately, the square inside the circle. "One scholar has suggested that, since the compass, which is used to draw circles, points towards the bowl of the sky, and that the square, which is used to draw squares, points towards the earth, that the combination of the two symbols represents the powers of God in creating the bowl of the starry heavens and the four corners of the earth."[146]

The circle within the square can also symbolize the spirit encased in a mortal tabernacle or veiled in flesh.[147] Something like this idea may have been behind DaVinci's Vitruvian Man, which was drawn within a circle and square. It was meant to give an ideal to the dimensions of mankind, but also served as a scale model of the universe.

Beyond these common meanings, the square and the circle can also reference related pairs such as time and eternity, earth and heaven, man and woman, temporal and spiritual, or even the Father and the Son.[148] When combined into one, the circle and square can indicate a junction between heaven and earth, a point in which time and eternity meet, the union of a man and woman in marriage, etc. It is therefore an apt symbol for unity, oneness, or completion.

The combination of the circle and the square has fascinated many throughout history. The concept shows up in diverse places, even in mathematics: "The 'squaring the circle' method of understanding pi has fascinated mathematicians because traditionally the circle represents the infinite, immeasurable, and even spiritual world while the square represents the manifest, measurable, and comprehensive world."[149] As another example, one of Masonry's goals was to "square the circle" or, in other words, to harmonize the physical and spiritual sides of mankind.

With these ideas in mind, it is interesting to note that the circle and square are combined in the order of prayer and again, in the ritual embrace at the veil at the conclusion of the endowment. Here we glimpse another meaning. It is perhaps only through Christ and His Atonement that any true "squaring of the circle" or "circle encompassing the square" in unity becomes possible.

A Tale of Two Trees

The ceremony at the veil is the spiritual highlight of the endowment and its most sacred part. In one sense, the endowment is God's explanation of our life's condition, purpose, and journey through mortality using the symbols of two trees. The ceremonial figures of Adam and Eve represent each of us. Like Adam and Eve, we were also created of the dust. God gave us the breath of life. We entered mortality through the veil of our mother's womb, forgetting our previous life. We grow up in a state of innocence, like Eden, but eventually fall through our own individual choices.

With Adam and Eve, we symbolically partake of the fruit of the tree of knowledge at the beginning of the endowment. In our actual lives, we do this through the use of our agency and by the consequences of our actions and those of others. We sin and partake of the bitter fruit that we might know to prize the sweet. We are here to gain knowledge and to learn good from evil through our own mortal experience (see Moses 6:55–56). We find ourselves separated from God and living in a lone and dreary, telestial world. Our task is to find our way back home. We make mistakes but are given time to repent and to prepare to pass the angelic sentinels set there to guard the way back to God's presence and the tree of life (see Alma 12:24; Genesis 3:24). These angels not only serve as guardians, but once we are sufficiently prepared, they help us return (see D&C 77:11).

In his vision, Lehi saw that there are many ways to become lost in mortality but only one path back to the tree of life. He came to know that the fruit of the tree of life is most "desirable above all other fruit" (1 Nephi 8:12). Nothing else life offers us can compare. Near the end of his record, Nephi gave some further explanation about the path leading to this tree. He labeled the path the "doctrine of Christ" (see 2 Nephi 31 & 32) and testified that it is the only way back (2 Nephi 31:21). The final part of the doctrine of Christ is enduring to the end. The endowment ordinances, in one sense, are ordinances associated with enduring to the end. The temple endowment and the doctrine of Christ are inseparably connected.

After explaining how we find ourselves in our current state, the endowment further clarifies this path back, as we discussed in chapter

5. As the ceremony concludes at the veil (as a symbol of the tree of life), we have finally come full circle. Once cast out of God's presence, we are preparing to return. It is significant that we are not given the name of the second token of the Melchizedek Priesthood until this point. It is figuratively describing the fruit of the tree of life. The ceremony at the veil is our petition to be given this fruit. Actually, receiving the promised blessings must involve Christ directly and personally. He alone is the keeper of the Gate.

In this way, the endowment story is the tale of two trees, the tree of knowledge and the tree of life; it is God's explanation of our purpose and journey in mortality using these two symbols.

Keys of the Kingdom

To conclude and recap quickly: six days before administering the endowment for the first time, while addressing the Relief Society, Joseph Smith declared that the keys of the kingdom were about to be given to the sisters to enable them to detect every thing false.[150] A few days later, he further defined the keys as "certain signs and words by which false spirits and personages may be detected from true, which cannot be revealed . . . till the Temple is completed."[151] Therefore, according to Joseph, the keys of the kingdom are given in the endowment. And the sisters hold them as well as the brothers. If you are endowed, you potentially hold the keys of the kingdom, provided you understand them. The question you need to answer is what exactly does that mean? How do those keys function? What do they access? How does one use them?

Do these keys construct or possess some inherent magic? Magic functions by getting all the elements of a spell exactly right. Even if the wielder does not understand how the spell works, as long as all the crucial elements are present, it still functions. Some may view the endowment this way, as granting an authoritative hall pass for the next life. Brigham Young seemed to believe that the garment had magical properties.[152] His statement about the endowment can be viewed to convey a similar view of it.[153] If that is the case, then it does not matter if you understand the keys or not—it is enough to possess them.

On the other hand, is it rather that the keys are primarily symbols meant to teach and instruct us? Is the real "key" not the symbol, but rather obtaining the information or the experience that the symbol is meant to convey? In what manner are we to understand these keys? Joseph Smith's declarations that we cannot be saved in ignorance and that we are saved no faster than we gain knowledge would seem to support this view and refute the first.

A third possibility is that the keys are a combination of both. Do these tokens and keys have inherent value but only function for one with proper understanding? For example, a seer stone in Joseph's hand aided in the translation of the Book of Mormon and gave him greater access to God. In the hands of another, the same stone may have been just a rock and nothing more. Another example might be the Liahona. It functioned according to the heed and diligence given it and did not work when those who possessed it were negligent. Do the temple keys operate in a similar manner?

I am simply raising questions that seem important. I leave it to you to seek answers.

CHAPTER 8

HISTORICAL CONTEXT

Two men went up into the temple to pray.
—Luke 18:10

SOMEONE ONCE ASKED ME about some wording in the endowment that troubled them. At the heart of their question was the real issue: Is the endowment we have today perfect? And if not, does it really matter? This chapter will briefly review some of the endowment's history to provide some perspective. By the end, I hope you will be able to reach your own conclusion to these questions.

For some members, the temple is not a good experience. While these brothers and sisters may be a minority, their feelings are very real. Some concerns might be alleviated by better understanding the endowment's history. We will begin there, but this chapter will conclude with questions relevant to all patrons. So please do not skip it, if you have only had a positive experience with the temple.

The reasons members sometimes struggle with the temple are varied. It may evoke something from their past that was unpleasant or difficult. Others may perceive the ordinances contain something that fundamentally goes against their core beliefs. Some see inequality or remnants of polygamy and patriarchy in the ceremony. A few may simply have been offended by an insensitive temple worker. Whatever the reason, if you are one who struggles, I would humbly plead with you to please look at the temple with new eyes after reading this chapter. There is so much good that can be gained there. We risk depriving ourselves when we focus on a problem to the exclusion of other things. That is not to minimize concerns, but it may be possible to consider a new approach.

History of the Endowment

Joseph Smith repeatedly pressed the Saints in Nauvoo to complete the temple. Eventually, knowing that he would not live long enough to see it finished, he introduced the endowment to a group of nine men in May of 1842. Years later, Brigham Young recalled the event:

> When we got our washings and anointings under the hands of the Prophet Joseph at Nauvoo, we had only one room to work in with the exception of a little side room or office where we were washed and anointed, and had our garments placed upon us and received our New Name. After he had performed these ceremonies, he gave the Key Words[,] signs, tokens and penalties. Then after this we went into the large room over the store in Nauvoo. Joseph divided upon the room the best that he could, hung up the veil, marked it, gave us our instructions as we passed along from department to another, giving us signs, tokens, penalties with the key words pertaining to those signs.[154]

Thus endowed, this initial group became known as the Holy Order.[155] Over the next eighteen months, Joseph continued to add to the basic endowment. He introduced separate prayer circle meetings, sealing for time and eternity of a husband and wife, and along with sealing, the law of adoption[156] and, finally, a capstone two-part ritual called the second anointing (sometimes referred to as a second endowment).

On September 28, 1843, this second anointing was first administered to Joseph and Emma.[157] Emma became the first female member admitted to the Holy Order and the first to be given both the first and second endowments. Shortly after, other women were initiated into the order and Joseph endowed and sealed them and their husbands. "Those who received the second anointing had their feet washed, were anointed as priests and kings, priestesses and queens, and their exaltation and promise of eternal life . . . was sealed upon them."[158] This was the full extent of the endowment ordinances introduced by Joseph. By the time of his death in 1844 at Carthage, he had endowed thirty-seven men and thirty-two women.[159]

It appears that Joseph planned to introduce the endowment to the general Church membership as soon as the Nauvoo Temple was completed. Unfortunately, he never had the finished temple to work with, and he seemed to have been somewhat dissatisfied with the endowment as it was then administered in a single room partitioned with canvases.[160] He left Brigham Young a charge to complete the work. Brigham recalled: "Bro. Joseph turned to me and said: 'Brother Brigham this is not arranged right but we have done the best we could under the circumstances in which we are placed, and I wish you to take this matter in hand and organize and systematize all these ceremonies with the signs, tokens, penalties and key words.' I did so, and each time I got something more, so that when we went through the temple at Nauvoo I understood and knew how to place them there. We had our ceremonies pretty correct."[161]

In December of 1845, about a year and a half after Joseph's martyrdom, Brigham began to introduce the endowment to the general Church membership. This was done in the attic of the still-unfinished Nauvoo Temple, again using canvas partitions. As these endowments proceeded, Brigham made additions, changes and alterations to the ceremony Joseph had introduced. William Clayton kept a temple diary. Early accounts of the Nauvoo ceremony indicate that initiatory washings and anointings were done in large tubs in separate men's and women's rooms. The entire body was washed. The anointing was then done by pouring perfumed, consecrated oil from a horn over the head and allowing it to run down over the whole body.[162]

Clayton recorded that the Nauvoo members participated in the endowment drama.[163] Male initiates played the role of Adam while female initiates the role of Eve. Only four other roles were included (Elohim, Jehovah, Michael, and the Devil), and these were played by

Church leaders.[164] On December 13, 1845, just three days after commencing the Nauvoo temple endowments, Brigham introduced three new characters (Peter, James and John) to the drama. Clayton wrote:

> Last evening an arrangement was made establishing better order in conducting the endowment. Under this order it is the province of Eloheem, Jehovah and Michael to create the world, plant the Garden and create the man and give his help meet. Eloheem gives the charge to Adam in the Garden and thrusts them into the telestial kingdom or the world. Then Peter assisted by James and John conducts them through the Telestial and Terrestrial kingdom administering the charges and tokens in each and conducts them to the vail where they are received by the Eloheem and after talking with him by words and tokens are admitted by him into the Celestial kingdom.[165]

These characters are still present in the modern ceremony, although patrons now sit as a company rather than participating directly in the role of Adam and Eve. Christian ministers were added in the 1850s, reduced to one minister in 1905, and removed completely in 1990.[166] Originally, all initiates were taken through the veil one at a time by a single Church official at the conclusion of the ceremony. The practice of a husband taking his wife through did not start until 1856.

Between December of 1845 and February of the following year, over 5,000 members received their endowment in the Nauvoo Temple, of these, more than half were women.[167] Just under 600 couples also received their second anointings or second endowments in the Nauvoo Temple.[168] "In addition to [Brigham] Young, at least nineteen other men were authorized to perform second anointings. On a typical day, six to twelve couples received this ordinance."[169] Church leaders also began performing adoption sealings, intended to organize families based upon priesthood rather than biological associations. Baptisms for the dead, first introduced by Joseph in 1840, resumed in the Nauvoo Temple.[170] Additionally, some marriage sealings of living men and women to deceased men and women occurred. Beyond these, no vicarious endowments or other ordinances are recorded for the dead in Nauvoo.

Following the exodus, ordinances resumed in Utah in 1852 in the Council House and then in the Endowment House that was completed in 1855. The Endowment House was the first building designed specifically for administering temple rituals, with ordinance rooms including a creation, garden, world and celestial rooms.[171] Previously, only canvas partitions had been used in the Red Brick Store and in the Nauvoo Temple. Between 1855 and 1884, approximately 54,000 received their endowments in the Endowment House.[172]

It was not until 1877, with the completion of the St. George Temple, that the endowment ceremony was finally committed to writing. For nearly 35 years (from May 1842 to April 1877), it had existed and been transmitted only orally. Variations, then occurring, between the endowment sessions concerned President Young who wanted to standardize the ceremony. On January 14, 1877, Brigham tasked a committee, comprised of Wilford Woodruff, Brigham Young Jr., John D. T. McAllister and L. John Nuttall, with this charge: "write out the Ceremony of the Endowments from Beginning to End."[173] The process took several months to complete with changes, revisions, and much discussion ensuing over the specific wording. As part of this written endowment, Brigham introduced a 30-minute lecture which was delivered at the veil at the conclusion of the endowment. The lecture outlined some of Brigham Young's Adam-God theory that has since been renounced by the Church.[174] By the time Brigham finished working on the endowment, he may have left fingerprints in places Joseph never intended.[175] Some of those may remain to this day.

Even after all this work, Brigham Young never seemed completely satisfied with the ceremony. For example, he felt that the endowment should be administered in two parts: first the Aaronic portion and then at a later date the Melchizedek portion, after the initiate had gone forth into the world and proven himself or herself worthy of more.[176] In other aspects, Brigham seemed to have remained uncertain as to how to proceed. He concluded that things would be fixed in the Millennium:

> After Joseph comes to us in his resurrected body he will more fully instruct us concerning the Baptism for the dead and the sealing ordinances. He will say be baptized for this man and that man and that man be sealed to that man and such a man to such a man, and connect the Priesthood together. I tell you their [sic] will not be much of this done until Joseph comes. He is our spiritual Father. Our hearts are already turned to him and his to us. This [is] the order of the Holy Priesthood and we shall continue to administer in the ordinances of the kingdom of God here on Earth.[177]

President John Taylor similarly concluded: "Had Joseph Smith lived he would have had much more to say on many of those points which he was prevented from doing by his death."[178] This view of the ceremonies as being unfinished left the door open to continued changes and modifications both to the ceremonies themselves and to the Church policies surrounding them.[179] Church leaders, following Brigham Young, continued to make changes and refinements.

The next major revision included the removal of an oath of vengeance originally inserted into the endowment by Brigham Young in response to the martyrdom of Joseph and Hyrum.[180] This oath may have partly contributed to the tragic Mountain Meadows Massacre. Between 1904 and 1906 much of the endowment was subjected to public scrutiny as part of the Congressional hearings for LDS senator-elect and Church Apostle, Reed Smoot. The concern centered around this oath of vengeance and the endowment's covenants and whether such conflicted with a senator's obligation of loyalty to the Constitution of the United States. This was a very uncomfortable moment in Church history. Partly in response to this situation, Heber J. Grant appointed a committee in 1919 to revise the endowment.

Between 1919 and 1927, this committee proposed a number of changes to the endowment which were approved and accepted. Salt

Lake Temple President, George F. Richards chaired the committee from 1922 on and was behind many of the revisions. These changes included removing the oath of vengeance, discontinuing temple choirs, eliminating descriptions accompanying the penalties, several changes to the garments worn outside of the temple, and reducing the number of times that priesthood robes were changed from shoulder to shoulder. Changes were also made to the wording of the ceremony and some of the ordinances, including codifying some of the previously "unwritten" parts of the ordinances. His journal entries describe many of these changes.[181] Richards summarized his work as follows:

> I can say that since I became the President of the Salt Lake Temple *we have re-written those temple ceremonies and ordinances which ha[d] been heretofore written*, first at the time of the Dedication of the St. George Temple, and have put them into leatherback covers as loose leaves and provided each Temple President with a copy. Later those ceremonies known as unwritten ceremonies, i.e. the covenants and the instructions given in forming the [prayer] circle and at the veil, were written and copies furnished on loose leaf sheets for the Presidents of Temples Book. A list of 83 rules and decisions has been written[,] also for the guidance of Temple Presidents[,] *supplanting all former rules not in full harmony*.[182]

These revisions were not received unanimously. George Q. Cannon, who was serving as president of the St. George Temple at the time, balked at implementing the changes and was severely criticized by Richards. Cannon replied, ""We are not controlled by [the] Salt Lake Temple. . . . This temple has the original of these endowments which was given by President Brigham Young and we have not nor will we change anything thereof unless dictated by the President of the Church."[183] Richard's changes were not implemented in St. George until 1926 when Edward H. Snow replaced Cannon as the president. Even as late as 1927, Richards was still finding resistance in some temples to his changes, which he saw as improvements. The primary criticism was that he, and not the First Presidency, had initiated the changes. Richards responded by stating the First Presidency "could not be expected to be in touch with all the details of Temple work & with the needed changes only as these things are brought to their attention."[184] His final influence over the temple ceremonies was extensive.

In addition to the endowment ceremony, changes were made to the policies and procedures surrounding temple work. For example, it was in 1921 that adherence to the Word of Wisdom became a mandatory requirement for admission. Other revisions continued over the following decades. The explanation of the symbolism of the marks on the veil was added in 1936 at the suggestion of David O. McKay. The first Spanish language endowment was administered in 1945 in the Mesa Arizona Temple. The first filmed versions of the ceremony were released in the 1950s, in part to accommodate various languages needed for the Swiss and New Zealand Temples. The films also allowed future temples to administer the endowment in a single room rather than having the participants move among several rooms.

The next major revisions came in 1990 following a survey sent to some 3,400 Church members ascertaining their feelings on the ceremony. The 1990 changes were extensive and involved a complete removal of the penalties, eliminating the character of the Christian minister, changes to two of the signs and to wording of the covenants of obedience and chastity, removal of the five points of fellowship, dropping the lecture at the veil, and numerous revisions to the wording of the entire ceremony.[185] Updated temple films were released in conjunction with these changes and added music and better cinematography to the presentation.

The most recent direct modifications occurred in 2005 when the initiatory ordinances were changed to a symbolic washing and anointing. Clothing in the garment is now done prior to the initiatory by the patron rather than as part of the ordinances. These changes were made following a lawsuit filed against the Church by a disgruntled patron.[186] These alterations made the experience more comfortable for many patrons and participation in the initiatory ordinances dramatically increased, thereafter.

Finally, in 2013 and 2014, three new endowment films were released. Some members view the acting and increased cinematic interpretations of these most recent temple films as changing the endowment in subtle ways. These nuances, in some cases, may have theological implications and perhaps change the meaning of certain phrases without altering any wording. Emotion, facial expressions, tone of voice and body language are all important parts of nonverbal human communication and contribute to the message being conveyed. Whether these types of artistic touches constitute actual changes is probably a matter of personal opinion. Some members like the new films better. Others prefer the old ones and perhaps find the increased emotional content distracting.

Prayer Circles

Another area of the endowment that has seen multiple changes in its practical application is the prayer circle. The early Saints who were personally administered to by Joseph Smith formed a select group known as the Quorum of the Anointed.[187] Initially, this group was comprised solely of men, but by 1843 it was expanded to include women.[188] The first male members of this "quorum" were not chosen from any particular Church quorum.[189] Nor did this quorum appear to function in any sense as a priesthood quorum in governing administrative matters within the Church.[190] The common trait shared by most of this group was having received their second anointings, in addition to the endowment.

It appears that the primary purpose of this quorum was to meet in prayer circles, which occurred fairly regularly.[191] While Joseph still lived, these prayer circles also practiced the ordinances that were subsequently administered in the temple.[192] This may have provided a valuable review and assisted with learning since the temple endowment was not performed for the dead in Nauvoo. They did not have the opportunity to repeat the ordinances for the deceased that members do today.

As the endowment began to be administered more widely among the general body of the Saints, some members were given their second anointings along with their endowments, but many were not. In December of 1845, only about ten percent of those who were then being endowed were also invited to join the quorum and its weekly prayer circle meeting.[193] However, this distinction quickly became clouded, and within a few months membership in the Quorum of the Anointed gradually expanded to include most, if not all, endowed members.[194] As a result the original quorum soon grew too large to meet as a single body and appears to have broken into smaller groups.

From the available historical records, it seems that this order of prayer was not restricted to a full group, but that individuals also practiced it alone. For example, Heber C. Kimball recorded in his journal on June 6, 1844: "Last nite I clothed my self and offerd up the Sines of the Holy Preasthood—and called one the nam of the Lord he hurd me for my heart was mad comfortable."[195]

Following the exodus from Nauvoo, special prayer circles were commonly held in Salt Lake City and other settlements from 1851 until 1929. These prayers were held in various locations, often in members' homes.[196] The primary participants were men, but participation was not based on ecclesiastical positions; rather, many were simply groups of friends and family and often crossed ward or stake boundaries. Women also held their own prayer circles. Under the direction of Eliza R. Snow, sisters met during the exodus and in the early settlements of Utah.[197] Some ward Relief Societies also held occasional prayer circles.[198] These prayer circles were discontinued by the First Presidency in 1929.[199] In part, this decision was made because these circles had become somewhat exclusive and created an inequality with those who were left out. It was therefore decided to limit them to the temple where all could participate.[200]

During the same time period, special ecclesiastical prayer circles were held in many stakes. Participation in these circles depended upon one's position in the stake. Most included the stake presidency, high council, and stake clerk.[201] Some stakes expanded them to include other officers as well. These ecclesiastical circles were organized or authorized by a member of the First Presidency or Quorum of the Twelve Apostles. Sometimes they were extended to wards, priesthood quorums, or other groups, such as a temple presidency.[202] Many of these were held in regular Church buildings outside of the temple. This practice was discontinued by President Kimball in a letter dated May 3, 1978 as the growth of the Church made it too difficult for the First Presidency to approve all the stake and ward requests to convene these circles. Since that time, the prayer circle has been restricted to the temple endowment.

Within the temple, in the past, the prayer could be voiced by a patron, whereas today it is always offered by an ordinance worker who is given strict guidelines as to the content of the prayer. Some have wondered why members are taught this order of prayer but then are not permitted to use it, except in such a limited, restricted manner. This brief overview provides part of the explanation.

Sealing Practices

Sealing practices and policies have also changed over time. When Moroni ministered to Joseph Smith on the evening of September 21, 1823, he reiterated a promise the Lord had made earlier: "Behold, I will reveal unto you the Priesthood, by the hand of Elijah the prophet, before the coming of the great and dreadful day of the Lord. And he shall plant in the hearts of the children the promises made to *the fathers*, and the hearts of the children shall turn to *their fathers*. If it were not so, the whole earth would be utterly wasted at his coming" (D&C 2:1–3; emphasis added). Notice there are two distinct groups referred to in this prophecy. We sometimes conflate them into one. The first group is "the fathers." This is a reference to the ancient patriarchs which include a line from Adam and Eve down through Abraham, Isaac, and Jacob. The second group is "their fathers," referring to our ancestors or kindred dead.

In 1842, Joseph gave part of the meaning of this verse as relating to baptism for the dead (see D&C 128:18). Within another year, the Prophet had expanded this "welding" link to include the sealing of a husband and wife and their children in an eternal family. However, it should be noted that these family sealings went beyond biological, familial connections to create families grouped by priesthood lines and covenant.[203]

Orson Pratt explained that God had joined Adam and Eve for eternity and placed them at the head of the human family. Because their union was under the authority of God, their children naturally became "heirs of the priesthood" and were "born in the covenant," meaning they were recognized by God as legitimate members of His family and heirs to His kingdom.[204] Each new faithful family became a link in this chain stretching through the "fathers (and mothers)" back to Adam and Eve who were linked to God. Exaltation, in part, depended upon being part of this familial chain.

The problem was this patriarchal and matriarchal chain had been broken through apostasy. By the time of the Restoration, no new links had been formed for thousands of years. It was necessary for an "adoption" to occur, thereby "grafting" a new branch into this patriarchal order and creating a new link with the patriarchal fathers.[205] In a similar manner, Abraham had come out of a generation of apostasy and was grafted into this priesthood familial chain, becoming one of "the fathers." He was given a promise that all those thereafter who received the same patriarchal priesthood that Abraham held would be accounted as his seed (see Abraham 2:10–12). Sarah participated in these promises as a matriarch. It was to her posterity, Isaac, that these promises continued. Joseph Smith became a new link in this chain at the time he was promised exaltation (see D&C 132:49). Abraham became his "father" (and Sarah his "mother"), and Joseph became a "son" and heir to all the promised blessings. Once Joseph had established a link between himself and Abraham as one of these patriarchal fathers, he was then able to extend exaltation to others by sealing them to himself.[206]

In the Nauvoo era, there seem to have been two distinct sealing concepts. One was the sealing of a husband and wife in an eternal union. The second was the sealing or adoption of a man or woman or a couple into this patriarchal/matriarchal chain or priesthood family of God. The subject is further clouded and complicated by polygamy which is a topic beyond the scope of this book. I would simply point out that sealing does not always equal marriage, though we often tend to conflate the two in the topic of polygamy. A second major purpose of sealing was to organize priesthood-based families.[207]

Following Joseph's death, prominent men in the Church, primarily those holding the apostleship, were allowed to have persons adopted or sealed to them as sons. This was meant to secure one's eternal future but soon had temporal ramifications as well. Between 1846 and 1848 many such adoptions of "fathers and sons in the priesthood" occurred.[208] Problems soon ensued. This system of temporal social organization resulted in "fathers who demanded too much of their sons" and "children who in turn expected too much from their fathers."[209] It also led to quibbles over men seeking to be sealed to the "highest" priesthood authority and to those who sought to bypass others in trying to attain a higher position. Brigham Young counseled the brethren to advance by "boosting up . . . instead of trying to pass."[210] The situation soon proved as dysfunctional as attempts to live the United Order.

In truth, no one understood the doctrine well or how to implement it. The oft-cited incident where Joseph Smith appeared to Brigham Young in a dream and told him to "tell the people to be humble and faithful, and be sure to keep the spirit of the Lord and it will lead them right" came in response to Brigham seeking to better understand this law of adoption.[211] Shortly thereafter, the practice was largely discontinued for several decades before seeing a resurgence with the completion of the St. George Temple.

In 1877, the same year the endowment was first written, several policies and rules were established in relation to sealings and priesthood adoptions. With these new rules in place, the practice resumed.[212] Problems and dissatisfaction ensued, once again. Wilford Woodruff resolved things permanently by changing the practice to seal families together along biological lines as far back as was practical and then sealing the last man in the chain by adoption to Joseph Smith.[213] The response to this change by the general Church membership was favorable, but left a question as to the status of the more than 13,000 adoptions that had already occurred. The First Presidency ruled that the records of these adoptions would remain and that problems would be straightened out in the hereafter.[214]

Years later, the practice of sealing the end of familial lines to Joseph Smith was dropped, leaving behind the current policy of only sealing genealogical lines back as far as available records permit. This practice seals "their fathers" (our ancestors) to us but does not create a link with "the fathers" (the patriarchal / matriarchal family chain bound to God) if such is required.

Perspective

Having traced this history, the question remains: does it all matter? One reason it might is in response to some members' concerns with the temple. If we view the endowment as perfect in its present form, then parts of it remain troubling for some. If, instead, we recognize these revisions and changes as an ongoing effort by Church leadership to improve and perfect the temple ceremonies then perhaps, in their present form, they can be viewed more fluidly and open, and less rigidly and dogmatic. Wilford Woodruff, who helped write the first 1877 version, seems to have felt that the underlying principles in the endowment were more important than the specific wording of the ceremony.[215] I agree with that sentiment. That view would caution against placing too much weight upon specific phrases or wording.

In my experience, sometimes revelation comes from the Lord in precise words. At other times, the message is delivered through sudden understanding or insight that I am then left to try to put into words or describe on my own. Hopefully, you have experienced both in your life. When it comes to the endowment, we do not know whether Joseph Smith was given exact words or if he received information that he then was left to put into language and ceremony. What I have been able to study and learn suggests the latter. Therefore, when I approach the endowment I am careful about putting too much weight on specific wording but rather look for the underlying message: what is the Lord trying to teach me?

When something is troubling, perhaps we should do as the endowment instructs and seek for further light and knowledge from the Lord. By way of example, prior to 1990, the covenant of obedience was worded so that women submitted to the "law" of their husbands and to his counsel in righteousness. Sisters are also anointed to become queens and priestesses to their husbands rather than unto God. When interpreted literally, these phrases leave some sisters feeling like they are placed in a subservient role or that their husbands are intermediaries between them and the Lord. Furthermore, because the "law of the husband" was never defined, some men exercised unrighteous dominion (see D&C 121:39). While the covenant of obedience for the women was reworded in 1990, other areas of the temple ceremonies were not altered. Differences in the wording of the sealing ordinance for a man and a woman remain to this day. Some interpret these variations as antiquated remnants of patriarchy and polygamy and find them offensive.

Frankly, if we consider the historical context at the time the endowment was first put in writing in 1877, there may be some merit to that notion. At the time, an external battle was heated and growing with the U.S. government over the issue of polygamy. Part of Brigham

Young's strategy was to gain constitutional protection of polygamy by enshrining it as an essential part of the religion and therefore protected under freedom of religion. At the same time, internally within the Church, many members, including some polygamist wives, were unhappy with the hardships and lifestyle. Some had an increasingly difficult time in their families and home life.

Given these circumstances, which existed while producing the first written version of the endowment, it may have been very easy for those involved to word the covenants in a way intended to help address these contemporary problems. If an unhappy polygamist wife was troubling her husband with her complaints, a covenant to obey her husband may have provided an easy solution. Like Brigham's Adam-God theory or his oath of vengeance that were both inserted into the endowment and then subsequently removed, perhaps this wording did not belong either. Brigham's fingerprints may have been left in other areas of the endowment as well.

It is possible that Joseph administered a covenant to obey God worded exactly the same way for both men and for women. He may also have ordained both men and women as kings and queens unto God. But what was eventually written down and recorded was somewhat different. It is probably impossible to know from the historical records whether this was the case. On the other hand, these things may not have been altered by Brigham Young but simply reflected some of the culture of the time.

In either case, if we look for the underlying principles, we see the need for both men and women to obey God. The challenge is the same for both sexes. The covenant of obedience was later explained by President David O. McKay as making God the center of our lives.[216] This view of the covenant seems more consistent with the gospel as a whole. The notion that God would treat his sons differently from his daughters or that he would require his sons to be an intermediary is not reflected in scripture. In fact, we find precisely the opposite. When God clothed Adam and Eve in the Garden of Eden, He made a coat of skins for and clothed each of them personally. He did not clothe Adam and then tell him to go clothe Eve (see Moses 4:27). God ministered to both equally.

Furthermore, He tells us that the image of God is male and female together (see Genesis 1:27). This truth was once openly reinforced in the endowment. In the 1931 version, when Elohim asks Jehovah if it is good for man to be alone, Jehovah responded: "It is not, Elohim, for we are not alone."[217] If we really understood the truth that God is male and female, then we might see that a better way to possibly dramatize the endowment would be to actually have a man and a woman speaking together in unison whenever Elohim is voice in the dialogue.

While I do not wish to minimize the abuse or hurt that many women have experienced, the goal of equality between the sexes ultimately misses the point. The real goal is something much greater—the unity of the male and the female as a complete whole. The Book of Mormon plainly teaches that all are alike unto God, both male and female (see 2 Nephi 26:33). The very idea of a husband "ruling" over his wife is contrary to and offensive to the instructions given in the great revelation on priesthood authority which explicitly states: "*No power or influence* can or ought to be maintained by virtue of the priesthood" (D&C 121: emphasis added).

With this background and understanding, it may be completely appropriate for women and men who are troubled by the wording of a particular covenant to view the underlying meaning and intent rather than interpreting the words literally, especially if that helps them see the overall endowment in a more positive light.

We potentially risk overlooking the good that could be gleaned from the ceremony, if we get hung up on a perceived negative element. In all of this, please understand that I am not suggesting that we willy-nilly adjust the endowment to suit our personal preferences and whims. Not at all. But I do think we should approach the endowment prayerfully, seeking additional help and insight from the Lord, recognizing that there may be something we can glean even from things with which we initially disagree.[218]

Do the Changes Matter?

Members familiar with the history might answer the question of whether these changes matter in a variety of ways. The issue is complicated by a statement Joseph Smith left. He instructed: "ordinances instituted in the heavens before the foundation of the world, in the priesthood, for the salvation of men, *are not to be altered or changed.* All must be saved on the same principles."[219] If the temple ordinances are salvific, this charge does not seem to leave any room for modification. On the other hand, if the temple ordinances are meant to instruct and help bring us unto Christ, like the ordinances under the law of Moses, then changes may be permissible, unless they dilute or lose part of what the original was able to teach.

Church leaders are aware of this caution by the Prophet Joseph. It is used in the current training videos for temple workers to encourage strict adherence to temple policies and to avoid "temple drift."[220] Temple drift is a term coined to refer to minor variations in performance of the ordinances. Great care is taken to ensure that temple workers do not innovate. The concern over temple drift is understandable. Minor modifications over time led to changes of ordinances in historic Christianity. As an example, the difference between baptism by immersion and the baptism of infants by sprinkling can be traced to small steps, taken over time for seemingly good reasons.

God is not bound to honor that which varies from His word or what He has established. Isaiah testified of the last days: "The earth also is defiled unto the inhabitants thereof; because they have transgressed the laws, *changed the ordinance*, broken the everlasting covenant. Therefore, hath the curse devoured the earth, and they that dwell therein are desolate: therefore the inhabitants of the earth are burned, and few men left" (Isaiah 24:5, emphasis added). This dire prediction is reminiscent of the warning Moroni gave Joseph Smith recorded in Doctrine and Covenants 2, which is a foundation of our modern temple work: "If it were not so, the whole earth would be utterly wasted at his coming" (D&C 2:3).

It is clear that covenants and ordinances are a serious matter with the Lord and not something to trifle with. Some view the cumulative changes to the endowment and initiatory as significant enough to render the current versions corrupted and in direct violation of Joseph's warning. One the other hand, Joseph left Brigham a charge to finish up and refine the original ceremony. Joseph also never had the completed Nauvoo Temple to work with. He began the work but did not seem to complete it. (From the description of Facsimile No. 2 in the Book of Abraham, it appears that there was and is yet more to come. Whether that would have been given by Joseph in the Nauvoo Temple is unknown.) In any case, it appears that the endowment we have today is not fully complete or finished (see, for example, Figures 8–11, Facsimile No. 2). Brigham completed the charge received from Joseph and felt that things were "pretty correct" but not perfect, even towards the end of his life. Future leaders continued to make refinements to the ceremonies in the same spirit.

Other members believe, or assume, that these changes were all made by direct revelation and therefore in full accordance with the Lord's will. This could provide a nice solution to the dilemma. However, a potential problem with this approach is that, with only one exception, none of those responsible ever claimed a revelation dictating the changes.[221] Even in the case of the 1990 changes, a letter was read explaining that changes were made by those who held the keys to do so but no mention was made of any revelation or direction from the Lord. It, therefore, requires an assumption to take the position that these changes were all dictated by the Lord.

If everything was given by direct revelation, then why did Brigham Young add things that were later denounced and removed? Why was there need for ongoing revision, if it was all by revelation from the start? One could argue the Lord reveals things line upon line, but that process is usually additive in nature. We are given more over time. In this case, many things have been eliminated. We have less than earlier generations, not more. And with all of these changes, corrections, additions, and subtractions, we might wonder if the endowment is perfect today? Or will more be corrected or changed in the future?

On one occasion, I heard a temple president express his opinion that these changes do not matter. I agree and disagree with him. In some respects, the endowment has not ever been and is probably still not perfect or complete. Removing some things, such as the oath of vengeance which never belonged in the first place, seems completely appropriate. Likewise, some feel that there are still vestiges of patriarchy and polygamy that similarly do not belong and should be changed. Viewing the endowment ceremony as an imperfect work in progress certainly might help resolve these concerns.

On the other hand, some of the changes seem to more directly alter the ordinances as established by Joseph Smith. For instance, the original penalties of the endowment were later modified and then completely removed. In the process, we may have lost something of importance. As another example, the initiatory ordinances have been significantly altered. Personally, I prefer administering them in the new manner and am happy to see the vastly increased participation in these beautiful ordinances as patrons are more comfortable now. But I am also grateful that I received the initiatory for myself in the old manner. I do not know if I would have understood it as well if I had only experienced it after 2005.

The question as to whether these changes matter is one you should ponder for yourself and take to the Lord. I do not feel, or wish to seem, critical of those who have had stewardship of these things in the past or the decisions they made. I raise these questions because the answers may not be as cut and dried as we might assume. The Lord's feelings and views may be very different from our own. And I think these things are worth careful thought and consideration.

Regardless of how you see these issues, great value can be obtained in the temple ordinances and in temple worship today. The Lord's Spirit is there and those who attend regularly can attest to the blessing the temple is in their lives. We cannot change and are not responsible for the past, but we are responsible for how we receive the things that are made available to us now. We need to accept in faith all that we have been left by Joseph Smith. We cannot expect to receive anything more from the Lord if we are unwilling to receive what is already here. The present temple ceremonies may not be perfect, but they are what is offered us today. Our faith in receiving them matters. For many years, I have attended the temple weekly. That experience changed my heart, made me a better person, blessed my marriage, and brought me closer to my Savior. It will similarly bless all who come to worship there regularly and sincerely.

As we conclude this topic, I would also remind you of the situation the Lord's apostles at Jerusalem found themselves in after His death. At that point in time, the existing church hierarchy and priesthood leadership had become so corrupt that they opposed Christ. Caiaphas was serving as the High Priest, and he and his father-in-law, Annas, had been active participants in the events culminating in the Lord's death. The temple itself had become defiled and corrupted. Twice during the Lord's ministry, He had personally cleansed it. He lamented over Jerusalem and declared that their house was left desolate (see Matthew 23:27). And in less than 40 years, their temple would be completely destroyed by the Romans.

Yet, in the midst of this awful condition, in the days following the Lord's death, his disciples were "continually in the temple, praising and blessing God" (Luke 24:53). Despite the corruption and apostasy, for these disciples the temple remained a holy place where they could worship God. The situation is reminiscent of the Lord's parable concerning the Pharisee and the publican who went up to the temple to pray (see Luke 18:10–14). One was accepted and the other was not. Our individual faith and sincerity in seeking God matters greatly.

Perhaps the same temple can be a holy place for one, while being profaned by another as the Lord deals with us individually.

Which version of the ordinances you received may ultimately be far less important than how you receive and act upon what you are offered in the temple. Our individual attitude and response matters. To some, the temple rites are meaningless. This is more a reflection of their own spiritual preparedness, or lack thereof, than it is of the inherent value of the endowment. Others may view the endowment as imparting an authoritative hall-pass for the afterlife and give little thought to further effort beyond learning things well enough to pass through the ceremony. A few may feel that some superior status is bestowed by temple ordinances. They see themselves as being chosen or better than others by virtue of being endowed and are thus lead to pride and arrogance. That attitude separates us from God and from light and truth. It potentially turns the rites into a tragic misstep rather than a divine blessing.

On the other hand, if you understand that the temple rites communicate information through symbols and are designed to instruct us in the things of God, and if you approach the temple in a spirit of humility with a desire to learn, then the endowment is a great blessing. Once we grasp the meaning, however, we must actually live the endowment in our daily lives in order to receive the promised blessings. Seeking further light and knowledge is essential in this process. So is actually conversing with the Lord, not just through ritual but in reality. The endowment is to give us faith and confidence to make the journey.

HOMEWORK

1. For those interested, a comparison of past and present versions of the endowment scripts is available online at ldsendowment.org. The author of this site is undisclosed, but he or she has carefully omitted those parts of the endowment that are most sacred and covered by covenants of non-disclosure, leaving behind the remaining textual body for study.

CHAPTER 9

LIVING YOUR ENDOWMENT

But it must needs be done in mine own way.
—Doctrine and Covenants 104:16

THE CROWNING COVENANT of the endowment, one that prepares us to enter the Lord's presence, is consecration. This covenant is not only a precursor to receiving the Lord, but is necessary for the establishment of Zion. We tend to think of consecration as an economic law, but economic consecration is only a part of it. Full consecration requires giving ourselves wholly to the Lord. We are to become one with Him (see John 17:21). The sacrifice that is required of all who become accepted of the Lord is in part a test of our ability to live the law of consecration. It will require us to place upon the altar that which we most value and is most difficult for us to let go.

CONSECRATION

Consecration is a topic that is not very clear to many members. It may be the least understood of all the endowment covenants. I hope that you will give some careful thought to what it means in your life. What follows is my current thinking on this topic and is shared only as my opinion and from a desire to be helpful.

The endowment dialogue directs us to receive the law of consecration as outlined in the Doctrine and Covenants. It then defines this law as meaning that we are to consecrate ourselves, our time, talents, and everything which the Lord has or may bless us with in the future to the Church. This is for the stated purposes of building up the kingdom of

God and establishing Zion. One immediate problem, however, is that this definition, given in the endowment, does not match up with the law of consecration as outlined in the Doctrine and Covenants. The endowment's definition is much broader.

A second dilemma stems from the fact that a careful study shows the Doctrine and Covenants contains instructions that the Church no longer tries to implement. Since the Church is not attempting to implement the full law of consecration as outlined in the revelations, how are the endowment's instructions to be understood and lived by its members? It is not possible to fully do so at present as described in the Doctrine and Covenants.

Some have, therefore, concluded that this law has temporarily been replaced by the law of tithing and that at some future point consecration will again be required. This view seems to be supported by the language of the endowment. With the prior covenants of obedience and sacrifice, initiates promise to "observe and keep" these laws. But with the covenant of consecration the wording is different. We agree to "accept" this law as it is contained in the Doctrine and Covenants. This can be interpreted to mean that we are simply accepting the law in concept but are not currently required to live it. However, this approach ignores the remaining language of the endowment which requires us to consecrate ourselves, our time, talents, and everything to the Church. That obligation seems to relate to here and now, not to some distant future.

The law of consecration is first outlined in section 42 and was given in Kirtland in 1831(see D&C 42:30–36, 70–73). Early efforts to live this law failed. Further attempts to live the law of consecration under the United Order were later rekindled in Utah under Brigham Young but again met with failure. In 1838, the Lord clarified the law of tithing which was to be a "standing law unto [my people] forever" (D&C 119:4). This law required a one-time consecration of all surplus property to the Church and then those who had thus been tithed should thereafter "pay one-tenth of their interest annually" (D&C 119:4).

The Church no longer requires a one-time consecration of all surplus property of new members.

Given this ambiguity, it is not surprising that there is some confusion over consecration. Per our discussion from the last chapter, this is an area of the endowment that I believe needs clarification and could be better understood by looking at the underlying principles. I would like to suggest an alternative way to view consecration—one, perhaps more consistent with the Doctrine and Covenants as a whole and with the rest of scripture and that better fits within the overall context of the endowment.

In considering this topic, we tend to focus on the economic aspect of consecration. The underlying principles are outlined in section 104, as follows:

1. Everything belongs to Him. The Lord built the earth and "all things therein are mine" (D&C 104:14).

2. The earth is full, and there is enough and to spare (vs. 17). We should have an abundance versus a scarcity mentality.

3. We are stewards over the blessings we receive (vs. 13).

4. We are free to act as independent agents, but are accountable to the Lord for how we use what we are given (vss. 13, 18).

5. The Lord's way is to exalt (or improve) the poor through the rich being made low (i.e. sacrificing to bless the poor) (vs. 16).

We will look at these principles in greater detail later, but it should be apparent that they can apply to more than material blessings. They can apply to our time, talents, or anything else that we perceive as ours. Consecration, then, is much greater than simply an economic law. But because wealth tends to be a problematic area a lot of focus is placed there. In the Sermon on the Mount, the Savior teaches us to lay up treasures in heaven rather than on earth and cautions that we cannot serve both God and mammon (see 3 Nephi 13:19–24). In one sense, consecration is a very real test of where our heart is and what we treasure.

One may wonder why the endowment covenants are necessary since we essentially agreed to all of them at baptism. That is true enough, however, when the covenants are considered within the context they are presented, then it becomes apparent that the Lord is trying to teach and instruct us. There is a progression to the covenants which should be tied to our own spiritual growth. As such, consecration is the pinnacle—the crowning covenant of the endowment. It is received along with the most sacred token and ordinances of the endowment.

The present wording requires patrons to consecrate themselves to the Church. In the last chapter, we discussed historical changes that have been made to the endowment in an effort to improve it. The covenant of consecration is an area that could perhaps be clarified. I believe it is preferable to understand this covenant as consecrating ourselves unto Christ, rather than the Church. At first glance that might seem the same, but upon closer consideration an important distinction emerges.

If my covenant is with the Church alone, then I am essentially off the hook unless and until the Church requests something of me; only then am I obligated to give it. On the other hand, if I am consecrating myself to Christ, then the burden falls upon me to prayerfully seek to understand His will in my life and then live it day by day. The responsibility shifts. One the Church controls, the other I am responsible and accountable for. This view does not preclude me from responding to the request of a Church leader or to a calling from the Church as per the current wording, but, in addition, it also places upon me the responsibility of being a steward over my time and all that the Lord blesses me with. It is a broader application and potentially extends to all areas of life, such as education, career, family, recreation, etc., and not just to our spiritual life in the Church.

Giving ourselves to Christ also seems to be more closely aligned with the context in which the covenant is presented. This final covenant is given in conjunction with a token that represents receiving the Second Comforter and being redeemed from the Fall. It is a token tied directly to the crucifixion and the Atonement. It therefore has a direct connection to our Savior. The accompanying covenant does as well.

Additionally, our covenant and bond with Christ should be very direct and personal. Potentially, it will endure far longer than the institutional Church will exist. Christ would like to seal us as His (see Mosiah 5:15). He is the true vine, and we are to be branches grafted into Him (see John 15:1–5). We are to take upon us His name. And we are to have His Spirit abide with us. The very notion behind of all of our gospel covenants is to become one with our Savior. For all of these reasons, I prefer to understand this law as consecrating myself to Christ.

Another reason I believe the current wording of this covenant is too narrow is because past prophets also lived this law independent of having any formal church organization. We can see many examples in the scriptures. Nephi, in fact, had some important things to say about the law of consecration (see 2 Nephi 32:9, 33:4). It is easy to see in the stories and example of his life how he lived this law. And we could cite many such examples, but in each of these cases the men and women in scripture were consecrating themselves to the Lord, not to an institution. So, consecrating ourselves to Christ also seems to be more in harmony with the overall principle of consecration found throughout the scriptures.

Finally, it is difficult, if not impossible, from the currently available public records to trace how or when the current wording of this covenant was placed within the endowment. If we assume that it was included in the original 1877 version, then the historical context may again help explain the wording. There had been a renewed effort in the 1870s to live the United Order. Brigham Young had also led a reformation effort for many years aimed at whipping the Saints into shape.

He and succeeding Church presidents often encountered resistance to policies and changes they wanted to implement. It may have proven an easy solution to simply word the covenant in a manner that gave the Church greater control. The unfortunate side-effect, however, may be that it reduced the law of consecration to something less than the scriptures indicate it to be.

Consecration is the capstone covenant of the gospel and is much greater than an economic law or system. The word consecrate means to make something sacred or holy or to devote it to a particular purpose. The Savior's life is the ultimate example. He declared: "I came into the world to do the will of my Father, because my Father sent me" (3 Nephi 27:13). This is true consecration. It is worthy of our best efforts to emulate as we seek to become one with Christ. Consecration connects us with Christ in doing the work of the Father and extends to all aspects of our lives.

Zion

One of the endowment's stated purposes for consecration is to establish Zion. Consecration is a necessary foundational element of Zion, but this raises the question: what exactly is Zion?

The scriptural definition of Zion is given in the book of Moses: "And the Lord called his people Zion, because they were of one heart and one mind, and dwelt in righteousness; and there were no poor among them" (Moses 7:18). The result of this condition was that the "Lord came and dwelt with his people" (Moses 7:16). Zion includes three elements:

- The Lord's presence.
- No poor among the people.
- People of one heart and mind living in righteousness.

It is easy to see how consecration is required to bring about the necessary conditions. We are now over 170 years past Joseph Smith's death and yet are we any closer to establishing Zion (based on these criteria) than the Saints in his day?

It is true that the Church has grown in numbers, wealth, influence, and even somewhat in acceptance by mainstream society. But are we any closer to being of one heart and mind? Or are we becoming increasingly fractured and divided? Are we closer to economic equality? Or is the gap between the wealthy and poor members of the Church increasing? Do we receive the Lord's presence and the gifts of the Spirit? Or do we generally find a lack of them? We want to believe that "all is well" and that "Zion prospereth," but the reality is we are no closer to Zion today than we were in 1844.

Perhaps the best place to practice and prepare is within our own families. The ideals of Zion must begin first in our marriages and then extend outward. What better place to learn to follow Christ? For example, think of our baptismal covenants that require us to bear one another's burdens and then apply them at home (see Mosiah 18:8). Husbands, are you aware of your wife's burdens? Are you helping her to bear them or adding to them? Wives, ask the same questions toward your husbands. What better way is there to consecrate ourselves to the Lord than by serving our spouses and children within our own families?

Furthermore, we are to stand as witnesses of God (see Mosiah 18:9). Parents, have you done this with your children throughout their lives? Have you taught them the gospel and shared your testimony in word and by example? Ultimately, "the eternal contest between good and evil is not fought with great armies, but one life at a time."[222] That battle can be greatly aided or hindered within our homes.

Is there contention or discord in our families or extended families that we could help resolve (see 3 Nephi 11:29–30)? Are there broken hearts we could help mend or forgiveness we have withheld and need to extend? If we truly wish to become a king or a queen as we are anointed to become, then perhaps the best place to begin is by following the example of humility and service of the King within our own homes and families. We must humbly seek His direction and help as we do so. Let us first in our homes begin to have one heart and mind and live together in righteousness.

Care for the Poor

A second characteristic of Zion is their care for the poor. This care extends to their needs until there are no poor remaining. The scriptures make it clear that we have an individual obligation to care for the poor. It is not something we can pass off to the Church and feel we have done enough. This is an area where I have needed to do some repenting over the past few years. This section is primarily addressed to readers who are living in North America or other areas of economic affluence.

The Lord has repeatedly expressed his concern for the poor. He has also said that their needs are to be addressed in His way which is to elevate them through the rich being made low (see D&C 104:16). In other words, those who have are to sacrifice in order to lift and bless those who have not. How are we to do this? Is paying tithing and a generous fast offering enough?

Tithing is not our only obligation. Everything we have comes from the Lord and belongs to Him. He has directed how ten percent of what we have is to be used (tithing), but that still leaves us as stewards over the remaining ninety percent, which can also be used to further God's purposes. For some, the remaining amount is fully needed for the support of their families. But many have a surplus and it is to this surplus we shall speak further.

In the Book of Alma, we find an example of the law of consecration in practice. The people of the church "did impart of their substance, every man according to that which he had to the poor and the needy, and the sick, and the afflicted; and they did not wear costly apparel, yet they were neat and comely" (Alma 1:27). This sounds very much like the principles of the law of consecration in practice. Notice that they did not spend beyond what they needed (costly apparel) but rather sought to bless the poor and the needy in addition to taking care of their own needs.

The result of this practice is very interesting. They began to become wealthy and have a surplus of everything they needed. When this occurred, they did not set their hearts upon their riches, but rather expanded the good they were able to do with their wealth. "And thus in their prosperous circumstances, they did not send away *any* who were naked, or that were hungry, or that were athirst, or that were sick, or that had not been nourished; and they did not set their hearts upon riches; therefore *they were liberal to all*, both old and young, both bond and free, both male and female, whether out of the Church or in the Church, having no respect to persons as to those who stood in need" (Alma 1:30, emphasis added). What a wonderful example of consecration in action, not just the temporal care provided, but also the charity and love and compassion that is developed in the hearts of the people.

The end result is most curious. It defies the laws of modern economics. "And thus they did prosper and become far more wealthy than those who did not belong to their Church" (Alma 1:31). These people are giving away their money and resources. Their hearts are set on loving and serving their fellowmen rather than on riches. They refuse to buy the latest designer clothing and the newest chariots. But as a result, they become wealthy. How is that possible? It does not make sense based upon our economic laws. But He who is able to take five loaves and fishes and feed a multitude is able to bless these people with increased wealth as a result of their wise stewardship of their resources. These are the principles upon which Zion is to be built.

These people reached a point where they only saw the needs and sought to fill them. They did not care if the person in need was a member or a non-member, whether they were male or female, black or white. They only saw their suffering and ministered to them. They were generous in addressing these needs. It was not a stingy, begrudging, judgmental effort. These descriptions are giving us a glimpse into the hearts of these people. It is where our own hearts need to grow to and emulate.

Where had these people been taught this doctrine and learned this behavior? It came from the instructions left by King Benjamin. He reminded us that we are all beggars before God, and told us to not suffer any beggar to petition us in vain (see Mosiah 4:16). Do not ignore their pleas or turn them away empty-handed. We are instead to remember our own status as a beggar before God and have compassion on our fellowmen. We are not excused by the convenient thought that their condition is their own fault or that they deserve their suffering (see Mosiah 4:17). If that is our attitude, then we have no interest in the kingdom of God and have great cause to repent (see Mosiah 4:18). We simply cannot judge or always know the full situation. We are to minister where we see a need. Despite how plainly this is put, we often feel it does not apply in our modern society.

Outside the walls of the Salt Lake Temple, there are often a handful of beggars asking for money. Because I lived in a community where encountering such beggars was not common, when I visited the Salt Lake Temple the situation often left me uncomfortable. I hurried by and ignored them. But that lack of compassion on my part was so wrong. I did not see the bitter irony in attending the temple, participating in a prayer circle, and begging God for blessings that I needed, while I had just ignored the pleas of some of His children waiting outside. Alma taught of our need to cry unto the Lord for mercy, salvation, and for His blessings in our lives (see Alma 34:18–27), but then cautioned that if we then turn away the needy, our prayer is in vain and we are as dross which is good for nothing but to be thrown out (see Alma 34:28–29).

In our day, it is easy to justify our lack of compassion with the thought that the beggar we encounter in the street is just going to waste our money on drugs or alcohol. And, in some cases, that may happen. But the problem is we cannot judge because we rarely see or know the entire situation. A few years ago, I decided to repent of my prior attitudes and to begin seeking opportunities to bless the lives of the poor and needy. This started with small, simple efforts but has since become a great blessing in my life.

Initially, it sometimes felt awkward. I questioned myself and often wondered if I was doing the right thing. Was I helping or enabling? In response, the Lord reminded me that when we serve the least, we are serving Him. My attitude today towards so many of these issues is completely different than it used to be. I have learned through my experiences that many who are reduced to begging on the streets feel humiliated and would rather not be there but often have legitimate needs and feel they have no other option to address them. I have had many sweet experiences with people who are homeless or very poor.

For example, one young man I met had struggled with drug addiction. At one point in his life, he had traveled to Las Vegas with his dealer. Like the prodigal son, this young man had partied with "friends" until his money ran out and he found himself abandoned and on the street. With no other way to return home this young man had begged on the road with a cardboard sign until strangers had compassion upon him and he obtained enough for a bus ticket. Once home, he checked himself into a drug recovery program. When I met him, he had been sober for several months and was working to rebuild his life. I do not know who gave him some help when he was in the gutter, but I am grateful they had compassion in a critical moment in his life.

Some may feel that our obligation to the poor is fully met by paying a generous fast offering. While that is important, we can do more. Like the good Samaritan, we need to be directly and personally involved in relieving the suffering of others. He did not just donate to a good cause. If all of our efforts to relieve poverty are distant and removed, e.g. just donating money to the Red Cross, the LDS Humanitarian fund, etc., we may miss the opportunity of developing compassion and real charity for others that is possible by being more personally involved.

One month as Fast Sunday approached, I challenged my grown children to pay a double fast offering that month. Half of it they were to pay to the Church as they normally would. With the other half, they were to find someone during the week that they could help with the money. Then on Sunday, they were to fast specifically for that person or family. This exercise made fasting and paying fast offerings a much more meaningful experience that month because they were able to see the person who was blessed by their sacrifice. When we simply make a contribution to the Church, we do not always see the connection with the recipient on the other end. I would encourage you to try the same idea this next Fast Sunday and see if it changes things for you.

Apart from tithing, the Lord has not given specific rules for how we are to care for the poor. Rather, He taught principles and then makes us as stewards and agents of His resources. We should seek for the Lord's Spirit to direct and help us, but should also do much good of our own free will. Take a step of faith and try, even if it seems awkward or unnatural at first.

The Lord explained: "Behold this is the way that I, the Lord, have decreed to provide for my saints, that the poor shall be exalted, in that the rich are made low. For the earth is full, and there is enough and to spare; yea, I prepared all things, and have given unto the children of men to be agents unto themselves. Therefore, if any man shall take of the abundance which I have made, and impart not his portion, according to the law of my gospel, unto the poor and the needy, he shall, with the wicked, lift up his eyes in hell, being in torment" (D&C 118:16–18). He also stated, "For it is expedient that I, the Lord, should make every man accountable, as a steward over earthly blessings" (D&C 118:13). We are stewards over whatever blessings we receive. We will be accountable for that stewardship. And if we have not been good stewards, we will find ourselves in hell.

We are left with two somewhat opposing principles to work through. One is that all these things are to be done in wisdom and in order and that we do not need to run faster than we have strength (see

Mosiah 4:27). The other principle is that in the Lord's way, we are to lift the poor by being made low. In other words, we are to sacrifice to bless others. This obligation does not leave us off the hook until we have everything we possibly want, to then work with anything left-over. There never seems to be anything left. The principle is that we do not need to spend excessively or extravagantly on our own needs. To the extent we do so, we are robbing the poor. In other words, we are spending money on ourselves that should be used to help them (see 2 Nephi 28:13).

Alma's people did not spend money on expensive clothes. Instead, they dressed affordably and used the difference to help others. With this approach, nearly everyone can do something to help the poor, no matter how meager their monthly budget. To put it in a more modern context, suppose I need a new vehicle. I want a pickup truck for my job, for use in Scouting, and for things around my home with my family. The truck I would really like to buy is the fancy, top end model with a diesel engine that can tow almost anything. It would cost about $60,000 to purchase a new one where I live. But I don't really need a diesel truck, nor do I need the fancy leather seats, or even a brand-new vehicle. Everything I need can be done just fine with a more basic truck. A really good model that is a year old is available for about $30,000. Let's assume that I have saved the $60,000 and can afford either truck. If I choose the truck that really meets my needs instead of the nicer one I would like, then I am "making myself low" and through that small sacrifice will have $30,000 remaining that I can use to bless others.

That does not permit me to judge another who drives around in a more expensive diesel truck. Some may have work or needs that are different from mine. I am not to worry about what others may do, but am simply to be a good steward over the resources that the Lord has blessed me with. What I choose to do with my resources shows the Lord where my heart really lies. C. S. Lewis once observed that if our charitable giving is not truly costing us something then we are probably not giving enough. That thought is in harmony with the principles the Lord is trying to teach us in the scriptures. The truck example is just a simple illustration of these ideas. Each of us is left to figure out how to implement these ideas in our own lives.

Money itself is not the problem. It is only a tool and is to be used for good. The problem lies in the intentions of our hearts. The Book of Mormon plainly warns: "For behold, ye do love money, and your substance, and your fine apparel, and the adorning of your Churches, *more than ye love the poor and the needy*, the sick and the afflicted" (Mormon 8:37, emphasis added). That hits close to home. The sin of Sodom is still found in many of our communities: "Behold, this was the iniquity of thy sister Sodom, pride, fulness of bread, and abundance of idleness was in her and in her daughters, *neither did she strengthen the hand of the poor and needy*. And they were haughty, and committed abomination before me: therefore I took them away as I saw good" (Ezekiel 16:49–50, emphasis added). The solution is found in living the covenants of the temple endowment. Consecration is aimed at fixing our hearts and helping us develop and exercise charity.

Another principle taught in the Doctrine and Covenants is that temporal and spiritual blessings are tied together. "Nevertheless, in your temporal things you shall be equal, and this not grudgingly, otherwise the abundance of the manifestations of the Spirit shall be withheld" (D&C 70:14). If you are not receiving the spiritual experiences you desire, it may be due in part to the way you manage your temporal blessings. Study out the principles taught in the scriptures and begin living them.

As I began to repent and live these principles better in my own life, blessings followed. I could see the effects in the lives of others and could see the Lord blessing me in return. I felt happy about my progress and what I was doing. Then one day while serving at a homeless shelter, I met a woman who is a modern-day example of the widow and her mite. This woman is homeless, living in her car. She is old enough to receive a social security check from the government each month. Despite her own need, she had saved these checks until she had enough to buy a small mobile home in a rural area for another man who was also homeless to get him off the streets. She continued to live in her car. When I learned of her sacrifice, I felt utterly ashamed of my own efforts. Like the rich men in the Savior's parable, I had cast into the treasury out of my abundance while this woman had cast in all of her living.

These principles are so important that the Savior stated that when He comes again to divide His sheep from the goats, the basis upon which His judgment will be made is threefold: did we feed the hungry, clothe the naked, and minister to the sick and imprisoned (see Matthew 25:31–46)? His regard for the least among us is such that He considers this ministry or neglect as if it were done unto Him personally (see Matthew 25:40, 45).

The Church cannot meet all the needs. They are simply too great. And our full duty to the poor cannot be discharged simply through paying tithing and fast offerings and feeling that is enough. We must bless others as wise stewards of the resources and blessings we have been given. This is the essence of the law of consecration. In doing so, we bring ourselves and potentially others unto Christ and thereby build His kingdom.

Beyond those in our own neighborhoods and communities who may need our help, there are many, around the world, who cannot help themselves. It is easy to preach self-reliance, but in some parts of the world that is simply not possible because the opportunities to become so do not exist. Others, such as children or those critically sick or injured, may not be in a position to help themselves.

A year or two ago, I became aware of a group called the Liahona Foundation. The sole purpose of this organization is to address the needs of LDS children in developing nations who are not getting adequate nutrition in their formative years. This often presents lifelong ramifications and limitations. In some extreme cases, these LDS children are so malnourished that they are literally starving to death.

When I first learned of this, I was incredulous. Is it really possible that there are LDS children who have starved to death in this day of economic prosperity?

I did some research and found it was sadly true. Gratefully, such cases are extreme and not common, but there are many, many LDS children who are malnourished. The Liahona Foundation was founded by Brad Walker, a physician who wanted to address this need.[223] For about $50 they can feed a child a nutritional supplement for a year. Nursing students from BYU and other humanitarian volunteers visit many of these children on an annual basis to track their growth, height, and weight. Thanks to these supplements, many of these children are able to get their physical development back on track to normal. Fifty dollars is such a little amount for someone living in North America, yet for these children it may make a lifetime of difference. For $6,000 the Liahona Foundation can feed and supply the needs of an entire stake. They currently serve about 185 stakes, but have about 200 more stakes they cannot yet serve because of a lack of funding.

Some of the physicians who are part of their organization regularly work an extra shift at the hospital rather than take a day off so they can donate the additional funds to the children. This is another great example of the law of consecration in action. We must do more as individuals. We cannot wait for the Church to do it all. "For behold, it is not meet that I should command in all things; for he that is compelled in all things, the same is a slothful and not a wise servant; wherefore he receiveth no reward" (D&C 58:26). Consecrate yourself to Christ, and let Him direct your path.

The Lord's Presence

The final characteristic of Zion is that the Lord's presence is found there. These things are all tied together. Becoming of one heart and mind in righteousness, eliminating poverty among us, and having Christ's presence are integrally tied to consecration. Actively consecrating ourselves to Christ allows Him to sanctify us to where He can receive and dwell with us. The temple endowment teaches us this truth, if we have eyes to see it.

The temple covenant of consecration is received in conjunction with a sign and token that are tied to receiving Christ as the Second Comforter. We did not discuss the physical ordinances accompanying this blessing. But here within the sacred context of what we are discussing, I would like to detour for a moment to talk about the sacrament.

The sacrament is an ordinance that is perhaps greater than we may realize. Baptism connects us with the Holy Ghost—the third member of the Godhead. We typically talk about the sacrament as a renewal of that covenant. While that is not inappropriate, consider that the sacrament may be something altogether higher and holier. The sacrament potentially connects us with Christ—the second member of the Godhead.

The emblems of the sacrament are His flesh and His blood. We ingest them as a witness that we are willing to take His name upon us. And we are promised that we may live so as to always have His (meaning Christ's) spirit to be with us. If you recall the discussion on covenants from *Understanding Your Endowment*, you recognize these elements as a symbolic merging of our identities. Christ is becoming part of us and we of Him. The sacrament is an ordinance of becoming one. It is also a bond between a community of believers as we all work to become united as one in Christ.

We are reminded of His promise: "Behold, I stand at the door and knock: if any man hear my voice, and open the door, I will come in to him, and will sup with him, and he with me" (Revelation 3:20). It is significant to me that Christ's promise includes a supper—or sacrament with Him. Can you imagine how you would feel having Christ personally minister the sacrament to you? And look at how many times He does exactly that when He visits with the Nephites. Despite being in His immediate presence, He administers the sacrament to them on at least two occasions.

Likewise, when Moses and seventy of the elders of Israel ascended the mount into God's presence, they ate and drank with him (Exodus 24:9–11). We find it again in the instructions Joseph received with respect to the ordinance of washing the feet in Doctrine and Covenants 88:138–141. At the time, this was the crowning ordinance in the Church, a witness that those who received it were clean before the Lord and were sealed up to eternal life. This sacred ordinance was to begin with prayer, followed by the sacrament, and then their feet were washed clean (D&C 88:141).

Finally, as He instituted the sacrament, Christ instructed His disciples that the ordinance was to remind them of that hour when He was present with them (see JST Mark 14:20–25). Thereafter they were to remember it whenever they partook anew (ibid., verse 24). The sacrament therefore can remind us of either a time we spent with Christ or that we will spend with Him in the future.

For all of these reasons, I believe the sacrament to be a higher and holier ordinance, not just a renewal of prior covenants. Excepting small children, the sacrament is only to be taken by those who have previously entered the waters of baptism. We are to partake of it worthily, with real intent. It is something we partake of frequently. We receive it as newly-baptized disciples and it is found in the final crowning, sealing ordinances assuring eternal life.

The sacrament is an ordinance tied to the Second Comforter, as a reminder of that visit if we have already received it, or as the potential for us to qualify for such in the future. It is a fellowship (oneness) with Christ so that we may approach the Father. No flesh can dwell in the presence of God save through the merits and mercy and grace of the Son (see 2 Nephi 2:8). The sacrament prepares us.

Conclusion

In conclusion, we are stewards over blessings that the Lord has given us. Everything we have, ultimately, belongs to Him. We are to use those resources to bless our families and others of God's children.

The strong are to bless, serve, and lift the weak. And each of us will eventually be accountable to God for how we utilize what we have been given. These principles are the basis of the law of consecration as outlined in the Doctrine and Covenants. It is easy to see that these principles can apply to any blessing we receive including our time, talents, and other gifts we are given.

These principles of consecration are the very opposite of Babylon, where every person conquers according to his or her own strength, and where the strong often prey upon the weak (see Alma 30:17). That is Satan's model and we see it being lived in the world all around us. In stark contrast, consecration is one of the foundations of Zion. Charity is developed and exercised through these principles of consecration and is aimed at lifting and blessing the lives of the poor until no poor remain. Some of this work has to be done as a group effort (e.g. through the Church), but some of it also needs to be done individually as we bring to pass much good of our own free will (see D&C 58:26).

Beyond all of this, consecration is ultimately about giving our hearts unto God and becoming His. It is about becoming one in heart, mind, and spirit with Him.

HOMEWORK

1. How could you better live the law of consecration? How would the Lord have you bless the lives and ease the burdens of the poor?

2. Read "Spreading Zion Southward" an article by Brad Walker, founder of the Liahona Children's Foundation, addressing the problems and needs of Church members in third world countries. The article is in two parts: "Part I: Improving Efficiency and Equity in the Allocation of Church Welfare Resources" and "Part II: Sharing Our Loaves and Fishes." Both articles were originally published in Dialogue: A Journal of Mormon Thought 35, no. 4 (Winter 2002): 91–109 and are available online.[224] You can learn more about their work at *liahonachildren.org*.

CHAPTER 10

CONCLUSION

And the end of all our exploring will be to arrive where we started
and know the place for the first time.
—T. S. Eliott

WE NOW RETURN to a question raised at the beginning of this book: what was the purpose for the expanded endowment introduced in Nauvoo? And where did it all come from? If we consider Joseph's life up to that time, several key influences converge. These would include, at least, the following:

- The prophecy that the fathers and the children needed to be connected through Elijah's ministry before the Lord's return (see D&C 2). This was quoted by Moroni at the onset of Joseph's ministry. In Nauvoo, nearing the end of it, Joseph was concerned about this "welding link."
- He had translated the Book of Abraham and obtained therein some of what is contained in the endowment, along with some things he was not permitted to reveal (see Facsimile 2, Figures 3, 7, 8, 9–21).
- He was concerned that the Saints were growing dependent upon their leaders and were not learning to receive revelation and direction for themselves.[225]
- The Saints had largely failed to receive the blessing of the Lord's presence in Kirtland. Joseph may have recognized that more time was required for learning, growth, and development before the people could be prepared for this blessing. There needed to be intermediate steps

between the initial rites of accepting the gospel through baptism and the later crowning ordinances of the gospel.

- The Lord had placed the entire Church under condemnation in Kirtland, but had given them another chance to make things right in Nauvoo (see D&C 84:54–56; 124:28).

- Joseph may have known that his remaining time was short and that the temple would not be completed before his death. He seemed to have a sense of urgency about putting into place what he could even before the temple was finished.

- Two months prior to inaugurating the endowment, Joseph entered the Masonic Lodge in Nauvoo. He quickly learned and moved up through their ceremonies and degrees.

- Joseph had been in the presence of the Father and the Son on multiple occasions, and had also been taught by Moroni, Michael, Peter, James, John, Gabriel, Raphael, and others (see D&C 128:20–22). He saw a vision of the degrees of glory and knew many of the mysteries of God (see D&C 76). He wanted the Saints to share in these experiences. On one occasion, he lamented: "It is my meditation all the day, and more than my meat and drink to know how I shall make the Saints of God comprehend the visions that roll like an overflowing surge before my mind."[226]

- Historic Christianity had been condemned by the Lord for having a form of godliness but lacking real power (see JS–History 1:19). Joseph wanted a people empowered with spiritual gifts, holding genuine priesthood authority and power, and manifesting the miracles and blessings promised the true followers of Christ (see Mark 16:17).

Given all of these influences, he certainly would have been thoughtful about what he left behind to help the generations who would follow.

Origins of the Endowment

Joseph never left a direct explanation of the origins of the Nauvoo endowment. This led to later speculation as to where it came from. Similarities between elements of the endowment and the ceremonies of Freemasonry have added to the debate. The relationship of Masonry to the temple endowment is a complex topic. Opinions on the matter run the gamut from Joseph Smith plagiarized the entire ceremony to he took nothing from Masonry and any resemblance is purely coincidental. The truth probably lies somewhere in the middle of these extremes. Some elements of the endowment are identical to symbols in Masonry, and it is easy to argue that Joseph borrowed them. But it is also apparent that much of the endowment was known to Joseph long before his involvement in Masonry.[227] There are also many differences between the two ceremonies, including the overarching purpose for each. So, it is a vast oversimplification to simply claim Joseph plagiarized the endowment.

There is also compelling evidence that many of the common symbols are found in cultures predating both Mormonism and Masonry. As a result, some have argued that both Masonry and the endowment derive from common but more ancient sources. These commonalities have led others to conclude that Joseph recognized in the Masonic Temple remnants of truths that he was subsequently able to restore and correct to their original forms.[228] This idea seems supported by the fact that Joseph was interested in Abraham, ancient Egypt, Enoch and Zion, and other things which pre-dated historic Christianity. The full religion which existed with Adam and Eve in the beginning of the world is prophesied to return at the end of the world (see Moses 6:7). Joseph seems to have been focused on that restoration during the latter part of his ministry.

Another possibility is that Joseph borrowed symbolic elements from Masonry but then redefined their meanings within a new context. This would not be without historic scriptural precedence. When the destroying angel visited Egypt, the Lord took a well-known cultural practice of the time (marking the door with sacrificial blood) and adapted it to the Israelites' circumstances. He gave new meaning to an existing rite through Moses.[229] In a similar manner, Christ took the emblems of the Passover (unleavened bread and wine) and redefined them in establishing the sacrament (see Mark 14:14–26). The symbols of the Passover now had an entirely new meaning. Joseph may have done essentially the same thing.

This idea seems supported by his explanation of Masonry. Joseph is reported to claim: "Freemasonry, as at present, was the apostate endowments, as sectarian religion was the apostate religion."[230] This statement could be interpreted to mean that the symbols of Masonry were correct but their meaning and purpose were not. The fact that the endowment reaches back to a more ancient time is apparent from the description of the inaugural endowment at the Red Brick Store: "In this council was instituted the Ancient order of things for the fir[s]t time in these last days."[231] While Joseph included symbols from Masonry, the meaning and purpose of these symbols was very different within the new endowment. His followers, many of whom were experienced Masons, accepted this explanation.[232]

Perhaps a more interesting question would be how much of the endowment came from direct revelation and how much was left to Joseph to piece together on his own? It is probably impossible to know with any degree of certainty. It appears to have developed a piece at a time over several years. But did it come as ideas, thoughts, and principles or in a form more concretely defined? As we discussed earlier, sometimes the Lord gives specific words and information, while at other times, revelation comes as "pure-intelligence" in the form of concepts or sudden understanding, which we are then left to put into our own words.

Based upon the fact that Joseph appears to have borrowed elements from Masonry, I would suggest that it was the latter approach. Joseph understood concepts and ideas that he was trying to communicate and preserve. Masonry provided him with an example of a ritualistic framework to which Joseph could attach many of these principles. It may have been the spark needed to help him know how to approach the task of what he could leave behind after his departure.

In the end, however one views this topic, choosing to worry over the origins of the endowment's symbols while missing what is being communicated may be a little like quibbling over the elements Christ chose to use in His parables rather than focusing on the message He was trying to relay. It focuses on the wrong thing. Which brings us back to the really important question: what was Joseph trying to leave us in the endowment? The answer to this question is what matters.

Ancient and Modern Israel

The parallels between ancient and "modern" Israel (speaking of the Church as such) are striking. As members of the Church today, we tend to think of ourselves as superior to the ancient saints under Moses, but that may be a hasty conclusion. In a revelation received in Kirtland, the Lord explained the problem and failure of ancient Israel. Moses had stood in the presence of the Lord and spoken with Him face to face. Rather than have his people envy his position, he sought diligently to sanctify them so that they might experience the same blessing (see D&C 84:23). Joseph Smith explained, "Moses sought to bring the children of Israel into the presence of God, through the power of the Priesthood, but he could not."[233]

Ancient Israel received multiple experiences to help them prepare but ultimately refused the blessing. Their final rejection became known as the Day of Provocation.[234] On that day, the Lord withdrew from them telling Moses: "I have sworn in my wrath, that they shall not enter into my presence, into my rest, in the days of their pilgrimage" (JST Exodus 34:2). As a result, they lost the Holy Order or fulness of the priesthood, and its associated ordinances (see JST Exodus 34:1).

Like Moses, Joseph Smith had also stood in the Lord's presence. He too sought diligently to sanctify his people in Kirtland. Though a rich spiritual endowment occurred in Kirtland, for most of the Saints it fell short of the promised blessing of beholding the Lord. Modern-day Israel under Joseph had fared no better in obtaining the promised blessing than ancient Israel had under Moses. Undeterred by this failure, Joseph tried again in Nauvoo to bring the Saints to know their Lord. Once again, failure ensued. There is not a single account of the Lord's appearance in the Nauvoo Temple, despite His promise to visit that house (see D&C 124:27–28).

As a result of ancient Israel's failure, the Lord took Moses and the higher priesthood but left behind a lesser priesthood and ordinances (see D&C 84:25–26). After Moses, Israel primarily functioned under the Aaronic Priesthood with the High Priest as its head. Despite their rejection, the Lord continued to work with and through ancient Israel. Can you imagine the Lord's disappointment with these people? He had freed them from slavery, led them out of Egypt through a series of miracles into the wilderness, and then offered to walk with them personally. They were invited to return to His presence. An opportunity to create a Zion existed. A few responded, but most did not.[235] Instead, they listened to their fears and asked Moses to speak to God for them (see Exodus 20:18–21). It was easier that way.

Here we find a very interesting situation, one which seems to apply to us as well. The Lord offered these people a higher way. He wanted to give them a fulness of the priesthood, return them to his presence, and make of them a kingdom of priests (see Exodus 19:6, D&C 84:19–26). Moses wanted all to reach the same prophetic status that he enjoyed. He did not want to be a permanent intermediary. He lamented, "Would God that all the Lord's people were prophets" (Numbers 11:29). The higher way required these people to sanctify themselves, receive personal revelation and direction, and learn to walk with God. That is what both God and Moses wanted for ancient Israel.

When they refused, the Lord gave them a lesser way. He left them a law of carnal commandments and outward ordinances. The priesthood was restricted to a single tribe, the Levites. What remained instead of the fulness was a preparatory gospel. Eventually, the Israelites forgot that what they had was merely preparatory. Future generations, rather than rising up and *becoming* what the Lord had desired for their forefathers, got caught up in endless routines of *doing* and lost sight of the higher path.

Over time, many lost sight of the reasons for the rites and ordinances of the law of Moses and began to see them as ends in themselves, rather than as a means to an end. The end, of course, was to testify of and to bring them unto Christ. They began to think salvation came through the ordinances of the law of Moses. They became lifted up in pride and considered themselves God's chosen people because of their lineage and ordinances, believing that they alone were saved while all others would go to hell. They developed a hierarchy of rabbis and authorities, and added traditions and rules to the Lord's commandments. They focused on outward appearances of cleanliness and purity and did not notice the disappearance of spiritual gifts among them. Eventually, such a degree of apostasy ensued that, by the time Christ came on the scene, they rejected the very God who gave the law and ordinances to Moses in the first place. It is a bitter irony!

As Latter-day Saints, we potentially face the same problems. We like to think of ourselves as modern-day Israel, and in many ways, we mirror them. Their problems began with wanting Moses to speak to God for them. Joseph Smith saw the same conditions developing among the early Saints in Nauvoo. In his first public discourse given after introducing the endowment, he read "the 14th Chap. of Ezekiel—Said the Lord had declared by the prophet that *the people should each one stand for himself [or herself]* and depend on no man or men in that state of corruption of the Jewish Church—that righteous persons could only deliver their own souls—*applied it to the present state of the Church of Latter Day Saints*—Said if the people departed from the Lord, they must fall—that *they were depending on the prophet hence were darkened in their minds from neglect of themselves.*"[236] This sermon preserves an insightful view into some of Joseph's mindset at the time he introduced the endowment.

The Saints were becoming too dependent upon him for revelation and direction and not rising up to develop the ability to receive revelation for themselves. It was essentially the same problem that ancient Israel experienced when they told Moses to go talk to the Lord for them and then tell them what he said. Modern Israel had just substituted Joseph for Moses. The endowment addresses these problems fairly directly. There we are taught to "stand for ourselves" by looking to God to supply further light and knowledge. We are shown there how "righteous persons can deliver their own souls." Joseph left a loud and clear message to us in the endowment, but we often ignore or fail to grasp it.

Joseph taught openly and plainly during his ministry: "It is the privilege of the Children of God to come to God & get Revelation. . . . When any person receives a vision of Heaven, he sees things that he never thought of before. . . . The Father could not be glorified in the Son on any other principle than *we coming to God, asking, receiving, heavens open visions &c.—They are done away because of unbelief.*"[237] Unbelief is always the problem! It is not that we are unable or unauthorized to seek these things. Nor is it our lack of Church office or position—it is simply our own unbelief. Joseph continued, "It is our privilege to pray for & obtain these things. . . . God is not a respecter of persons, we all have the same privilege. Come to God weary him until he blesses you &c—we are entitled to the same blessings."[238]

That the Lord had concerns with the early Church is plainly evident from scripture. In Kirtland, He had placed them under condemnation for neglecting the Book of Mormon (see D&C 84:54–58). This came just a few months prior to the Lord's invitation to build a temple in Kirtland and the promise that they could behold His face there (see D&C 88). How was this condemnation and invitation linked through the Book of Mormon? The Book of Mormon contains example after example of those who lived under the limitations of the law of Moses but who rose up individually to return to the Lord's presence and then received the fulness from Him (see Alma 13:1). Despite living under the lesser law or preparatory gospel of their time, these individuals entered into the higher way. We discussed earlier how Lehi was one of these.

Despite the endowment of power that was given in Kirtland, for most, it still fell short of receiving the Lord. More time and spiritual preparation were needed. The Saints were given another opportunity in Nauvoo. The Lord told them to build another temple and issued a sobering decree: "For there is not a place found on the earth that *he [Christ] may come to* and restore again that which was lost unto you, or *which he hath taken away*, even the fulness of the priesthood" (D&C 124:28; emphasis added). By the time this revelation was given in 1841, the Lord had taken the fulness of the priesthood from the Church. (That does not mean that it was taken from Joseph, as an individual, but the Church as a group had already lost the higher path.) We see the beginning of the exact same condition that plagued ancient Israel—the fulness is being withdrawn and something lesser is being left behind. However, they were being given another chance.

The Lord promised to come visit them at the temple in Nauvoo and complete the restoration: "And verily I say unto you, let this house be built unto my name, that *I may reveal* mine ordinances therein unto my people; for I deign to reveal unto my Church things which have been kept hid from before the foundation of the world" (D&C 124:40–41; see also vs. 28; emphasis added). The Saints could correct things but this had to be accomplished within a given time-frame. "And I give unto you a sufficient time to build a house unto me . . . and if you do not these things at the end of the appointment *ye shall be rejected as a Church*" (D&C 124:31–32; emphasis added). That is a pretty dire warning from the Lord. In this revelation, He gave very specific requirements for the temple. He promised blessings for completing it and cursings for failing to do so.

The deadline for accomplishing this work is not specifically defined in the revelation (see D&C 124:33). While he lived, Joseph pushed the Saints to complete the temple with a sense of urgency. For example, in June of 1843, roughly a year prior to his death he admonished: "I will now ask this assembly and all the Saints if you will now build this house and receive the ordinances and blessings which God has in store for you; or will you not build unto the Lord this house, and let Him pass by and bestow these blessings upon another people? I pause for a reply."[239] As late as January of 1844, he lamented: "if the whole Church should go to with all their might to save their dead, seal their posterity, and gather their living friends and spend none of their time in behalf of the world, they would hardly get through before night would come, when no man can work; and my only trouble at the present time is concerning ourselves, that the Saints *will be divided, broken up, and scattered,* before we get our salvation secure."[240]

Despite this concern, work on the temple proceeded slowly. By the time of Joseph's death in June of 1844, approximately 3½ years had passed from the date of the revelation commanding the temple be built. At the time of the martyrdom, the outer walls were only completed to the second story. Was three and a half years, sufficient time to build the Nauvoo temple? The Kirtland Temple had been completed in a similar time frame (January 1833 to March 1836), so it seems the Nauvoo Temple could have been finished before Joseph and Hyrum were killed. Furthermore, during the same time period the Saints had constructed a number of buildings of lesser importance including a Cultural Hall, a Seventies Hall, and a Masonic temple or lodge.

Did the Church meet the requirements in completing the Nauvoo Temple within the allotted time frame or not? Did the Nauvoo Saints succeed or fail?[241] This is a critical question, one that has largely been forgotten by modern Mormons. Some, who understand these events, believe that the Nauvoo Saints met the conditions, just in the nick of time before being driven out. They argue the lost fulness was restored because Joseph introduced the endowment and other temple ordinances before his death and because of the keys he delivered. The Lord's hand has been evident in much of the work of the Church since then, so it may seem a safe conclusion that the deadline was met.

However, if we consider the possibility that we have been mistaken in our traditional view of these events, then a closer look at the available evidence suggests a very different conclusion.[242]

Perhaps many members today assume that the Nauvoo Temple was completed before the endowment was administered there beginning in December of 1845, roughly 18 months after Joseph's death. The historical fact is that the exterior was complete at the time, but the interior was not. Following the deaths of Joseph and Hyrum, and fully aware of the Lord's dire warning, the Saints resumed construction on the temple with greater dispatch. However, when the endowment was finally administered therein, it was done in the still-unfinished attic, which had been partitioned off with canvas curtains in a makeshift fashion. While the attic area was temporarily dedicated for the purpose of endowing as many as possible before the Saints were driven from Nauvoo, much of the interior of the temple remained incomplete. When the exodus began in earnest in February of 1846, a small crew remained behind to finish up the temple until it was considered complete enough to be dedicated on April 30, 1846. By then most of the Saints had departed, and by September of that year the temple was lost to the mob. (For a more detailed chronology of the Nauvoo Temple refer to this endnote.[243])

Even in April when the temple was finally dedicated, it was consider only just good enough. The reality is that the interior was never fully completed.[244] Elder Hyde, who offered the dedicatory prayer, fully aware of the Lord's deadline, concluded that the work had been done just "by the skin of our teeth."[245] His view has become the official position of most Church historians since then. But what really matters is how the Lord saw their efforts. The best indication of how the Lord felt may be seen from the events that followed.

The Lord had promised to visit the Nauvoo Temple to restore the fulness which had been lost (see D&C 124:28). This never occurred. Unlike Kirtland, there is not a single account of Christ visiting the Nauvoo Temple. That fact would seem to indicate failure on the part of the Nauvoo Saints to meet the deadline and conditions. The promised blessing was not given. Furthermore, the Lord had also promised that if the people would labor with their might, He would make the place holy to them and they would not be moved out of their place (see D&C 124:43–45). Instead, the Saints were not allowed to remain in Nauvoo, but were once again driven out, as had previously happened in Missouri and Ohio. This would be a second indication of failure to meet the required time frame.

God plainly warned that if they did "not do the things that I say, I will not perform the oath which I make unto you, neither fulfil the promises you expect at my hands, saith the Lord. For instead of blessings, ye, by your own works, bring cursings, wrath, indignation, and judgments upon your own heads" (D&C 124:47–48). One has to wonder: were the Saints blessed as the Lord had promised or were they instead, as the revelation warned, driven out of their place, suffering cursings, wrath, and judgments? An objective review of the historical events suggests that the Saints did not meet the deadline in time.

Finally, clear evidence of the Lord's displeasure may be seen in a sign He sent. Anciently, the Lord's presence was symbolically manifest in the camp of Israel through a pillar of fire at night and a cloud by day as He led them (see Exodus 13:21). These same two signs of the Lord's presence were again seen in Nauvoo, but this time they were manifest following the Saints' departure and in conjunction with the destruction of the Nauvoo Temple. Sometime around midnight on October 8–9, 1848, the temple caught fire and burned until only the four exterior walls remained. The temple itself became a pillar of fire at night. No one knows how it started; historians simply claim it was by the hand of an unknown arsonist.

Following this fire another group, the Icarians, made plans to reconstruct the temple and made some effort toward that end. However, on May 27, 1850, a tornado toppled the remaining exterior walls. "One source claimed the storm seemed to 'single out the Temple,' felling 'the walls with a roar that was heard miles away.'"[246] A cloud by day, following the pillar of fire at night, completed the destruction of the Nauvoo Temple. Here the ancient symbols of the Lord's presence in the camp of Israel were manifest in the destruction of the Nauvoo Temple. What clearer sign could the Lord have given of his displeasure and the reasons therefore?

One might argue that the Lord destroyed the temple in response to it being desecrated after the Saints left Nauvoo rather than as a sign of His displeasure. However, the Kirtland Temple had likewise passed into the hands of various groups and was used for a variety of other purposes after the Saints departed. At one point, it fell into such a state of disrepair that sheep and hogs roamed freely within its walls.[247] Unlike Nauvoo, the Kirtland Temple had been sanctified by the actual presence of Jesus Christ. And yet it stands today. The Lord did not destroy it, as He did the Nauvoo Temple. So, the argument does not match the history. It also does not account for the other conditions set out in section 124, which were not met, namely that Christ would visit the Nauvoo Temple and that the Saints would not be driven from that place (see D&C 124:28, 45).

Loss of the Fulness

If we, therefore, conclude from the historical evidence that the Church did not meet the conditions within the allotted time frame, then where does that leave us today? We find ourselves in much the same condition as ancient Israel when they angered the Lord and were likewise "rejected" by Him. That rejection did not mean that He stopped working with them entirely, but rather that they had lost the higher way and were left with a lesser preparatory gospel.

When Joseph was taken from our midst, as a Church, we likewise lost the fulness, just as ancient Israel had when Moses was taken. Even if we have more than the ancient Israelites, what we have left is still less than what God was willing to bestow. But, one might object, didn't Joseph leave behind the fulness in the ordinances and the keys? That argument ignores the language of the revelation which required

Christ personally to come to restore the fulness (see D&C 124:28). It also ignores what happened in Kirtland as a historical precedent.

In Kirtland, Joseph began administering ordinances outside of the temple before it was completed. Those physical ordinances were in preparation for the endowment of actual spiritual power which followed with the Pentecostal outpouring upon the Saints when Christ, Moses, Elias, and Elijah visited. In Nauvoo, in a similar manner, Joseph again began to administer ordinances outside of the temple before its completion. These should have been followed by a corresponding outpouring of spiritual gifts in Nauvoo. That did not occur. Even if we assume that Joseph left behind a fulness in the capstone ordinances (referring to the second endowment or second anointings), those physical ordinances are still not complete without the corresponding spiritual component, namely the ministry of the Second Comforter.

Baptism is clearly not complete without both the physical ordinance of submersion in water and the ensuing spiritual baptism of fire and the Holy Ghost. The full ordinance requires both the physical and the spiritual components. It is the same in all salvific gospel ordinances. Likewise, it is the same in the final, crowning ordinances that Joseph left behind. In fact, probably more so. The fulness of the priesthood cannot be received without or apart from the personal ministry of Jesus Christ. Joseph could administer the physical portion, but the spiritual component necessarily comes from Christ.

The scriptures plainly testify that Christ is the keeper of the gate and that He "employeth no servant there" (2 Nephi 9:41). You cannot get a fulness without Christ and the Father (see Alma 13:1). This is why the Second Comforter is necessary. None of those who received ordinances from Joseph could claim to possess the fulness without also receiving the personal ministry of the Second Comforter. Christ had promised to visit them in the Nauvoo Temple and finish what Joseph started, but it never happened.

Furthermore, we know that Joseph did not leave everything behind. This is evidenced from Facsimile No. 2 of the Book of Abraham.

Figures 9 through 21 are not given to us but "will be given in the own due time of the Lord." In the Vision of Glory recorded in Doctrine and Covenants 76, Joseph learned mysteries of the kingdom which surpass all understanding but which he was not permitted to leave behind (see D&C 76:114–115). He is reported to have said that he could reveal a hundred times more about these kingdoms if he were permitted to do so. And, yet, we are promised that we can know these things for ourselves, if we will go to the Lord (see D&C 76:116–118). It should be clear from these scriptures that Joseph was not able to leave behind the fulness that he himself possessed.

Sadly, since losing this fulness, in many ways we have followed the same path as ancient Israel. That is, we assume that we have everything we need and have lost sight of the fact that we do not. We are lifted up in pride as God's chosen people and neglect further pursuit of the higher path He still offers. Today, we even resist the very idea that we are invited to return to the Lord's presence (see D&C 93:1). Like those who thought salvation came from the ceremonies under the law of Moses, many Latter-day Saints see salvation as coming through the ordinances of the temple, not recognizing they are utterly incomplete as currently administered. We have also developed a hierarchy of authorities, and have added our own traditions, rules, and customs to the Lord's commandments contained in scripture. We focus on outward appearances and tend to ignore our collective lack of spiritual gifts and power. We have not yet learned to walk and talk with God.

We do not like to hear this and tend to resist it. We prefer to think all is well and that Zion prospers (see 2 Nephi 28:21). We ignore the fact that President Benson reiterated in the 1980s that the Church remains under condemnation. That has not been renounced by any Church president since. However uncomfortable it may be, we need to recognize the truth of what has happened, so that we can begin to repent of our plight. We cannot hope to rise up to receive something higher, if we do not first recognize that what we have left today is something lesser. God has continued to work with and through the

Church since Nauvoo, but it has been in a lesser manner, just as in ancient Israel, and not in the higher way God wanted to walk with us.

In the end, whether you agree or disagree with this view of our history, the current state of the Church as a group is not the most critical thing. Ultimately, it is your individual standing before God that matters most. If the Church is in perfect standing today (and everything in this chapter is wrong), how does that save you? On the other hand, if the Church as a group is under some degree of condemnation or rejection by the Lord and is laboring under a lesser gospel, then how does that damn you? We are each responsible to work out our own salvation with fear and trembling before God. This is what Joseph was trying to teach at the time he introduced the endowment: "*the people should each one stand for himself* and depend on no man or men . . . —that *righteous persons could only deliver their own souls.*"[248] That is not possible if we are too dependent upon any person or organization to lead us. If we do that, then Joseph warned we will be "darkened in [our] minds" for neglecting the things which ultimately fall upon us to do.[249] We must learn to receive personal revelation and guidance, develop a relationship with the Lord, and eventually walk the higher path by returning to His presence. He can then complete our endowment.

What Might Have Been

Before concluding, I want to return to the Book of Mormon to look at two events there that may be relevant to our discussion. First is the visit of Christ to the Nephites which occurred at the temple in Bountiful. LDS Scholar, John W. Welch, has insightfully shown how the Savior's sermon delivered there, in that setting, relates to our own temple endowment and the covenants thereof (see 3 Nephi 12–14).[250] Christ's sermon is well worth studying in that light. And continuing in that same line of thought, what happened next with the Nephites is very interesting. After delivering the sermon, Lord observed that the people were weak and not prepared to understand all of the message

He had been asked to deliver. He was ready to depart (see 3 Nephi 17:2–4). But the people did not want Him to leave, and so, filled with compassion for them, He stayed.

Not only were the people physically weakened, Christ also lamented their spiritual condition: "Jesus, groaned within himself, and said: Father, I am troubled because of the wickedness of the people of the house of Israel" (3 Nephi 17:14). While Christ may have been referring to others as well, He was speaking of these people gathered in the crowd around Him. For a long time, I missed that point. Despite the fact that these people were more righteous than those who were destroyed in the events preceding His visit, these people were still in need of repentance and spiritual healing (see 3 Nephi 9:13). And as a result, they were not prepared to receive His full message. The way He went about addressing these problems is very interesting.

First, Christ healed all of their sick (see 3 Nephi 17:7). This remedied the physical weakness, but still left the spiritual condition. He then called for their little children to be brought forth and seated around him. Christ stood in the middle (see 3 Nephi 17:12–13). Essentially, He formed a prayer circle. The adults may not have been fully worthy, so He worked with their little children who were without sin. Their parents remained outside the circle but were permitted to watch. He is using these children to help minister to, heal, and save their parents.

After forming the circle, Christ then knelt upon the ground and prayed to the Father. The record continues: "The eye hath never seen, neither hath the ear heard, before, so great and marvelous things as we saw and heard Jesus speak unto the Father; and no tongue can speak, neither can there be written by any man, neither can the hearts of men conceive so great and marvelous things *as we both saw and heard* Jesus speak; and no one can conceive of the joy which filled our souls at the time we heard him pray for us unto the Father" (3 Nephi 17:16–17, emphasis added).

Prayer is the portal that opens the veil. There is more going on here than the scriptural record states. These people are both seeing and hearing things which they cannot share but which fill them with such joy they are overcome (see 3 Nephi 17:18). Christ then brought the children forward one by one and blessed them individually (vs. 21). As He concluded, the heavens opened, angels descended encircling the children with fire and ministered to them, while their parents and the others watched (vss. 24–25). Following these miraculous events, and in this sacred setting, Christ then introduced the sacrament before departing. This should be another indication of just how sacred the sacrament really is.

The healing that Christ had promised these people in the aftermath of the destruction of their land, He provided here within the context of a prayer circle (see 3 Nephi 9:13, 17:11–18). That prayer also parted the veil and opened the heavens. The prayer circle in our temple ceremony is also to bless and heal the sick and occurs immediately prior to the patrons being presented at the veil. Our symbols are reflective of the reality that these Nephites experienced.

The visit of the angels is also significant. Those beings who attend Christ in His ministry are part of the Church of the Firstborn. Joseph Smith explained their purpose: "What object was gained by this communication with the spirits of the just? *It was the established order of the kingdom of God: The keys of power and knowledge were with them [the Church of the Firstborn] to communicate to the Saints [on earth].*"[251] Joseph knew this because he had received such revelation for himself.[252] He explained that the purpose of the ministry of these angelic beings is to bring us up to their level of knowledge and understanding.[253]

Joseph also affirmed that such blessings are available to us if we will qualify ourselves to receive them: "We cannot be made perfect without them, nor they without us . . . . *we may come to an innumerable company of angels, have communion with and receive instruction from them.*"[254] The knowledge thus gained cannot be written but can only be received from heaven in the manner being shown through these scriptural accounts.

Following the personal ministry of Christ and these angels, the Nephites were subsequently able to establish a Zion society that lasted for about two centuries before it was destroyed by pride (see 4 Nephi 1:24). Joseph likewise sought to establish Zion among his people. The Saints in Nauvoo were commanded to build a temple for Christ "to dwell therein," with the explanation that "there is not a place found on earth that he [Christ] may come to and restore again that which was lost unto you, or which he hath taken away, even the fulness of the priesthood" (D&C 124:28).

Sadly, that promised visit never occurred. But it leaves us to wonder what might have happened if Christ had visited the Nauvoo Temple. Would He have ministered in a manner similar to what occurred in Bountiful among the Nephites? Clearly, the fulness the Nephites received is greater than what we currently possess in our endowment. And if Christ had ministered in Nauvoo, could the Saints then have subsequently established a Zion society that would have endured? We can only speculate as to what might have been, and how great was the Lord's disappointment in the missed opportunity.[255]

The original floor plan of the Nauvoo Temple was constructed in a manner similar to the Kirtland Temple, with large assembly halls on the first and second floors to accommodate the people gathering. Joseph did not live long enough to utilize the temple, but if his intended purpose was primarily to administer the ordinances restored above his Red Brick Store, then why didn't the temple's interior architecture reflect that, as more modern temples do?[256] It wasn't until the St. George Temple in Utah that a temple was completed with rooms specifically designed for the endowment ceremony.

The original Nauvoo Temple had a baptismal font in the basement, an assembly hall on the first floor similar to the one in the Kirtland Temple, another assembly hall on the second floor, and a council room and offices in the attic. There were no Creation, Garden, World, Terrestrial or Celestial rooms in the first Nauvoo Temple.[257] This is very curious, unless, Joseph was following the same pattern established

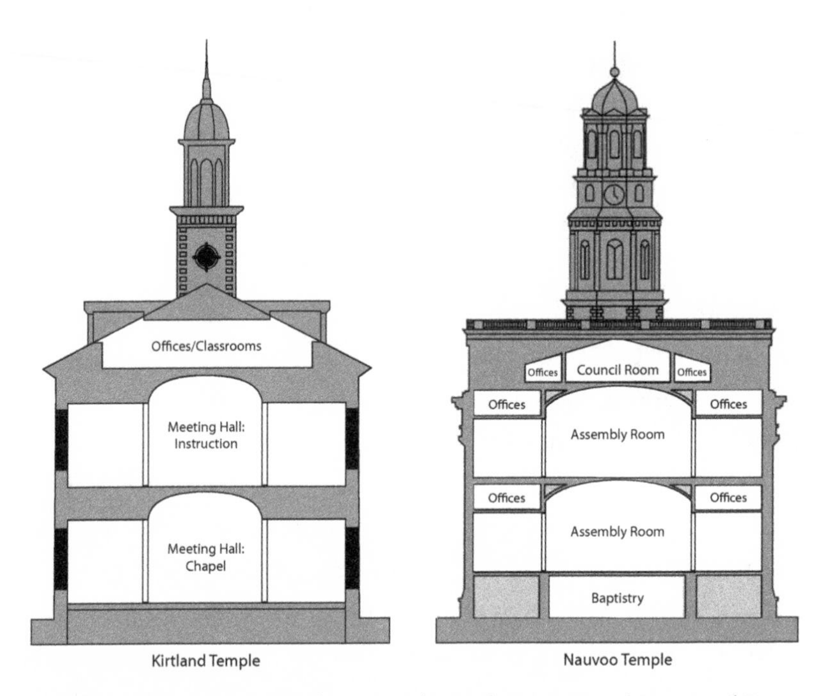

Richard O. Cowan, *Temples To Dot the Earth: Inspirational Stories and Facts Concerning the Lord's House* (Springville, Utah: CFI, © 1997, 2011), 53. Used by permission of Cedar Fort, Inc.

in Kirtland, where he administered the outward ordinances in order to prepare the people for the real endowment of power which was to be provided by heaven and the visit of Christ. The revelation required Christ personally to restore the fulness which had been lost (see D&C 124:28).

With this in mind, consider a second example from the Book of Mormon, namely the brother of Jared. His story is also relevant here. Once again, we find Christ ministering personally, though this time to an individual rather than to a group. In the brother of Jared's story, we can find all the elements of our temple endowment—not in a ritualized format but rather as they unfold in the events of his life. Let's review them quickly.

At the tower of Babel, Jared and his brother had to recognize and reject the error and apostasy around them. Like Adam and Eve, they sought the Lord's word rather than heeding the philosophies of men. The scattering of the people at the great tower is symbolic of the Fall and being driven forth from the presence of the Lord. In response, the brother of Jared cried unto the Lord in mighty prayer, not only for himself but he also sought to intercede on behalf of others (their friends and families).

As a result of his knocking, the Lord had compassion upon them, blessing them "because this long time ye have cried unto me" (Ether 1:43). He promised to lead them to a land "which is choice above *all the lands of the earth*" (Ether 1:42). This is speaking of the promised land that the Jaredites were to inherit, but it also prefigures being led back to heaven, a return to God's kingdom, a place which is choice above all the lands of the earth. We find symbols in this story of both the Fall and the Redemption.

Thus, the Jaredites commenced their long journey through the lone and dreary wilderness. Here, sacrifice and obedience were required. The brother of Jared sought direction from the Lord at each stage of their journey, consecrating himself to accomplishing the Lord's will in his life. He was "continually directed by the hand of the Lord" (Ether 2:6). We see him returning to report. "O Lord, I have performed the work which thou hast commanded me" (Ether 2:18). Their journey was a time of testing, learning, and growth. It was difficult but with each phase his faith and trust in the Lord increased.

The final test for the brother of Jared was encountered as he prepared for their voyage across the ocean. Here he had two problems that he apparently had not solved in the barges he had previously built (see Ether 2:6). He pled with the Lord to not suffer them to cross the great sea in darkness, implying that they may have done exactly that in prior barges crossing smaller bodies of water (see Ether 2:22). The brother of Jared recognized that the Lord's chastening hand throughout their journey was for their benefit and blessing and he was willing to make any sacrifice required but also pled for and made intercession for the others in order to bless them (see Ether 2:22, 3:2).

The Lord gave him a solution to the air, but did not solve the lighting problem. Instead God ruled out the only two sources of light the brother of Jared would have known (e.g. they couldn't have sunlight or fire) and told him to come up with a solution. The story here may not seem very remarkable to us because we have electric lights and are reading the account in hindsight, but put yourself in his shoes for a moment. He was left to conceive of something that had never been envisioned before and then to convince the Lord to empower his plan. The Lord's purpose here was to help the brother of Jared's faith finally be sufficient to part the veil. In similar manner, the problems and challenges we face are given to help us grow and develop.

We are also invited to the veil of the temple to learn something from the Lord. The brother of Jared approached the Lord again and again throughout his journey, frequently conversing with Him to receive direction and instructions, until finally his faith was sufficient for the Lord to part the veil and bring him back into His presence. The entire account is well worth studying in the light of our temple endowment ceremony.

The purpose for discussing it here is that this story should give each of us hope. Despite the apostasy and failure of the world around him, the brother of Jared was able to lay hold upon these blessings for himself by his diligence and faith. We can do the same by following his example. And to make sure that we do not miss that point, the Lord, speaking specifically of our day, states that if we will repent of our iniquity and "exercise faith in me . . . even as the brother of Jared did, that they may become sanctified in me, then will I manifest unto them the things which the brother of Jared saw, even unto the unfolding unto them all my revelations, saith Jesus Christ, the Son of God" (Ether 4:6–7). The whole point of the story is to invite us to go and do likewise.

The brother of Jared's endowment was completed by receiving the personal ministry of Christ. He was given by our Savior the endowment Joseph described in Kirtland, namely "that wisdom, that intelligence, and that power, which characterized the ancient saints, and now characterizes the inhabitants of the upper world."[258] Christ has promised us the same blessings, if we will follow the path outlined. Despite whatever limitations may exist among a society or within a group, it is clear from the scriptural record that the fulness is always available to individuals who will rise up to receive it from the Lord (see Alma 13:1).

What Joseph Left Behind

To summarize, modern Israel's failure to receive the blessings promised in Nauvoo once again provoked the Lord's ire. He left a clear sign of his displeasure in the destruction of the Nauvoo Temple. Just as Moses had been taken from ancient Israel, Joseph was taken from modern Israel. Like Moses, Joseph also left behind ordinances. Despite our early failure as a group, within the ordinances Joseph left behind lies an authorized invitation for us to rise up as individuals and claim the blessings that he wanted to bestow upon all the Saints.

The group failure of the Israelites did not prevent the success of some individuals. Even after Moses was taken and within the remaining limitation of functioning under the Aaronic Priesthood, we find many examples in the Old Testament and in the Book of Mormon of those who rose up to receive the fulness of the Melchizedek (or patriarchal) Priesthood directly from the Lord.[259] Through the temple ordinances, we have the same opportunity in front of us.

In the endowment, Joseph essentially left a trail of breadcrumbs marking the way. Joseph knew his remaining time was short and that he could not leave behind the fulness he possessed, so he did the next best thing. He left a path we could follow to obtain the fulness for ourselves! As we have discussed, that fulness can only come from and through Christ.

The endowment is to help us rise up to the higher way and to learn to walk with God. Instead of viewing it as an invitation and a teacher, we too often see it as an end in itself. In so doing, we make the same mistake in approaching our ordinances that the children of Israel so often made in approaching theirs. The ordinances and rites of the law of Moses were primarily intended to testify of Christ and His future Atonement. Our rites likewise testify of Christ, but primarily invite and prepare us to return to His presence in this life.

How do we receive the fulness today? How can we walk the higher path? First, we should honor and respect everything we were left by Joseph Smith. There is tremendous value in the temple ordinances we have today. The Lord's Spirit is there and it is my testimony that regular, consistent temple worship will bless and sanctify your life in ways you may not anticipate at first. Go to the temple regularly, consistently, and ask the Lord to teach you. It is not reasonable to want something more from Him if we neglect what has already been given.

But beyond that, Joseph left a statement that may be helpful. He said: "[God] set the ordinances to be the same forever and ever and set Adam to watch over them, to reveal them from heaven to man, or to send angels to reveal them."[260] He then went on to cite Hebrews 1:14 and explained that angels would be sent to minister to all who shall be heirs of salvation. Those angels operate under the direction of Michael who acts under Christ. Joseph concluded that this is the manner by which God will establish power, revelations, and glory and that God will not honor those He has not called, ordained, and chosen. Once, the endowment taught this doctrine more openly. In earlier versions Elohim stated plainly: "Adam, we will provide for you a Savior and *send you messengers to instruct you how you may return to our presence.*"[261] This truth is still manifest in the endowment, if we have eyes to see it, and is likewise attested to in scripture (see D&C 77:11, for example).

Finally, Joseph testified: "I assure the Saints that *truth, in reference to these matters can and may be known through the revelations of God in the way of His ordinances, and in answer to prayer.* The Hebrew Church 'came unto the spirits of just men made perfect, and unto an innumerable company of angels, unto God the Father of all, and to

Jesus Christ the Mediator of the new covenant.' What did they learn by coming to the spirits of just men made perfect? Is it written? No. *What they learned has not been and could not have been written.*"[262] That sacred knowledge is beyond what is written in our temple endowment ceremony and can only be obtained from heaven.

Moving Forward

If we are to obtain the higher path, it will necessarily involve the ministry of heaven through angels and the Holy Ghost, then through Christ and, finally, the Father. Joseph understood this. That is why he stressed the two important purposes for the endowment we discussed earlier (i.e., we would know how to ask and receive an answer and we would be able to detect false spirits and messages from true). Both purposes relate to this process of connecting with heaven. Salvation cannot come without it.[263]

Once obtained, we then become prepared to bless and assist others. Joseph clarified in a stunning and rather sobering statement, "No man [or woman] can be the minister of Jesus Christ, *except he has the testimony of Jesus* & this is the Spirit of Prophecy. *Whenever Salvation has been administered it has been by Testimony. Men at the present time testify of Heaven & of hell, & have never seen either—& I will say that no man knows these things without this.*"[264]

The endowment outlines the way and equips us to make the journey, if we have eyes to see it. It does not bestow the fulness but permits us to move forward individually to receive the fulness. As a group, we may be under condemnation, but ultimately the Lord deals with us and we are accountable to Him as individuals.

Looking back on the past, I have many Nauvoo pioneer ancestors that crossed the plains. I am very sympathetic to what they endured and recognize the great sacrifices they made. I feel no criticism for any who lived back then but rather acknowledge and honor their efforts and the noble lives that many of them lived. In some ways, their challenges were greater than ours. And in other ways, perhaps ours are equally great. Their failures and their successes leave me very humbled.

Rather than flattering ourselves today about being a royal, chosen generation and seeking to justify our past history, we should instead recognize the enormous challenge and opportunity that lies in front of us. We need to seek repentance and to find the Lord in a deeper and more personal manner than ever before. We ought never relent in our search to know Him until we too, like the brother of Jared, are able to abide in His presence. It is only through humility and meekness that we become fit for the Lord to work with us. We should be humbled by the failure of ancient Israel and by the failure in Nauvoo. Both groups had an opportunity to walk personally with the Lord and did not. We have the same invitation extended to us individually through the endowment and the Book of Mormon. The ultimate question is: will we fare any better?

That answer is up to you.

EPILOGUE

For a long time the narrative outlined in the last chapter was difficult for me to accept because it runs so counter to everything I had previously cherished and believed. In many ways, it would have been easier to simply omit the material from this volume. However, we cannot repent, until first recognizing that something is amiss. We do not seek a cure, until acknowledging we are ill. We cannot hope to find a higher path, until we first see that we are traversing a lesser. Truth is sometimes a bitter pill.

I hope that you will take your questions and concerns to the Lord. He alone is qualified to teach and instruct. This book is intended as a beginning, not an ending. It is an invitation to a delicious feast the Lord has waiting. Completing your endowment requires you to return to the tree of life, partake of its fruit, and be healed from the battering of mortality. It is about coming personally to your Savior. You alone can make the trek. He alone can heal and save. He declared unequivocally, "I am the way, the truth, and the life" (John 14:6).

We do not need more busywork. We do not need another program to implement. What we do need is to strengthen our individual relationship with our Savior. That is the key. We must learn to better hear and recognize His voice and follow His direction in our lives (see 2 Nephi 32:3-6). It might actually require us to *do* a little less in order to make more time for praying, pondering, studying, and listening.

The temple can be an invaluable aid in our growth. For over fourteen years, I have attended weekly and can testify of the immense blessing of the temple ordinances and temple worship in my life. My marriage and family have been blessed and strengthened as a result of this service. My heart has been changed and I am a better person. The peace, refuge, and strength of the temple carried me through some of the most difficult periods of my life. The temple has taught and inspired me and brought me closer to my Savior. Many of the most sacred, spiritual experiences of my life occurred in the temple. I will always be grateful to the Lord and to Joseph Smith for these blessings. Many who serve consistently and regularly in the House of the Lord can testify of similar blessings in their own lives. The Lord's hand and Spirit are manifest there.

Having partaken of the fruit of the tree of knowledge and finding ourselves in this fallen world, the temple endowment outlines in symbolism our path back to the tree of life. It gives us an invitation and a map, but it is up to us individually to make the journey. Accept what we are offered in the temple in faith, but do not mistake the symbol for the reality. Your endowment is not complete until you are redeemed into Christ's presence. Though not easy, it is possible. The door and invitation are open:

"Therefore, ask, and ye shall receive; knock, and it shall be opened unto you" (3 Nephi 27:29).

ENDNOTES

1. *Teachings of the Prophet Joseph Smith*, comp. Joseph Fielding Smith (Salt Lake City: Deseret Book, 1976), 306. Hereinafter cited as *TPJS*.
2. *TPJS*, 217.
3. Dieter F. Uchtdorf, "Acting on the Truths of the Gospel of Jesus Christ," Worldwide Leadership Training, February 11, 2012.
4. John A. Widtsoe, "Temple Worship," *Utah Genealogical and Historical Magazine*, Apr. 1921, pp. 58, 63.
5. Ibid, 63.
6. *TPJS*, 364.
7. *TPJS*, 137.
8. Joseph Smith, *History of the Church of Jesus Christ of Latter-day Saints*, 7 volumes (Salt Lake City: Church of Jesus Christ of Latter-day Saints, 1951), vol. 1:316-317. Hereinafter cited as *HC* volume:page.
9. *HC* 2:197; emphasis added.
10. Damon Smith has outlined the neglect of these early members in his book, *A Cultural History of the Book of Mormon, Volume 1: Setting, A Foundation, of Stones to Stumble Over*, (San Bernardino, CA: Self-published work), 2013.
11. See Doctrine and Covenants 84 and Doctrine and Covenants 88, given in September and December of 1832 respectively.
12. See the introduction to the Book of Mormon.
13. As recently as 1986, President Benson affirmed that the Church may remain under this condemnation for continuing to neglect the Book of Mormon. Since that day, I am unaware of any Church leader stating that this condemnation has been removed. Regardless of the status of the Church as a whole in the Lord's eyes, individually we are under an obligation to correct these things in our own personal lives. See Ezra Taft Benson "Cleansing the Inner Vessel," *Conference Report*, April 1986; also "The Book of Mormon: Keystone of Our Religion," *Conference Report*, October 1986.

14. *HC* 2:379-380. The original record states: "At about 3. oclock P.M. I dismissed the school and the [First] presidency, retired to the loft of the printing office, where we attended to the ordinance of washing our bodies in pure water, we also perfumed our bodies and our heads, in the name of the Lord at early candlelight, I met with the presidency, at the west school room in the Chapel [Kirtland temple] to attend to the ordinance of annointing our heads with holy oil- -also the [high] councils of Zion Kirtland and Zion, met in the two adjoining rooms, who waited in prayer while we attended to the ordinance,— I took the oil in my < left > right hand, father Smith being seated before me and the rest of the presidency encircled him round about.— we then streched our right hands to heaven and blessed the oil and concecrated it in the name of Jesus Christ— we then laid our hands on our aged fath[er] Smith, and invoked, the blessings of heaven,— I then annointed his head with the concecrated oil, and sealed many blessings upon him, head, the presidency then in turn, laid their hands upon his head, beginning at the eldest, untill they had all laid their hands on him, and pronounced such blessings, upon his head as the Lord put into their hearts— all blessing him to be our patriarch, and < to > annoint our heads, and attend to all duties that pertain to that office.— I then took the seat, and father annoint[ed] my head, and sealed upon me the blessings, of Moses, to lead Israel in the latter days, even as moses led him in days of old,— also the blessings of Abraham Isaac and Jacob.— all of the presidency laid their hands upon me and pronounced upon my head many prophesies, and blessings, many of which I shall not notice at this time, but as Paul said, so say I, let us come to vissions and revelations,— The heavens were opened upon us and I beheld the celestial kingdom of God, and the glory thereof, whether in the body or out I cannot tell,— I saw the transcendant beauty of the gate that enters, through which the heirs of that Kingdom will enter, which was like unto circling flames of fire, also the blasing throne of God, whereon was seated the Father and the Son,— I saw the beautiful streets of that Kingdom, which had the appearance of being paved with gold— I saw father Adam, and Abraham and Michael and my father and mother, my brother Alvin that has long since slept, and marvled how it was that he had obtained this an inheritance < in > that Kingdom, seeing that he had departed this life, before the Lord < had > set his hand to gather Israel < the second time > and had not been baptised for the remission of sins— Thus said came the voice < of the Lord un > to me saying all who have died with[out] a knowledge of this gospel, who would have received it, if they had been permited to tarry, shall be heirs of the celestial kingdom of God— also all that shall die henseforth, with < out > a knowledge of it, who would have received it, with all their hearts, shall be heirs of that kingdom, for I the Lord < will > judge all men according to their works according to the desires of their hearts— and again I also beheld the Terrestial Kingdom I also beheld that all children who die before they arive to the years of accountability, are saved in the celestial kingdom of heaven— I saw the 12, apostles of the Lamb, who are now upon the earth who hold the keys of this last ministry, in foreign lands, standing together in a circle much fatiegued, with their clothes tattered and feet swolen, with their eyes cast downward, and Jesus < standing > in their midst, and they did not behold him, the Saviour looked upon them and wept— I also beheld Elder [William E.] McLellen in the south, standing upon a hill surrounded with a vast multitude, preaching to them, and a lame man standing before him, supported by his crutches, he threw them down at his word, and leaped as an hart, by the mighty power of God Also Eld[er] Brigham Young

standing in a strange land, in the far southwest, in a desert place, upon a rock in the midst of about a dozen men of colour, who, appeared hostile He was preaching to them in their own toung, and the angel of God standing above his head with a drawn sword in his hand protec[t] ing him, but he did not see it,— and I finally saw the 12 in the celestial kingdom of God,— I also beheld the redemption of Zion, and many things which the toung of man, cannot discribe in full.— Many of my brethren who received this ordinance with me, saw glorious visions also,— angels ministered unto them, as well as myself, and the power of the highest rested upon, us the house was filled with the glory of God, and we shouted Hosanah to the God and the Lamb I am mistaken, concerning my receiving the holy anointing first after father Smith, we received < it > in turn according to our age." Dean C. Jesse, ed., *The Papers of Joseph Smith* (Salt Lake City: Deseret Book, 1993), 2:155-159.

15. *Oliver Cowdery Sketch Book*, January 16, 1836, archives, Historical Department, Church of Jesus Christ of Latter-day Saints, Salt Lake City, Utah, pp. 21-22 as quoted in David John Buerger, *The Mysteries of Godliness* (San Francisco: Smith Research Associates, 1994), 22.

16. There are several good summaries of the events surrounding the dedication and the spiritual manifestations which occurred. See, for example, Steven C. Harper, "A Pentecost and Endowment Indeed: Six Eyewitness Accounts of the Kirtland Temple Experience," *Opening the Heavens: Accounts of Divine Manifestations 1820-1844*, edited by John W. Welch (Provo: BYU Press, 2005), 327-371.

17. For example, William McLellin, David Whitmer and William Harris later denied any such angelic ministrations (see Buerger, Mysteries, 28-29.) While their accounts may be biased by their subsequent disaffection, it seems reasonable to assume that some of the Saints may have left disappointed or not having received what they anticipated.

18. *HC* 2:432, emphasis added.

19. I recognize there is some controversy over the contents and events of Doctrine and Covenants 110. For our purposes here, however, we will simply accept it as is commonly understood among LDS Church members. Regardless of whether Moses, Elias, and Elijah visited with Joseph and Oliver on this occasion or not, it appears that Joseph's understanding increased during this time and that this increased knowledge was later incorporated into the rituals of Nauvoo. These keys, whether given by Moses, Elias, and Elijah, or simply given by Christ during His visit seem to form the basic structure for the Nauvoo ordinances.

20. Clearly the work for the dead was a later addition that was not developed in Kirtland.

21. Matthew Brown argues that there were up to eight components of the Kirtland endowment including: "1) solemn assemblies for receiving instructions on the doctrines, principles, and laws of the gospel, (2) the ordinances of washing and anointing, (3) a sealing ritual, (4) the making of covenants, (5) partaking of the sacrament in commemoration of the Marriage Supper of the Lamb, (6) the employment of ritual gestures and language, (7) the ordinance of the washing of feet, (8) the reception of "power from on high" in the form of various spiritual mani-

festations." (Matthew Brown, *The Gate of Heaven: Insights on the Doctrines and Symbols of the Temple* (American Fork, UT: Covenant Communications, 1999), 209. This would make the Kirtland ceremony closer to the Nauvoo endowment, but it is still clear that Nauvoo was a significant expansion from the earlier period.

22. For a more detailed exploration of these ordinances see David John Buerger, "The Fulness of the Priesthood': The Second Anointing in Latter-day Saint Theology and Practice," *Dialogue: A Journal of Mormon Thought* vol. 16 (Spring 1983): 10-44. www.dialoguejournal.com/wp-content/uploads/sbi/articles/Dialogue_V16N01_12.pdf.

23. *HC* 1:323.

24. Although the basic ordinance of washing the feet was also greatly expanded in Nauvoo in the Second Anointings, the core purpose of these ordinances remains the same. In this sense, the expansion again serves to further teach, clarify, and instruct but the essential purpose is still to seal the recipient up unto eternal life.

25. *TPJS*, 308.

26. For more on this topic see *Understanding Your Endowment*, 16-19.

27. *TPJS*, 238.

28. *TPJS*, 150.

29. *TPJS*, 308.

30. Ibid.

31. *The Words of Joseph Smith*, comp. Andrew F. Ehat and Lyndon W. Cook (Salt Lake City: Bookcraft, 1988), 328. Hereinafter cited as *WJS*. Because this volume is out of print but remains available in e-book formats cites will also include the date of the sermon to assist those using electronic versions, e.g., (Sermon 10 March 1844).

32. The sealing rooms are an extension of the celestial room of the temple. This is not always immediately apparent in the newer temple designs but is nevertheless true. In some of the older temples of the Church, for example, the Salt Lake City and Manti Utah temples, at least some of the sealing rooms are directly connected to the celestial room.

33. See *Understanding Your Endowment*, chapter 4.

34. It is generally accepted in LDS Church theology that Elijah restored the sealing power on April 3, 1836, as recorded in Doctrine and Covenants 110. For the purposes of this book, we accept that position. However, that position is not without some controversy, which others have documented and explored. It is clear to me personally that Joseph Smith held the sealing power. When and where he received it is not as important to me. However, it is interesting to note from a scriptural perspective that Doctrine and Covenants 110 makes no specific mention of the sealing power. It simply discusses turning the hearts of the fathers to the children and the children to the fathers. In addition, Joseph Smith was given the sealing power by the voice of Jehovah in Doctrine and Covenants 132:46. "And verily, verily, I say unto you, that whatsoever you seal on earth shall be sealed in heaven; and whatsoever you bind on earth, in my name and by my word, saith the Lord,

it shall be eternally bound in the heavens." We see another example of this sealing power being conferred by the voice of the Lord in the Book of Mormon. The Lord told Nephi, "Behold, I give unto you power, that whatsoever ye shall seal on earth shall be sealed in heaven; and whatsoever ye shall loose on earth shall be loosed in heaven; and thus shall ye have power among this people" (Helaman 10:7).

35. Doctrine and Covenants 88:138-141. See also *HC* 1:323-324. The original entry reads: "The President said after he had washed the feet of the Elders, as I have done so do ye wash ye therefee [therefore] one anothers feet pronouncing at the same time through the power of the Holy Ghost that the Elders were all clean from the blood of this generation," "Minutes, 22–23 January 1833," *Documents, Volume 2: July 1831-January 1833, The Joseph Smith Papers* (2013), 378-382, www.josephsmithpapers.org/paper-summary/minutes-22-23-january-1833/3.

36. For a more detailed exploration of this topic see David John Buerger, "The Fulness of the Priesthood': The Second Anointing in Latter-day Saint Theology and Practice," in *Dialogue: A Journal of Mormon Thought vol. 16* (Spring 1983): 10-44. Article available at www.dialoguejournal.com/wp-content/uploads/sbi/articles/Dialogue_V16N01_12.pdf. Additionally, a few months prior to his death, Joseph Smith gave further instructions related to this topic that are worth careful consideration: "The spirit, power and calling of Elijah is that [you] have power to hold the keys of the revelations, ordinances, oracles, powers and endowments of the fullness of the Melchizedek Priesthood and of the Kingdom of God on the earth and to receive, obtain and perform all the ordinances belonging to the Kingdom of God even unto the sealing of the hearts of the fathers unto the children and the hearts of the children unto the fathers even those who are in heaven." (*WJS*, 329. Sermon of 10 March 1844, Sunday).

37. Ibid., 28.

38. Ibid., 43.

39. Though I am aware of one who has received these ordinances and who confirmed to me privately that they are still administered.

40. *TPJS*, 150.

41. *TPJS*, 151.

42. *TPJS*, 299.

43. *TPJS*, 151.

44. *WJS*, 254. (*Joseph Smith Diary*, by Willard Richards 15 October 1843).

45. *WJS*, 77. (Sermon 3 October 1841, *Times and Seasons*.)

46. *WJS*, 366. (Sermon 12 May 1844.)

47. *TPJS*, 345.

48. Bruce R. McConkie, *The Promised Messiah: The First Coming of Christ* (Salt Lake City: Deseret Book, 1978), 582.

49. *TPJS*, 335.

50. *WJS*, 10. (Before 8 Aug 1839 Willard Richard's Pocket Companion.)

51. *WJS*, 209. (James Burgess Notebook 21 May 1843.)

52. *WJS*, 329, emphasis added, (Sermon 10 March 1844). He also left a glimpse of how this might occur: "Let us suppose a case; suppose the great God who dwells in heaven should reveal himself to Father Cutler here by the opening heavens and tell him I offer up a decree that whatsoever you seal on earth with your decree I will seal it in heaven, you have power then, can it be taken of[f] No, Then what you seal on earth by the Keys of Elijah is sealed in heaven, & this is the power of Elijah, & this is the difference between the spirit & power of Elias and Elijah, for while the spirit of Elias is a forerunner the power of Elijah is sufficient to make our calling & Election sure" (WJS, 329-330.)

53. Though in my view, the Second Anointing ordinances are incomplete without also receiving the accompanying ministry of Christ as the Second Comforter, much like baptism of water is incomplete without the baptism of fire. In reality it is Christ's ministry that is the crucial part.

54. See David John Buerger, "The Fulness of the Priesthood': The Second Anointing in Latter-day Saint Theology and Practice." in *Dialogue: A Journal of Mormon Thought vol. 16* (Spring 1983): 10-44. In his article, Buerger cites evidence that these additional sealing ordinances were performed frequently in Nauvoo. Following the exodus of the Saints from Nauvoo, the practice appears to have ceased for about three decades. Brigham Young resumed these ordinances in January of 1867, about ten years before the St. George Temple was dedicated (see "The Fulness", 28). They continued to be performed in the various temples of the Church, often by temple presidents, until President Heber J. Grant dramatically curtailed the practice in 1926, changing the Church's policy to permit only the President of the Church to administer these ordinances in the future upon a recommendation from a member of the Quorum of the Twelve (see "The Fulness", 40). Thereafter, the frequency of these administrations slowed dramatically. Apparently, some fellow up in Idaho received these ordinances and then, contrary to instructions to not disclose the fact to anyone, went home and made a big to-do about it in his home ward, causing an uproar that eventually reached all the way to headquarters in Salt Lake. In response to disgruntled members who had not received these ordinances, their administration was drastically curtailed thereafter. It is my understanding that these ordinances are still performed on a very limited basis at present, though today there appears to be some question among general authorities as to whether they are essential or not (see "The Fulness", 43).

55. *HC* 5:1–2, emphasis added. Joseph's journal actually states: "4 May 1842 • Wednesday 4 In council in the Presidents & General offices with Judge [James] Adams. Hyram [Hyrum] Smith Newel K. Whitney. William Marks, Wm Law. George Miller. Brigham Young. Heber C. Kimball & Willard Richards. [illegible] & giving certain instructions concerning the priesthood. [illegible] &c on the Aronic Priesthood to the first [illegible] continueing through the day." (See Joseph Smith Papers, Journal December 1841–December 1842, 94). The entry in the History of the Church is expanded by content from Willard Richards' journal. Attached to the Joseph Smith journal entry is this explanation from the editors of the Joseph Smith Papers. "Richards, who participated in the events of 4 May 1842, made the

brief summary of JS's daylong temple instruction in this journal entry and also prepared the following description of the new endowment, which later became part of the JS multivolume manuscript history: JS instructed those present 'in the principles and order of the priesthood, attending to washings & anointings, endowments, and the communications of keys, pertaining to the Aronic Priesthood, and so on to the highe[s]t order of the Melchisedec Pristhood, setting forth the order pertaining to the Ancient of days & all those plans & principles by which any one is enabled to secure the fulness of those blessings which has been prepared for the chu[r]ch of the first-born, and come up, and abide in the prese[n]ce of Eloheim in the eternal worlds. In this council was institutd the Ancient order of things for the fir[s]t time in these last days.' According to Richards, JS's instructions "were of things spiritual, and to be received only by the spiritual minded: and there was nothing made known to these men but what will be made known to all saints, of the last days, so soon as they are prepared to receive, and a proper place is prepared to communicate them, even to the weakest of the saints; therefore let the saints be diligent in building the Temple and all houses which they have been or shall hereafter be commanded of God to build, and wait their time with patience, in all meekness faith, & perseverance unto the end, knowing assuredly that all these things refer[re]d to in this council are always governed by the principles of Revelation." (The Joseph Smith Papers, Joseph Smith History, Historian's Office, Draft Notes, ca. 1839—1856. CHL. CR 100 92. 4 May 1842; see also JS History, vol. C-1, 1328–1329.) For the purposes of this book, I assume that Richards' expanded statement was based upon or captures Joseph's fuller description of these ordinances. This assumption seems supported by Joseph's descriptions of the endowment's purpose as recorded in other sermons he gave around this time.

56. *WJS*, 59. (Sermon 5 January 1841.)

57. *TPJS*, 322. See also *WJS*, (Sermon, 27 August 1843.)

58. *TPJS*, 323.

59. Ibid.

60. *TPJS*, 308. Note, however, that obeying all the "commandments and ordinances of the house of the Lord" may mean something slightly different than appears on the surface. For starters, Christ lived under the law of Moses and so the "ordinances of the house of the Lord" would have been different for Him than they are today. That said, Christ certainly lived the covenants undergirding our modern endowment ceremony. The term "house of the Lord" can refer to His temple but can also refer to God's family. So another way to understand Joseph Smith's statement would be those who obtain the fulness of the priesthood are those who seek and do the will of the Father in their lives. Here again Christ is a perfect example (see 3 Nephi 27:13).

61. *TPJS*, 181.

62. See, for example *WJS*, Sermons on 27 Jun 1839; 1 May 1842; 14, 21 May; 11 Jun; 9, 16 Jul; 13 and 27 Aug; 9 Oct 1843; 21 Jan; 10 Mar; 7 Apr; 12 May; and 16 Jun 1844. Andrew Ehat, the editor of the *Words of Joseph Smith*, summarized these teachings in an unpublished paper he wrote entitled: "The Father Teacheth . . . The Covenant". In it he states: "Fulness of the Endowment (Gospel Covenant 17): The

ordinance points you to the spiritual experience that is the highest possible blessing of mortality when God, by his own voice, pronounces by an oath in His name a covenant—which He will not break—that you will attain to a fulness of the powers of the priesthood in eternity. If you seek His face by perfect faith, you will, in His presence, have these powers conferred upon you for time also."

63. *WJS*, 213. (Wilford Woodruff Journal, 11 June 1843.)

64. *TPJS*, 323.

65. *HC* 5:1-2. See also endnote 55.

66. *WJS*, 116-117. (Sermon 28 Apr 1842.)

67. Alan K. Parrish, "Keys of the Priesthood," *Encyclopedia of Mormonism*. Online at eom.byu.edu/index.php/Keys_of_the_Priesthood.

68. The same article in the *Encyclopedia of Mormonism* further states: "Latter-day Saints distinguish between holding the priesthood and holding keys to direct the work of the priesthood: one does not receive additional priesthood when one is given keys" (Joseph F. Smith, *IE* 4 [January 1901]:230). This clarifies that keys are not additional priesthood. President Joseph F. Smith further taught: "if it were necessary, though I do not expect the necessity will ever arise, and there was no man left on the earth holding the Melchizedek Priesthood, except an elder—that elder, by the inspiration of the Spirit of God and by the direction of the Almighty, could proceed, and should proceed, to organize the Church of Jesus Christ in all its perfection, because he holds the Melchizedek Priesthood." (*Gospel Doctrine*, 148.)

69. See, for example, Gordon B. Hinckley, "The Priesthood of Aaron", *Conference Report*, October 1982; also Bruce R. McConkie, "Only an Elder", *Ensign*, June 1975 and "The Ten Blessings of the Priesthood", *Conference Report*, October 1977.

70. *WJS*, 119. (Sermon 1 May 1842.)

71. See also Doctrine and Covenants 129:3-9; and notice that verse 9 is speaking of keys in the sense of being some knowledge or information we possess.

72. *TPJS*, 226. This statement in *Teachings* is a greatly expanded from what is recorded in the *Nauvoo Relief Society Minutes* book which simply states: "He spoke of delivering the keys to this society and to the Church—that according to his prayers God had appointed him elsewhere." (*WJS*, 28 April 1842, see also note 12 in that volume.) Apparently, George A. Smith for some reason felt justified in expanding this into the statement found in *Teachings* perhaps from other discussions or interactions he had with the Prophet. See also Andrew Ehat's note 19 to Sermon of 5 October 1840.

73. *WJS*, 42. (Sermon 5 October 1840.)

74. *WJS*, 108; emphasis added. (Sermon, 20 March 1842, *Wilford Woodruff Journal*.) For the sake of brevity, I omitted the remainder of the relevant portion quoted in his talk. However, it follows and confirms the connection between a sign representing or signifying an ordinance. "Their is a difference between the Holy Ghost & the gift of the Holy Ghost. Cornelius received the Holy Ghost before he was Baptized which was the convincing power of God unto him of the truth of the gospel

but he could not receive the gift of the Holy Ghost until after he was Baptized, & *had he not taken this sign ordinances upon him* the Holy Ghost which convinced him of the truth of God would have left him until he obeyed those *ordinances* & received the gift of the Holy Ghost by the laying on of hands according to the order of God he could not have healed the sick or command an evil spirit to come out of a man & it obey him, for the spirit might say to him as he did to the sons of Scava Peter I know & Christ I know but who are ye It matereth not whether we live long or short after we come to a knowlede of these principles & obey them, I know that all men will be damned if they do not come in the way which God has appointed" (emphasis added.)

75. For more discussion on the topic of names, see *Understanding Your Endowment*, 16-18.

76. Please recognize that what we are discussing here is a symbol. In our discussion, this symbol represents an "ideal" or a model and is not intended to disparage those who are born under or who have different circumstances in their personal lives. Mortal life rarely conforms to a perfect ideal, yet that does not mean a given path lies outside of God's perfect plan for that individual. Your individual circumstances may be the ideal for you. For example, some women are unable to bear children of their own despite greatly desiring that blessing. Others become mothers through adoption. Their love, care and sacrifice in raising their child is every bit as great, perhaps more so. There is great symbolism in all motherhood and in birth, and it is to this universal symbolism that I wish to speak in this present volume. In *Preparing For Your Endowment*, I wrote: "Mothers (inclusive of all women) are also types of Christ. They reflect Him in at least three important ways: 1) Like Christ, mothers also shed their blood and descend into the vale of death to bring forth new life. 2) Paul taught that the veil of the temple is a symbol of Christ's flesh (see Hebrews 10:19–20). Given that, if Christ is the veil through which we must pass to eternal life, then I would submit that a mother's womb is the veil through which all mankind passes to enter mortal life. Mothers are a veil on one end of our journey while Christ is the veil on the other end. The temple endowment provides us with an important reminder of this truth as the sisters are veiled as part of their temple clothing. 3) A mother's love is often the closest thing a child experiences to God's own love for us., and it is through a mother's love that we may first experience and begin to understand God's love. In these three ways, women are important types of Christ," (*Preparing For Your Endowment*, 99).

77. This entire section 88 of the Doctrine and Covenants is related to the temple. Or it may be better to say that the temple reflects the truths taught in section 88. Studying this section with that idea in mind can yield some fascinating insights.

78. The pattern is a type or symbol of Christ's birth. He was born of a mortal woman, Mary, and a spiritual Heavenly Father (reflecting our own mortal birth to a mother and spiritual re-birth by a father in baptism and confirmation).

79. *Journal of Discourses* 2:31.

80. The full text of this verse (D&C 132:19) discusses being sealed by the Holy Spirit of Promise by "him who is anointed, unto whom I have given the keys of this priesthood." At the time that person was Joseph Smith. He held the sealing power

and could function in the role of the Holy Spirit of Promise. Joseph performed this role only as directed by the Lord. Ultimately, it is the Lord alone who can judge our hearts and who can make and fulfill the promise of exaltation. As we discussed in chapter 3, the Lord holds these keys and can make the covenant and promise with whom He wills. We see this in the scriptures in Mosiah 26:20 and again in Doctrine and Covenants 88:3-4. This should give us confidence that the Lord can likewise extend the same Holy Spirit of Promise to our own marriages.

81. Our exaltation at that point is assured, unless of course we elect thereafter to willfully rebel and walk completely away from God (see D&C 84:41), thereby becoming a son of Perdition. However small that possibility may be, we always retain our agency and God always respects it. Therefore, this one provision must remain in the seals (see *WJS*, 330).

82. For more detail see Buerger, "The Fulness."

83. See endnote 54. It is my understanding that these ordinances are still performed on a very limited basis at present, though those who receive them are given the charge to not speak of them, and I would hasten to clarify that I have not received any such ordinances from the Church.

84. For example, Tom Phillips, is a well-known and documented case of one who received the Second Endowment ordinances and then subsequently lost his testimony and left the Church. He never received the Second Comforter, and therefore never received the full blessing. His case also illustrates the part of the difficulty of administering these ordinances. It is not just the problem of a worldwide organization, but also one of being able to judge when such an administration is merited and by whom. When men are involved, we are inevitably prone to error and mistakes. This is another reason why I think it is actually preferable to receive these things directly from the Lord. He cannot be deceived.

85. *TPJS*, 150.

86. *TPJS*, 346-347.

87. See, for example, Stephen D. Ricks and John Sroka, "King, Coronation, and Temple Enthronement Ceremonies in History," *Temples of the Ancient World* (Salt Lake City: FARMS & Deseret Book, 1994). For a broader non-LDS perspective of this topic, but one with fascinating insights, see A.M. Hocart, *Kingship* (Oxford University Press: London, 1927), pp. 70-98. Available online at www.bhporter.com/Porter%20PDF%20Files/Kingship%20by%20A.%20M.%20Hocart.pdf. Bruce Porter has also summarized these elements of kingship at www.bhporter.com/kingship_and_coronation_hocart.htm. See also Jeffrey M. Bradshaw and Roman James Head, "The Investiture Panel at Mari and Rituals of Divine Kingship in the Ancient Near East," online at templethemes.net.

88. Some years ago, I was praying earnestly for the Lord to teach me more about the endowment. I had attended the temple weekly for many years, studied all that I could find, but still felt that some critical things eluded me. I needed and sought the Lord's help. Around that time, a friend recommended a book to me entitled, The Serpent and The Dove: Messianic Mysteries of the Mormon Temple by Paul Toscano. I purchased a copy and began to read it. In the meantime, I continued

to pray each night for the Lord to teach me about the temple. One evening, the response came that He was teaching me through Paul's book. Until that moment, I had not recognized the book as part of the Lord's answer to my request. I share this story to point out that sometimes the message we are seeking may not come in the form or from a source we would expect.

At the time, I was unaware of Paul Toscano's history or his excommunication from the Church. Furthermore, I don't really know or care much about that history. As I concluded my study of his book, I found that I fundamentally disagreed with much of what his book contains. In my view, some of it counters scripture. However, I am also very grateful to Paul Toscano for his book because portions of it contained the answers I was seeking. It opened some portions of the endowment that had really puzzled me. Even many of the parts that I disagreed with were helpful because they forced me to reevaluate and reconsider my own beliefs and positions. This process was often accompanied by additional insights from the Spirit. It was a very helpful learning process. I am grateful for and acknowledge Paul Toscano's help in my understanding of the temple. While I don't believe the Lord's answer to me was a wholesale endorsement of the book (or that it would even be an appropriate answer for anyone else), it was what I needed at the time. It is quoted at several points that seem applicable in this chapter, and I want to acknowledge that many of the thoughts contained in this chapter were influenced by or originated with his book.

Some readers may be uncomfortable with Paul Toscano's book as a source. However, since reading it, I have also found support for the ideas taken from it in more mainstream Church sources such as BYU publications and the Maxwell Institute or FARMS (Foundation for Modern Research and Mormon Studies). I could have cited those sources instead to support the points made in this chapter, but doing so did not seem right. Those sources were not where I first learned of the ideas and, frankly, in some ways Paul Toscano outlines them in a clearer and more concise manner.

I share this in the hopes that we might all remain open to truths from whatever source they might come to us. It also helps to illustrate a tradition that has crept into our LDS culture. Sometimes rather than using the Holy Ghost to discern the truth of things as we are instructed to do in the scriptures (see Moroni 10:5; 2 Nephi 32:5), we instead rely upon the position or standing of the person who said it. WHO said something becomes more important than WHAT was said. We become dependent upon someone's position in the Church (or lack thereof) rather than the Spirit to discern truth.

89. *The Concise Oxford Dictionary of World Religions* (London:Oxford University Press 1997,) online entry at www.encyclopedia.com/religion/dictionaries-thesauruses-pictures-and-press-releases/kingship-sacral.

90. See for example, Isaiah 11:4 "But with righteousness shall he judge the poor, and reprove with equity for the meek of the earth: and he shall smite the earth with the rod of his mouth." See also Moses returning to Egypt with the rod of God in his hand (see Exodus 4:2-4, 17, 20). "The sceptre, a symbolic ornamental rod held by the monarch at a coronation, is most likely derived from the shepherd's staff, via the crozier of a bishop; it may, however, be a remnant of the ceremo-

nial spear that was presented to kings and queens at coronations in different parts of the world in early history." (Sir George Younghusband and Cyril Davenport, *The Crown Jewels of England*, 1st ed., Cassell, 1919, as cited from "Crown Jewels of the United Kingdom,"(en.wikipedia.org/wiki/Crown_Jewels_of_the_United_Kingdom#Sceptres) "The Was and other types of staffs were signs of authority in Ancient Egypt. For this reason, they are often described as 'sceptres', even if they are full-length staffs. One of the earliest royal sceptres was discovered in the 2nd Dynasty tomb of Khasekhemwy in Abydos. Kings were also known to carry a staff, and Pharaoh Anedjib is shown on stone vessels carrying a so-called mks-staff. The staff with the longest history seems to be the heqa-sceptre, sometimes described as the shepherd's crook. Use of a rod or staff as representing authority can be traced to the beginning of Classical Antiquity." (en.wikipedia.org/wiki/Sceptre). These same emblems can be likewise be found as recently as at the coronation of Britain's Queen Elizabeth II in 1953.

91. One example of such an orb from more recent Western history is the *globus cruciger*. "The globus cruciger (Latin, 'cross-bearing orb'), also known as the orb and cross, an orb (Latin globus) topped (Latin gerere, to wear) by a cross (Latin crux), has been a Christian symbol of authority since the Middle Ages, used on coins, in iconography, and with the sceptre as royal regalia. The cross represents Christ's dominion over the orb of the world, literally held in the hand of an earthly ruler (or sometimes it is held by an angel). In the iconography of Western art, when Christ himself holds the globe, he is called Salvator Mundi, (Latin, 'Saviour of the World')" from "Globus Cruciger," (en.wikipedia.org/wiki/Globus_cruciger).

In England, for example, the monarch is given a specific orb called the Sovereign's Orb during the coronation ceremony. "The Sovereign's Orb is a piece of coronation regalia. It was created for the coronation of Charles II in 1661 from the royal goldsmith Robert Viner. It is made of gold, sapphires, rubies, emeralds, amethyst, diamonds, pearls, and enamel. It has been used at all coronations after the one of Charles II. . . . During the coronation ceremony, the Archbishop of Canterbury places the orb in the right hand of the Monarch. . . . The Monarch leaves the coronation wearing the Crown, carrying the Sceptre, and holding the Orb." (simple.wikipedia.org/wiki/Sovereign%27s_Orb) It is interesting to me to note that in the English ceremony the orb "is handed to the sovereign during the investiture rite of the coronation and is borne later in the left hand when leaving Westminster Abbey" (en.wikipedia.org/wiki/Crown_Jewels_of_the_United_Kingdom#cite_note-148). [Public domain image by Cyril Davenport (1848-1941) via Wikimedia Commons.]

92. A modern example of such a sword is found in the Crown Jewels of the United Kingdom used in the coronation ceremonies of British monarchs. "The jeweled Sword of Offering, made in 1820, has a gilded leather sheath, a blade of Damascus steel, and is encrusted with 3,476 precious stones. George IV paid £5,988 for the sword out of his own pocket. It remained in personal ownership until 1903 when it was deposited with the Crown Jewels. The monarch is girded with the sword and

offers it at the altar as a promise to stop the growth of iniquity, protect the Holy Church of God, help and defend widows and orphans, restore the things that are gone to decay, maintain the things that are restored, punish and reform what is amiss, and confirm what is in good order throughout his or her reign. Afterwards, it is returned to the Keeper of the Jewel House by the abbey in exchange for a token sum of £5, and the sword is borne unsheathed for the rest of the ceremony." Cited from "Crown Jewels of the United Kingdom," (en.wikipedia.org/wiki/Crown_Jewels_of_the_United_Kingdom).

Furthermore, swords can also be used to denote the word of God (see Gaskill, *The Lost Language of Symbolism*, 68). For example, the scriptures state "the word of God is quick and powerful, and sharper than any two-edged sword" (Hebrews 4:12, see also D&C 6:2, 11:2, 12:2, 14:2 and 33:1.)

93. For a discussion of robes as a symbol of identity see *Understanding Your Endowment*, 3-4. In Medieval Europe the monarch's robes also had priestly connotations.

94. "Crowns, and the like represent authority, victory, wisdom and power" (Alonzo Gaskill, *The Lost Language of Symbolism*, Salt Lake City: Deseret Book, 2003, 69). Gaskill also notes that the crown is also a symbol of the reward awaiting the righteous as seen in scriptures such as Revelations 2:10, Doctrine and Covenants 20:14, James 1:12, etc. "A crown is a traditional symbolic form of headwear worn by a monarch or by a deity, for whom the crown traditionally represents power, legitimacy, victory, triumph, honor, and glory, as well as immortality, righteousness, and resurrection. In art, the crown may be shown being offered to those on Earth by angels. Apart from the traditional form, crowns also may be in the form of a wreath and be made of flowers, oak leaves, or thorns and be worn by others, representing what the coronation part aims to symbolize with the specific crown. In religious art, a crown of stars is used similarly to a halo. Crowns worn by rulers often contain jewels." See (en.wikipedia.org/wiki/Crown_(headgear)).

95. It is not known exactly when the spirit permanently enters the mortal body, if that is during the pregnancy or at birth. However, the scriptures allude to the fact that it may be at the moment of birth (see 3 Nephi 1:12-13). In any case, the point here is not when this happens in actuality but rather that birth symbolically represents a moment when time and eternity or earth and heaven meet.

96. *TPJS*, 272.

97. Ibid.

98. Learning to hear and heed the voice of the Spirit is crucial. It is one of the things the Lord says separates the righteous from the wicked: "And whoso receiveth not my voice is not acquainted with my voice, and is not of me. And by this you may know the righteous from the wicked" (D&C 84:52-53). This is a good spiritual thermometer for each of us: how often are we hearing the voice of the Lord in our lives?

99. Sir James George Frazer, The Golden Bough: A Study in Magic and Religion, abridged 1 volume (New York: Macmillan Publishing), 1922.

100. For example, see Stephen D. Ricks and John J. Sroka, "King, Coronation and Temple" in *Temples of the Ancient World*, Donald W. Parry, ed., (Salt Lake City: Deseret

Book and F.A.R.M.S), 1994, 249-253.

101. Hugh W. Nibley, "The Three Facsimiles from the Book of Abraham", unpublished paper dated 1980 (see portion entitled, "Facsimile No. 1"). Available online at:www.boap.org/LDS/Hugh-Nibley/TrFac.html#N_5_.

102. It is interesting that Joseph Smith also received the emblems of kingship in the sword of Laban, the golden plates (word of God), and a seer stone (the orb). In similitude of the sacrifice of the ancient kings, Joseph was likewise required to lay down his life.

103. dartmouth.edu/~humananatomy/resources/etymology/Pelvis.htm.

104. See, for example, "The Train of His Robe" online blog entry at jessikamayerblog.wordpress.com/2010/05/03/the-train-of-his-robe/.

105. The KJV simply states "his train filled the temple" (Isaiah 6:1). Other translations clarify this as the train of his robe. See:biblehub.com/isaiah/6-1.htm.

106. todaysrevelation.blogspot.com/2007/12/train-of-his-robe.html.

107. Toscano, Paul. *The Serpent and the Dove: Messianic Mysteries of the Mormon Temple* (SLC: Merrill & Toscano, 2014), 67. For a note on this source, please see endnote 88.

108. For example, I received an email from a friend who stated: "I have recently discovered that the current temple signs used to be connected to the penalties (removed in 1990) and that our current signs (the first 3) are an imitation of forming a knife to cut our neck, chest, and bowels. OK, I am disturbed by this. I have been able to forgive disturbing things in the past, but why oh why is this still practiced today? . . . I have a family file to do an endowment for this week and I'm afraid the whole ordinance will be forever tainted in my mind." While part of this statement is inaccurate, it reflects something of the questions that remained with many members with respect to the endowment's penalties. Many people misunderstood them and were uncomfortable with them. My response to this friend included some of the information discussed in this chapter.

109. For a more detailed discussion of this topic, see Covenant Blessings and Penalties, *Understanding Your Endowment*, 12-16.

110. There are scriptural examples of people who reached a point in their progression and accountability that God exacted a penalty from them when they knowingly violated the terms of their covenant. Ananias and Sapphira are one such example (see Acts 5:1-11). How and when such a penalty would be exacted is up to God, but it would probably involve someone who was very mature in the gospel and who was in deliberate rebellion.

111. *Understanding Your Endowment*, 12-16.

112. One might wonder, why there were two penalties in the Aaronic portion of the endowment? The answer is because they were both parts of a greater whole. Though they were separate, one was incomplete without the other. There was also some overlap in their symbolism. We find this duality in many aspects of the gospel. For example, the soul of man is comprised of a spirit and a body. Separately, they are

incomplete. Together, they are whole. There are two components. Likewise, the Fall was both physical and spiritual in nature. Christ's suffering and atonement involved both the garden and the cross. The garden alone was not sufficient without the cross. Because of this duality, we will primarily consider these penalties together as a pair.

113. The second penalty could also be viewed as foreshadowing our mortal death. Both penalties are appropriate as part of this symbolism. The head and heart are both related to life. When the heart stops beating and brain function ceases, mortal life ends.

114. This transition and change in the purpose of the penalties is consistent with Joseph Smith's teachings that the Aaronic Priesthood and law was associated with judgement and destruction but that the Melchizedek holds the keys of power and blessings. (See 27 Aug 1843 Sermon, *Words of Joseph Smith*, Joseph Smith diary by Willard Richards.)

115. "Taken in series, the four tokens outline the Messiah's mission from the pre-mortal realm, through the mortal and post-mortal realms, to the eternal realm signifying that the Messiah on high descended below all things to be in all things and through all things. Taken in series, the four names point to different stages of existence: past, present, future, and eternal. Taken in series, the four signs symbolize the rod, the orb (the reliquary of the seer stones), the scepter/ sword, and the crown, emblematic of the promised elevation of the initiates as kings and priests and as queens and priestesses of the kingdom of God possessing the gift of seership, illumination and wisdom to repent and forgive and to administer judgment justly and mercifully and the crowning gift of God's glory to be in and through, rather than over, all things. Taken in series, the three (former) penalties represented the blows of death inflicted upon and voluntarily received by the Christ-figure in taking responsibility for the creation of the imperfect mortal sphere and for the failings, imperfections, iniquities, and inequities of its inhabitants as declared by the prophet Abinadi in the Book of Mormon." (Toscano, *The Serpent and the Dove*, 68.)

116. The endowment wording simply presents the initiate to converse with the Lord through the veil and leaves ambiguous whether the title "Lord" is referring to the Father or to the Son. I am unaware of any official Church interpretation of this portion of the endowment, though admittedly one of the most recent endowment films does have the voice of the Father responding as the Lord during the instructions given before the company is presented. In the prior films, it was difficult or impossible to tell. Regardless, in my view, the ambiguous title "Lord" is most appropriately viewed as a symbol for both in this case. If we see the veil as representing Christ as the mediator, then the brother on the other side may appropriately be seen to represent the Father. If we instead see the veil as the division between the physical and spiritual realms, then the brother may be understood to represent Christ whom we will meet and converse with first before returning to the Father (see John 14:6, Ether 3:13-14). Another reason I believe the symbol can refer to either is because the Father and the Son are one (see 3 Nephi 11:27). Therefore, it seems completely appropriate to view the conversation at the veil as occurring between the patron and Christ.

117. A committee comprised of George F. Richards, Joseph Fielding Smith, Stephen L Richards, and Melvin J. Ballard recommended several changes to the garment to the First Presidency and Council of Twelve Apostles on April 22, 1936. These recommendations included: "that a definition be given in the temple of the symbolism and significance of the various marks in the garment. We believe that an understanding on the part of those entitled to wear the garment of these sacred makings will tend greatly to bring about more reverence for the garment itself. The best interpretation which has come to us up to this time has been supplied by President David O. McKay. It is as follows: A. The square: Honor, integrity, loyalty, trustworthiness. B. The compass: An undeviating course in relation to truth. Desires should be kept within proper bounds. C. The navel: That the spiritual life needs constant sustenance. D. The knee: Reverance [sic] for God, the source of divine guidance and inspiration. To this last one might be added that which is now in use: That every knee shall bow and every tongue confess that Jesus is the Christ." (George F. Richards, Joseph Fielding Smith, Stephen L. Richards, Melvin J. Ballard to the First Presidency and Council of Twelve Apostles, April 22, 1936, LDS archives, as quoted in Buerger, *Mysteries*, 153.)

118. Masonic Lodge of Education at: www.masonic-lodge-of-education.com/square-and-compasses.html. "The Square and Compasses (or, more correctly, a square and a set of compasses joined together) is the single most identifiable symbol of Freemasonry. Both the square and compasses are architect's tools and are used in Masonic ritual as emblems to teach symbolic lessons. Some Lodges and rituals explain these symbols as lessons in conduct: for example, Duncan's Masonic Monitor of 1866 explains them as: 'The square, to square our actions; The compasses, to circumscribe and keep us within bounds with all mankind.'" In Masonry, these two symbols are often pictured together and sometimes included the letter G in the center. "The letter has multiple meanings, representing different words depending on the context in which it is discussed. The most common is that the 'G' stands for God, and is to remind Masons that God is at the center of Freemasonry. In this context it can also stand for Great Architect of the Universe" (en.wikipedia.org/wiki/Square_and_Compasses.) In the temple, the square and the compass are appropriate symbols of Christ as the architect and creator of man and the universe.

119. See Covenant Marks or Tokens, *Understanding Your Endowment*, 19.

120. Ibid.

121. For a more detailed description of ancient covenant ceremonies and practices, see chapter 1 of *Understanding Your Endowment*. Elements of these ceremonies are found scattered throughout ancient civilizations around the world. It is my view that these practices descended from older gospel covenant practices between God and man. Though some of these practices were undoubtedly corrupted, traces of many of them can still be found in the Old Testament record as well.

122. Since its introduction, the temple garment has undergone several changes to its present form. Today, the marks are pre-sewn into the fabric and so the initiate

receives a pre-marked garment. See Devery S. Anderson ed., *The Development of LDS Temple Worship: 1846–2000 A Documentary History* (Salt Lake City: Signature Books, 2011), xxxix. Another apparent change to the garment involved the navel mark, which was originally in the form of an inverted arc, possibly representing our descent into mortality and subsequent return to God. Understanding this history helps us to see the correlation between these marks and the wounds of Christ.

"The marks on the veil and garment appear to be four because they cover four body parts, but they are in fact seven because they involve seven separate cuts of the cloth (2 cuts to make the square, 2 to make the compass, 2 to create the arc or inverted "V" at the navel, and 1 to create the rule at the right knee). These seven cuts represent Christ's seven wounded body parts (his four extremities, his side, his back— where he was flailed— and his head— where he was crowned with thorns). These seven wounded parts are also represented by the seven stars of the Pleiades and of the Big Dipper, the latter constellation appearing as a carving on the marble facing of the center west tower of the Salt Lake Temple" (Toscano, *The Serpent and the Dove*, 72). While this interpretation is Toscano's, his source for the inverted arc appears to be a document entitled, "History of the Garment" available at docslide.us/documents/history-of-the-garment.html. It is difficult, probably impossible, to know for certain how accurate this document is but it remains one of very few which attempts to preserve and trace this topic.

123. Toscano, *The Serpent and the Dove*, 70. For a note on this source, please see endnote 88.

124. The scriptures teach that at the final judgment day "every knee shall bow, and every tongue confess" that Christ is God (see Mosiah 27:31; Romans 14:11). He will then be recognized as the King, not only of the Jews, but of the whole earth. One of the endowment's symbols reminds us of this fact. But that same symbol is also a potent reminder of a King who first knelt to serve and lift all of His creation or kingdom. That required Him to leave his throne on high and descend below all things (see D&C 122:8).

125. Toscano, *The Serpent and the Dove*, 70. For a note on this source, please see endnote 88.

126. The brother on the other side of the veil is simply referred to as Lord and can symbolize either the Father or the Son. (Please see endnote 116, for further explanation). In this instance, the symbol is the Son.

127. See William Morgan, *Illustrations of Masonry*, as quoted in "The Sacred Embrace as Five Points of Fellowship," entry of April 4, 2012 on blog entitled "Wheat and Tares." These ideas are further developed and explained in the following poem, quoted on the same source:

By Brother N. A. McAulay

Foot to foot, that we may go,
Where our help we can bestow;
Pointing out the better way,

Lest our brothers go astray.
Thus our steps should always lead
To the souls that are in need.

Knee to knee, that we may share
Every brother's needs in prayer:
Giving all his wants a place,
When we seek the throne of grace.
In our thoughts from day to day
For each other we should pray.

Breast to breast, to there conceal,
What our lips must not reveal;
When a brother does confide,
We must by his will abide.
Mason's secrets to us known,
We must cherish as our own.

Hand to back, our love to show
To the brother, bending low:
Underneath a load of care,
Which we may and ought to share.
That the weak may always stand,
Let us lend a helping hand.

Cheek to cheek, or mouth to ear,
That our lips may whisper cheer,
To our brother in distress:
Whom our words can aid and bless.
Warn him if he fails to see,
Dangers that are known to thee

Foot to foot, and knee to knee,
Breast to breast, as brothers we:
Hand to back and mouth to ear,
Then that mystic word we hear
Which we otherwise conceal,
But on these five points reveal.

128. Richard Rohr, *Breathing Under Water: Spirituality and the Twelve Steps* (Cincinnati: St. Anthony Messenger Press, 2011).

129. *WJS*, lectures on 28 Apr 1842 and 1 May 1842.

130. *WJS*, 1 May 1842; emphasis added.

131. This point is also evident in James E. Talmage's description of the endowment: "The Temple Endowment, as administered in modern temples, comprises instruction relating to the significance and sequence of past dispensations, and the importance of the present as the greatest and grandest era in human history. This course of instruction includes a recital of the most prominent events of the creative period, the condition of our first parents in the Garden of Eden, their disobedience and consequent expulsion from that blissful abode, their condition in the lone and dreary world when doomed to live by labor and sweat, the plan of redemption by which the great transgression may be atoned, the period of the great apostasy, the restoration of the Gospel with all its ancient powers and privileges, the absolute and indispensable condition of personal purity and devotion to the right in the present life, and a strict compliance with Gospel requirements" (*The House of the Lord*, 83). There is perhaps yet another explanation for the presence of an embodied (resurrected) Peter, James and John, if the entire ceremony is viewed as revealing the future as well as the past. Seen in that light, the endowment has some startling ramifications, some of which seem alluded to in scripture and in Joseph's later Nauvoo discourses.

132. *WJS*, 4. (27 June 1839, Willard Richard's Pocket Companion.)

133. *TPJS*, 237-238.

134. *TPJS*, 238.

135. Ibid.

136. Wagoner, *Discourses of Brigham Young*, 135.

137. "A very serious conversation took place between President B. Young and Orson Pratt upon doctrine. O.P. was directly opposed to the President's views and freely expressed his entire disbelief in them after being told by the President that things were so and so in the name of the Lord. He was firm in the position that the President's word in the name of the Lord was not the word of the Lord to him." (*The Complete Discourses of Brigham Young*, Volume 2, 1061).

138. President Kimball in October 1976 general conference stated the following: "We warn you against the dissemination of doctrines which are not according to the Scriptures and which are alleged to have been taught by some of the General Authorities of past generations. Such, for instance, is the Adam-God theory. We denounce that theory and hope that everyone will be cautioned against this and other kinds of false doctrine" ("Our Own Liahona", Ensign, November 1976. See also, the entry for Adam God Theory in Mormon Doctrine).

139. April 30, 2017, blog entry, "You cannot believe everything you hear at Church" in the Exponent II at www.the-exponent.com/you-cannot-believe-everything-you-hear-at-Church/.

140. *HC* 5: 340.

141. James E. Talmage, *The House of the Lord: A Study of Holy Sanctuaries, Ancient and Modern* (Salt Lake City: The Church of Jesus Christ of Latter-day Saints, 1912), 99.

142. *TPJS*, 226.

143. For example: *Deseret News*, June 12, 1923; Joseph Smith, *History of the Church of Jesus Christ of Latter-day Saints,* ed. B.H. Roberts, 7 vols., (Salt Lake City: Deseret Book, 1970) 7: 390, 552, 554. Aaronic Priesthood Leadership Materials, 1973-1974 (Salt Lake City: The Church of Jesus Christ of Latter-day Saints, 1973), p. 7; Clark, *Messages of the First Presidency*, 6:256 as cited by D. Michael Quinn in "Latter-day Saint Prayer Circles", an article he presented at the Welch Symposium in honor of Professor Hugh Nibley, March 28, 1975. D. Michael Quinn was an assistant professor of history at Brigham Young University at the time. The prayer has been described in surprising detail in some official Church publications. For instance, the *Improvement Era* (August 1933) printed the following: "President [Lorenzo] Snow put on his holy temple robes, repaired again to the same sacred altar, offered up the signs of the Priesthood and poured out his heart to the Lord," cited in Quinn, "Latter-day Saint Prayer Circles." Quinn also quotes President Spencer W. Kimball who gave the following description: "Every Thursday the Council of the Twelve met in a room on the [Salt Lake] Temple's fourth floor. The apostles sat by seniority in twelve large oak chairs, in a crescent around an upholstered altar. Harold B. Lee played a small organ in the corner as they opened with a hymn. Then all twelve, dressed in temple clothes, formed a prayer circle around the altar. The prayer completed, they changed back to street clothes to handle the Quorum's business" (Edward L. Kimball and Andrew E. Kimball, Jr., *Spencer W. Kimball: Twelfth President of The Church of Jesus Christ of Latter-day Saints* [Salt Lake City: Bookcraft, 1977], 207). Quinn concludes, "Thus, through publications of the LDS Church, one may learn that an ordinance of the temple is known as the prayer circle, that it requires the participants to pray in a circle as they are dressed in holy temple clothing, and that the prayer is accompanied by offering certain signs of the priesthood at an altar" (Quinn, "Latter Day Prayer Circles," 80). The full article is available online at byustudies.byu.edu/content/latter-day-saint-prayer-circles.

144. For example, the current instructions include: 1) that the prayer is to be no longer than three minutes in length; 2) that no individual person is to be mentioned by name other than the President of the Church; 3) that phrases should be kept short enough to remember and repeat, etc. Other instructions are given as well, some of which concern wording that would not be appropriate to discuss outside the temple. The point is that the brother voicing the prayer is not just focused on the words but also trying to remember and follow directions he has received.

145. For one such example see Hugh W. Nibley, "The Early Christian Prayer Circle", *Mormonism and Early Christianity, vol. 4 of The Collected Works of Hugh Nibley* (Salt Lake City: Deseret Book and F.A.R.M.S., 1987), 45-99.

146. Brown and Smith, *Symbols in Stone*, 105, as quoted on ldssymbols.com.

147. Mason, W.L. Wilmshurst, stated: "The human body is the 'tomb of transformation'; the grave into which the soul descends for the purpose of working out its own salvation, for transforming and improving itself, and ascending out of it the

stronger and wiser for the experience."

148. See ldssymbols.com/squared-circle/ for a brief summary, although these symbols and interpretations can be found in many sources.

149. James Robert Brown, *Philosophy of Mathematics: A Contemporary Introduction to the World of Proofs and Pictures* (New York: Routledge 2008) as quoted on ldssymbols.com.

150. *WJS*, 117. (Sermon of 28 Apr 1842). Andrew Ehat adds this explanation: ""'Keys,' apparently meaning the keys of the kingdom, used in the next paragraph (at note 13; see also 1 May 1842, note 4). Apparently because the record says that the 'keys' would be given both to the Relief Society members and to the Church, and the 'keys of the Kingdom' referred to were to be given in the endowment, George A. Smith felt justified in amplifying this text as follows (italicized words are the amplifications): 'He spoke of delivering the keys *of the Priesthood* to the Church and *said that the faithful members of* the *Relief* Society *should receive them in connection with their husbands*, that *the Saints whose integrity has been tried and proved faithful, might know how to ask the Lord and receive an answer; for* according to his prayers, God had appointed him elsewhere' (*History of the Church* 4:604, or *Teachings*, 226). For further explanation, see *WJS*, Sermon 5 October 1840, note 19."

151. *WJS*, 119. (Sermon, 1 May 1842.)

152. Devery S. Anderson observed, "Brigham Young thought the garments had magical powers, saying that Willard Richards had been protected from bodily harm when he was shot at in Carthage, Illinois, standing alongside Joseph and Hyrum, who were assassinated. The Smiths had apparently removed their garments due to the heat, while Richards had not" (Devery S. Anderson ed., *The Development of LDS Temple Worship: 1846–2000 A Documentary History* (Salt Lake City: Signature Books, 2011), xxxix). His conclusion seems supported by Brigham Young's statement: "I recollect a promise Joseph gave to Willard at a certain time, when he clothed him with a priestly garment. Said he, 'Willard never go without this garment on your body, for you will stand where the balls will fly around you like hail, and men will fall dead by your side and if you will never part with this garment, there never shall a ball injure you.' I heard him say this [voice in the stand 'So did I'] It is true. When the mob shot Joseph, Willard was there and Br Taylor was in the room. I have nothing to say about the rest, you know about it. Willard obeyed the word of the prophet. He said, 'I will die before I part with this garment.' The balls flew around him, riddled his clothes, and shaved a passage through one of his whiskers." (Brigham Young, unpublished discourse, July 14, 1861, LDS archives, as quoted in Buerger, *Mysteries*, 148.)

153. Brigham Young described the endowment thusly: "Your endowment is to receive all those ordinances in the house of the Lord which are necessary for you, to enable you to walk back to the presence of the Father, passing the angels who stand as sentinels, being enabled to give them the key words, the signs, and the tokens pertaining to the holy priesthood and gain your eternal exaltation"(Journal of Discourses 2:31). On the surface, this statement appears to mean that you need to learn and memorize the signs and tokens given in the temple, and then you will be able to use them in the next life, thereby giving the temple's symbols magical properties.

Some members believe it is enough to memorize these things and then feel that they have obtained enough from their endowment. If we were to take Brigham's statement literally, then any man or woman can go to the temple and receive their endowment (or worse, just look it up online). They could carefully memorize and keep in their memory what they were taught, but could then come out of the temple, break all of their covenants, and live a wicked life. After death, as long as they remembered the temple's tokens and signs, they could pass by the angels and gain their exaltation in the next life despite having made no effort to keep their covenants. Such a notion is completely nonsensical, so the endowment must not mean that. Once we recognize that the temple's tokens and signs are symbols, then what is really important is coming to understand what the symbol represents and then receiving that actual thing in your life. If you receive not just the symbol, but also that which it represents, then you will be able to pass by the angels. Brigham's description is technically correct, but perhaps widely misunderstood.

154. From L. John Nuttal Journal, February 7, 1877, Special Collections, Harold B. Lee Library, Brigham Young University, Provo, Utah, as quoted in Buerger, *Mysteries*, 39.

155. This group met several times including reconvening the following month on June 27, 1842, for a prayer circle at the store.

156. For a discussion of this topic see Gordon Irving, "The Law of Adoption: One Phase of the Development of the Mormon Concept of Salvation, 1830-1900." Article available at byustudies.byu.edu/content/law-adoption-one-phase-development-mormon-concept-salvation-1830-1900. Gordon Irving was an associate for the Historical Department of the Church.

157. Joseph Smith's journal entry for September 28, 1843 records: "<28> Thursday 28 At 11.30, a.m. a Council conversed over the Store consisting of myself, my brother Hyrum [Smith], Uncle John Smith, Newel K. Whitney, George Miller, Willard Richards, John Taylor, Amasa Lyman, John M. Bernhisel, and Lucien Woodworth; and at 7 in the evening we met in the front upper room of the Mansion, with William Law and William Marks. By the common consent and unanimous voice of the Council, Baurak Ale <I> was chosen President of the Quorum, ~~and anointed and ordained to the highet and holiest order of the Priesthood. (with his companion)~~." *Joseph Smith Papers*, online entry at www.josephsmithpapers.org/paper-summary/history-1838-1856-volume-e-1-1-july-1843-30-april-1844/110?highlight=journal%20sept%2028%201843. Some weeks later, on October 19, 1843, William Clayton recorded that Joseph told him Emma "had been anointed & he [Smith] also had been a[nointed] K[ing]" (George D. Smith, ed., *An Intimate Chronicle: The Journals of William Clayton* [Salt Lake City: Signature Books and Smith Research Associates, 1991], 122, as cited in Michael W. Homer, *Joseph's Temples: The Dynamic Relationship between Freemasonry and Mormonism* (SLC: University of Utah Press, 2014), 215.

158. Michael W. Homer, *Joseph's Temples: The Dynamic Relationship between Freemasonry and Mormonism* (Salt Lake City: University of Utah Press, 2014), 215; also see David John Buerger, "The Fulness of the Priesthood": The Second Anointing in Latter-day Saint Theology and Practice," *Dialogue: A Journal of Mormon Thought* 16 (Spring 1983), 10-44.

159. Buerger, *Mysteries*, 64-65, gives a list of these men and women and the dates of their ordinances. Also see pages 72–73 for the dates and locations of the various meetings held during Joseph's lifetime.

160. In 1884, Lucius N. Scovil testified: "I can testify that on the 3rd day of May, 1842, Joseph Smith the Prophet called upon five or six, viz: Shadrack [sic] Roundy, Noah Rogers, Dimick B. Huntington, Daniel Cairns [sic] and myself (I am not certain but that Hosea Stout was there also) to meet with him (the Prophet) in his business office (the upper part of his brick store). He told us that the object he had was for us to go to work and fit up that room preparatory to giving endowments to a few Elders that he might give unto them all the keys of power pertaining to the Aronic [sic] and Melchisedec [sic] Priesthoods. We therefore went to work making the necessary preparations, and everything was arranged representing the interior of a temple as much as the circumstances would permit, he being with us dictating everything. He gave us many items that were very interesting to us, which sank with deep weight upon my mind, especially after the temple was finished at Nauvoo, and I had received the ordinances in which I was among the first, as I had been called upon to work in the Temple as one of the hands during the winter. Some weeks previous to the dedication he told us that we should have the privilege of receiving the whole of the ordinances in due time. The history of Joseph Smith speaks for itself. But I can and do testify that I know of a surety that room was fitted up by his order which we finished in the forenoon of the said 4th of May, 1842. And he gave us to understand that he intended to have everything done by him that was in his power while he remained with us. He said his work was nearly done and he should roll the burden of the kingdom upon the shoulders of the Twelve. I am the only one living that I know of, who helped to fit up that room, except Hosea Stout, [who] was there." ("The Higher Ordinances," *Deseret News Semi-Weekly*, February 15, 1884, as quoted in Buerger, *Mysteries*, 38.)

161. *L. John Nuttall Journal*, February 7, 1877, Special Collections, Harold B. Lee Library, Brigham Young University, Provo, Utah, as quoted in Buerger, *Mysteries*, 73. Nuttall was Brigham Young's secretary at the time.

162. Buerger, *Mysteries*, 81.

163. George D. Smith ed., *An Intimate Chronicle: The Journals of William Clayton* (Salt Lake City: Signature Books and Smith Research Associates, 1991), 203, as cited in Michael W. Homer, *Joseph's Temples: The Dynamic Relationship between Freemasonry and Mormonism* (Salt Lake City: University of Utah Press, 2014), 233.

164. Ibid.

165. Smith, *An Intimate Chronicle*, 210, as quoted in Buerger, *Mysteries*, 80.

166. Buerger, *Mysteries*, 80 see footnote 23.

167. Devery S. Anderson and Gary James Bergera, eds., *The Nauvoo Endowment Companies, 1845-1846: A Documentary History* (Salt Lake City: Signature Books, 2005).

168. Buerger, *Mysteries*, 90.

169. Ibid.

170. M. Guy Bishop, "'What Has Become of Our Fathers?' Baptism for the Dead at Nauvoo," *Dialogue: A Journal of Mormon Thought*. Available at www.dialoguejournal.com/wp-content/uploads/sbi/articles/Dialogue_V23N02_87.pdf.

171. en.wikipedia.org/wiki/Endowment_House.

172. Ibid.

173. Scott Kenney, ed., *Wilford Woodruff's Journal*, 9 vols. (Salt Lake City: Signature Books, 1984), 7:322, as quoted in Buerger, *Mysteries*, 110.

174. *L. John Nuttall Journal*, February 7, 1877, Special Collections, Harold B. Lee Library, Brigham Young University, Provo, Utah. The journal entry outlining the lecture is quoted in Buerger, *Mysteries*, 111-112.

175. For example, the endowment's oath of vengeance which Brigham Young inserted after Joseph's martyrdom, might have been understandable given the Saints' feelings at the time, but it seems contrary to the spirit of forgiveness that Joseph taught and demonstrated throughout his life. Another example concerns the endowment's treatment of women. Joseph ordained women to be queens and priestesses unto God, whereas Brigham apparently changed that in December of 1845 to ordain them queens and priestesses unto their husbands. This wording remains troubling to some members to this day.

176. "Most of you, my brethren, are Elders, Seventies, or High Priests: perhaps there is not a Priest or Teacher present. The reason of this is that when we give the brethren their endowments, we are obliged to confer upon them the Melchisedec Priesthood; but I expect to see the day, when we shall be so situated that we can say to a company of brethren you can go and receive the ordinances pertaining to the Aaronic order of Priesthood, and then you can go into the world and preach the Gospel, or do something that will prove whether you will honor that Priesthood before you receive more. Now we pass them through the ordinances of both Priesthoods in one day, but this is not as it should be and would if we had a Temple wherein to administer these ordinances. But this is all right at present; we should not be satisfied in any other way, and consequently we do according to the circumstances we are placed in" (*Journal of Discourses* 10:309 as quoted in Buerger, *Mysteries*, 117).

177. Richard S. Van Wagoner, ed., *The Complete Discourses of Brigham Young: Volume 2, 1853 to 1856*, (Salt Lake City, Signature Books), 1034.

178. *Salt Lake School of the Prophets Minute Book*, October 12, 1883, as quoted in Buerger, *Mysteries*, 116.

179. An entire book has been compiled to trace this topic since Joseph's death. See Devery S. Anderson, ed., *The Development of LDS Temple Worship: 1846–2000 A Documentary History* (Salt Lake City: Signature Books, 2011).

180. "One witness, disaffected Mormon and recently resigned Brigham Young Academy professor Walter M. Wolfe, testified that this oath was worded: "You and each of you do covenant and promise that you will pray, and never cease to pray, Almighty God to avenge the blood of the prophets upon this nation, and that you will teach the same to your children and your children's children unto the

third and fourth generations." On December 14, 1904 the Washington Times and the New York Herald featured front page photographs of a man in endowment clothing, depicting the signs and penalties. Testimony during this hearing as well as other previously published discussions of this oath indicate that, commencing with the Nauvoo Temple ceremony, the oath of vengeance was in fact required of all initiates. Most Latter-day Saints today would be uncomfortable taking such an oath or prayer, and the same was true of the general public at the time of the Smoot hearings. For Mormons in Nauvoo during the mid-1840s, the oath was a different matter. Encouraged perhaps by scriptural passages such as Revelation 6: 9-11, many Latter-day Saints hoped for revenge. Allen Stout, a former Danite, recorded in his diary after he watched the bodies of Joseph and Hyrum Smith being returned to Nauvoo: "I [stood] there and then resolved in my mind that I would never let an opportunity slip unimproved of avenging their blood. . . . I knew not how to contain myself, and when I see one of the men who persuaded them to give up to be tried, I feel like cutting their throats yet." Buerger, *Mysteries*, 133.

181. A number of Richards' journal entries from the time period describe some of these changes as follows:

 [3 June 1922:] I took 7:20 [a.m.] car for my work at the temple. This day [Saturday] I went before the [First] Presidency and presented to them an important change in the endowment ceremony by which the robes should be placed on the left shoulder first and then changed to the right shoulder once only before entering the Terrestrial room; also that Aaronic and Melchizedek be used instead of lower order of the Melchizedek and higher order of the Aaronic. I am to come back with a definite recommendation of the Presidency of the Temple. This is my own suggestion. Other members not accessible today.

 [7 June 1922:] I attended to my duties as usual at the Temple.... I presented the suggestions of a change in the order of robing and in the wording of the ordinances and lecture [at the veil] which were by vote approved.... The ceremonies and Lecture will be changed to conform. Full explanation will be given in Temple Historical Record. This will clarify some matters which at present are obscure and will shorten the services.

 [14 April 1923:] I spent 1-1/ 2 hours with the [First] Presidency where I read to them the ceremonies connected with the giving of the 1st and 2nd lectures of the Aaronic Priesthood as I had written them after hearing them repeated and after I had revised them. I asked if all the ceremonies could not be written, revised and approved and go into the Presidents' Book held only by the Temple Presidents. The [First] Presidency were all present and thought favorably of these [suggestions]. The matter is to be submitted to the Council of the First Presidency, the Twelve & Patriarch. This would give us a standard to go by that these ceremonies might be kept uniform. The subject of the garment was again brought up and considered and certain changes thought favorably of. The permisibility [sic] of dispensing with the collar, using buttons instead of strings, using the closed crotch and flop, and for the women wearing elbow[-length instead of writs-length] sleaves and leg length legs just below the knee. I spent about seven hours at the temple— President E. J. Wood was given a full set of Temple books to take home with him to Cardston for the Temple. [illegible] change.

[16 April 1923:] I spent at the temple writing what has heretofore been unwritten ceremonies of the temple. My son George assisted me all the afternoon." *George F. Richards Diary*, July 12, 1924, LDS archives, as quoted in Buerger, *Mysteries*, 136-139.

182. *George F. Richards Diary*, July 12, 1924, as quoted in Anderson, *Development of LDS Temple Worship*, xxxv (emphasis added).

183. *St. George Temple Minute Book*, December 14, 1911, as quoted in Buerger, *Mysteries*, 139.

184. *George F. Richards Diary*, July 12, 1924 as quoted in Anderson, *Development of LDS Temple Worship*, xxxv.

185. See www.ldsendowment.org for a side by side comparison of pre- and post-1990 texts minus the portions covered by covenants of non-disclosure.

186. This was confirmed by an attorney who represented the Church in the lawsuit.

187. D. Michael Quinn, "Latter-day Saint Prayer Circles" in *BYU Studies*. This is an article he presented at the Welch Symposium in honor of Professor Hugh Nibley, March 28, 1975. At the time, D. Michael Quinn was an assistant professor of history at Brigham Young University. The article is available online from Brigham Young University at byustudies.byu.edu/content/latter-day-saint-prayer-circles.

188. Emma was the first woman admitted to the order. She and Joseph were "anointed & ordained to the highest order of the priesthood" on September 28, 1843 (Quinn, "Prayer Circles" 4-5). "By the time Joseph Smith and Hyrum Smith were murdered in June 1844, more than sixty-five persons were members of the Quorum of the Anointed" (ibid., 5).

189. Joseph inaugurated the Nauvoo endowment rites with nine men on May 4, 1842. These men became the initial members of the Quorum of the Anointed. They are, together with their Church position at the time, as follows: Hyrum Smith (Presiding Patriarch), William Law (2nd Counselor First Presidency), Brigham Young (Apostle and President of the Quorum of the Twelve), Heber C. Kimball (Apostle), Willard Richards (Apostle and personal secretary to Joseph Smith), Newel K. Whitney (First [today we would say presiding] Bishop of the Church), George Miller (2nd Bishop of the Church), William Marks (Nauvoo Stake President), and James Adams (Branch President of Springfield, Illinois Branch and Church Patriarch). As this list illustrates, it is apparent that these men came from different quorums. Most are from the senior leadership of the Church; however, the inclusion of James Adams and George Miller is interesting. James Adams did not reside in Nauvoo at the time but lived in Springfield, Illinois, some 130 miles distant. James Adams was a Deputy Grand Master of the Masonic Grand Lodge of Illinois from 1840 to 1843. George Miller was the Worshipful Master of the Nauvoo Masonic Lodge (the senior local officer). Heber C. Kimball was the first Junior Deacon of the Nauvoo Lodge and one of the original petitioners to bring a Masonic lodge to Nauvoo. Others, including Hyrum Smith and Newel K. Whitney, also had close connections to Masonry.

190. Quinn, "Prayer Circles," 7.

191. "The Quorum of the Anointed met for the true order of prayer and for ordinance work at least weekly in four separate locations during Joseph Smith's lifetime: from September to November 1843 in the front upper room of the Mansion House, from November to December 1843 in the southeast room of Joseph Smith's Homestead, from December 1843 until June 1844 in the Assembly Room over Joseph Smith's store, and on a few occasions in January-February 1844 in Brigham Young's House" (Quinn, "Prayer Circles," 7).

192. Quinn, "Prayer Circles," 6.

193. Ibid., 10.

194. Ibid.

195. *Heber C. Kimball 1844-45 Journal*, June 6, 1844, as quoted in Quinn, "Prayer Circles," 8. See also entry of July 12, 1844, for another reference to this individual practice.

196. Quinn, "Prayer Circles," 12-14.

197. Ibid., 11.

198. Ibid.

199. Ibid., 14.

200. Ibid., 14-15.

201. Ibid., 15.

202. Ibid., 16.

203. For an examination of this topic, see Gordon Irving, "The Law of Adoption: One Phase of the Development of the Mormon Concept of Salvation, 1830-1900," 294. The full article is available online from BYU Studies at byustudies.byu.edu/content/law-adoption-one-phase-development-mormon-concept-salvation-1830-1900. Gordon Irving was an associate for the Historical Department of the Church.

204. Orson Pratt sermon, *Journal of Discourses* 1:58, HC 3:386-87, as quoted in Irving, "The Law of Adoption," 294.

205. Irving, "The Law of Adoption," 294.

206. Joseph may have sealed men as well as women to himself. Irving writes: "No consensus exists with regard to the date when the first adoptions were performed. Any conclusions as to whether the ordinance was practiced during Joseph Smith's lifetime must be viewed as tentative. It is certainly possible, perhaps probable, that Joseph Smith did initiate certain trusted leaders into the adoptionary order as early as 1842" ("The Law of Adoption," 295). Given the practice which followed, it seems a reasonable that it had been initiated by Joseph Smith.

207. It is possible that what Joseph was practicing in sealing women, and possibly men, to himself, and what became later Church practice with marriage and sealing of multiple wives may have been very different in purpose, scope, and intent.

208. Irving, "The Law of Adoption," 296.

209. Ibid., 301.

210. Ibid., 302.

211. Ibid., 303.

212. Ibid., 306.

213. Ibid., 312.

214. Ibid., 313.

215. Jennifer Ann Mackley, *Wilford Woodruff's Witness: The Development of LDS Temple Doctrine* (Seattle: High Desert Publishing, 2014).

216. David O. McKay, "David O. McKay Temple Address" (Salt Lake Temple Annex, Utah, September 25, 1941), BYU Library Special Collections.

217. www.ldsendowment.org/1931.html.

218. For instance, I believe there is a truth concealed within the sisters' covenant of obedience that should not be discarded without further thought. It is not that women should be subservient to men as some have supposed. That is not it! But there is some truth in the concept of submitting to and serving one another within the covenant of marriage. That submission should be the man to the woman and the woman to the man—it goes both ways. The idea is inherent in a covenant relationship. I am bound to my wife in a way that is different from my relationship to any other person because of our covenant. Paul taught that husbands are to love their wives as Christ loved the Church—even to laying down of his life (Ephesians 5:25). Ultimately, both spouses should sacrifice for each other and for their children. This voluntary submission of ourselves to another is one means to truly lift or change another. Think of Ammon and Lamoni in the Book of Mormon, as an example. Of course, this must be done prayerfully and carefully. It does not require that we submit to abuse.

219. *TPJS*, 308, emphasis added.

220. The current Church training video for temple workers attributes the statement that ordinances are not to be altered or changed to President James E. Faust; however, he was quoting the original statement from Joseph Smith.

221. The sole exception was when Wilford Woodruff discontinued the law of adoption, which organized families according to priesthood and instead replaced it with the practice of sealing to one's progenitors. He claimed this change was a result of revelation.

222. This is a line from the Warner Bros. 2014 movie, *Winter's Tale*.

223. For more information, visit their website at liahonachildren.org.

224. www.dialoguejournal.com/wp-content/uploads/sbi/articles/Dialogue_V35N04_105.pdf.

225. *TPJS*, 238.

226. *WJS*, Sermon 16 April 1843.

227. For a discussion of temple element's known to Joseph Smith before the introduction of the Nauvoo ordinances, see Jeffrey M. Bradshaw, "Freemasonry and the Origins of Modern Temple Ordinances," *Interpreter: A Journal of Mormon Scripture*, 2015. www.mormoninterpreter.com/freemasonry-and-the-origins-of-modern-temple-ordinances/.

228. For example, Eugene Seaich, "Was Freemasonry derived from Mormonism?", www.shields-research.org/General/Masonry.html#2.

229. H. Clay Trumbull, *The Threshold Covenant* (Kirkwood, Missouri: Impact Christian Books, 2000).

230. B. F. Johnson, *My Life's Review*, 85, as quoted in Bradshaw, "Freemasonry and the Origins of Modern Temple Ordinances."

231. *HC* 5:1–2.

232. The nine men first inducted into the endowment ceremony all had close ties to Masonry. See endnote 189 for further details.

233. *WJS*, 9.

234. Andrew F. Ehat, "Moses and Our Temple Blessings", unpublished paper of August 31, 2009. In the article, he lists "The Ten Tests in the Wilderness Leading to the "Dayof Provocation" as follows:

    (1) At Goshen: Exodus 5:19–21; 6:9–12; 5:1–6:12; 6: 28–7:6.

    (2) At the Red Sea (Pi-hahiroth): Exodus 14:10–12.

    (3) The Waters of Marah ("Bitter"): Exodus 15:22–24.

    (4) In the Wilderness of Sin (proving Israel by Manna and quail, between Elim and Sinai): Exodus 16:1–3, 19–20, 27–30.

    (5) Rephibim—Massah [Temptation] and Meribah [Contention or Strife]: Exodus 17:1–7; 8–16.

    (6) Incomplete Endowment at Sinai and False Worship of Golden Calf (KJV and JST): Exodus 19; 20:18–21, 1–19; 22ff; ch. 24; 32:1–35; ch. 33–34 (JST Ex 34:1–2); Deuteronomy 4:33–36; 5:4–5, 22–33; D&C 84:19–25.

    (7) Taberah ("Burning"): Numbers 11: 1–3.

    (8) Kibroth Hattaavah ("Graves of craving"): Numbers 11:4–34.

    (9) Hazeroth ("Settlement"): Numbers 12.

    (10) Final Day of Provocation (at Kadesh ["Holy"] in the Wilderness of Paran): Numbers 13–14.

235. Moses, Aaron, two of Aaron's sons and seventy of the elders of Israel entered the Lord's presence (see Exodus 24:9-10). It is possible there were others as well, as the next verse seems to indicate (see Exodus 24:11).

236. *WJS*, 120, emphasis added. (26 May 1842 *Nauvoo Relief Society Minutes.*)

237. *WJS*, 13-14, emphasis added. (Before 8 August 1839 *Willard Richards Pocket Companion.*)

238. Ibid.

239. *TPJS*, 312.

240. *TPJS*, 331. This may have been prophetic foresight as the Saints were broken up, divided and scattered in the events of the succession crisis and the exodus from Nauvoo.

241. The fact that the revelation does not specify a precise date for the completion of the temple has left this question open to discussion and interpretation. The length of the "sufficient time" (D&C 124:31) becomes a critical question. Was the 3 ½ years between the date of the revelation and the death of the Prophet Joseph Smith sufficient time? We are left to answer that for ourselves. However, the following facts are difficult to ignore: The endowments performed between December 1845 and February 1846 were administered in the unfinished attic which had temporarily been dedicated for that purpose. The last endowments were administered on February 7, 1846. The following day the Twelve met in the attic before departing Nauvoo and Brigham Young dedicated the temple as thus far completed. He prayed that the Lord would "enable them someday to finish the lower part of the building and dedicate it to Him and to preserve the temple as a monument to Joseph Smith" (Henry W. Bigler, Autobiography, Typescript, Lee Library, BYU). The next day, February 9, the roof caught fire at 3 a.m. and burned in the attic for a half an hour before being put out (*HC* 7:581). When the temple was finally dedicated in private and public services from April 30 to May 3, 1846, it was not actually a finished building but just considered "good enough". The roof had been repaired from the fire, but the charred attic space was never completely refinished. The stairway in the northwest corner was not finished. The main floor was finished, but the mezzanine half-story was not. This area was intended to be divided into seven rooms on each side of the building. These rooms were never permanently partitioned. Crimson draperies were planned to subdivide the whole main floor but these were never installed. The second floor assembly hall was only roughly completed. The best argument that can be made is that "from a functional point of view, the temple was completed. Every section of the structure had been given a rough finish and many areas a final finish as well" (Don F. Colvin, *Nauvoo Temple: A Story of Faith*, Brigham Young University, Religious Studies Center, 2002, p. 223). However, this argument is made with along with the admission that "there can be no doubt that had the Latter-day Saints remained in Nauvoo, they would have further embellished interior sections of the structure and given it a more perfect finish" (ibid.). Regardless of whether the temple was completed or remained unfinished, ultimately there is no historic record or account of Christ visiting the temple as He had indicated would happen (see D&C 124:27-28). And the language of the revelation states that Christ would be required to restore the fulness which had been lost.

     The historical arguments, that the fulness was restored by the rites performed by Joseph or by his passing of keys to the Twelve, ignore the specific language of the revelation. Christ was to come personally to restore that which had been lost. It can only be received by and from Him. Furthermore, revelation continues: "ye shall build it [the Nauvoo Temple] on the place where you have contemplated building it, for that is the spot which I have chosen for you to build it. If ye labor with all your might, I will consecrate that spot that it shall be made holy. And if my people will hearken unto my voice, and unto the voice of my servants whom I have appointed to lead my people, behold, verily I say unto you, *they shall not be moved out of their place.* But if they will not hearken to my voice, nor unto the voice of these men whom I have appointed, they shall not be blest, because they pollute mine holy grounds, and mine holy ordinances, and charters, and my holy words which I give unto them. And it shall come to pass that if you build a house unto my name, and do not do the things that I say, I will not perform the oath which I make unto you, neither fulfil the promises which ye expect at my hands, saith the Lord. For instead of blessings, *ye, by your own works, bring cursings, wrath, indignation, and judgments upon your own heads*, by your follies, and by all your abominations, which you practise before me, saith the Lord" (D&C 124:43-48, emphasis added.) The exodus from Nauvoo and the events which followed would seem to indicate that the people were moved out of their place and subjected to cursings, wrath, indignation, and judgments from the Lord as He had warned in 1841 would occur. In light of all of this, it is difficult to argue the Saints succeeded in meeting the deadline.

242. Denver C. Snuffer, Jr., *Passing the Heavenly Gift* (Salt Lake City: Mill Creek Press, 2011). Though others have also argued this alternate view of the events at Nauvoo, to my knowledge, Denver Snuffer was the first to publish it as an attempt to understand our collective history through the lense of the narrative outlined in Doctrine and Covenants Section 124.

243. The late Lisle G. Brown, curator of Special Collections in the Morrow Library at Marshall University, compiled an extensive and well documented chronology of key events and dates surrounding the construction, sale, destruction and reconstruction of the Nauvoo temple. His work, including cites to sources, is available online at users.marshall.edu/~brown/nauvoo/chrono.html. A cursory summary of the points most relevant to our discussion follows, but the interested reader would be well served to review Brown's compilation in detail:

NAUVOO TEMPLE CHRONOLOGY

• Winter 1839/40–Saints begin discussion of building a new temple and a site is selected.

1840

• August 1, 1840—The First Presidency writes: "...it is necessary to erect a house of prayer, a house of worship of our God, where the ordinances can be attended to agreeably to His divine will, in this region of country" (*HC* 4:186.)

• October 3, 1840—At the Church's General Conference, the Saints resolve to build a temple and a committee is formed to begin the work. Men agree to tithe their labor by working one day in ten on the temple (*HC* 4:205).

• October 19, 1840–Land for the site is selected from Daniel H. Well's property.

• Dec 1840—By this time, workers had begun quarrying stone. William Weeks had been selected that Fall to design the new building.

1841

• January 19, 1841—Joseph Smith, receives the revelation approving the location the Saints had selected and commanding the temple be built, along with specific promised blessings and cursings for accomplishing or failing to accomplish the work (see D&C 124).

• April 6, 1841—Cornerstone laying ceremony.

• October 3, 1841—At the Church's General Conference, Joseph Smith announced, "There shall be no more baptism for the dead until the ordinance can be attended to in the font in the Lord's House; and the Church shall not hold another conference, until they can meet in said house. For thus saith the Lord" (*Times and Seasons*, 2 [1 Oct 1841]: 578). Prior to this date, the Saints had been performing baptisms for the dead in the Mississippi river. For a more detailed examination of the introduction of baptism for the dead and its practice in Nauvoo see M. Guy Bishop, "What Has Become of Our Fathers? Baptism for the Dead at Nauvoo", *Dialogue: A Journal of Mormon Thought*, (www.dialoguejournal.com/wp-content/uploads/sbi/articles/Dialogue_V23N02_87.pdf).

• November 8, 1841–Brigham Young dedicated the wooden font centered in the basement and enclosed in a temporary structure to allow its use even as the construction proceeded around it. The basement was not yet completed. This font was temporary and was subsequently replaced with a stone one.

• November 21, 1841–First baptisms for the dead were performed in the new font (*HC* 4:454).

1842

• May 2, 1842–The *Times and Seasons* predicted the temple would be enclosed by the Fall.

• October 1, 1842–Joseph met with the Temple Committee to resolve complaints over the use of property and funds for the temple.

• October 11, 1842–The outer temple walls are about four feet high.

• October 24, 1842–A temporary floor is begun over the basement and the font.

• October 30, 1842–First meeting of the Saints in the unfinished temple. John Taylor is the first to preach therein.

1843

• April 7, 1843–During General Conference, another dispute arose concerning temple funds with accusation made that the temple committee was using temple funds for personal use. These accusations and questions continued to plague and delay the work for the remainder of the year.

1844

• June 12, 1844 Joseph Smith told a reporter that the temple's interior structure and arrangement had not been decided.

• June 20, 1844–Work ceased on the temple following the destruction of the Nauvoo Expositor press.

• June 27, 1844–By the time of the martyrdoms of Joseph and Hyrum, the exterior walls of the temple had not reached their final height, but were somewhere in the second story.

• June 28, 1844–Workmen employed to guard the temple walls. Work was suspended until July 8, 1844.

• August 15, 1844–The Twelve announce that the temple construction would continue according to the design and with all haste (*HC* 7:250).

1845

• May 24, 1845–Capstone Ceremony held completing the exterior walls. The services concluded with a Hosanna Shout. The attic was not framed and the roof not yet shingled.

• August 14, 1845–The last shingle is laid on the temple's roof.

• October 7-8, 1845–General Conference convened in the enclosed temple. Brigham Young had dedicated the partially completed structure on Sunday, October 5, 1845.

• October 31, 1845–Church leaders offer the temple and other Church properties for sale to the Catholic Church. The effort to sell the temple would continue over the next several years.

• November 30, 1845–The attic is completed and Brigham Young dedicated the attic rooms for ordinance work (*HC* 7:534-535).

• December 10, 1845–The administration of Endowments begins in the attic story (HC 7:541-543). Prior to commencing these ordinances the attic was partitioned into rooms using canvas which had originally been purchased and brought to Nauvoo for the purpose of constructing a tabernacle meeting place adjacent to the temple for the Saints to assemble. Potted plants, carpets, paintings and maps were also brought in as contributed by members.

1846

• January 1, 1846–Workmen began to plaster the first floor hall, the floor having been completed.

• January 7, 1846–Brigham Young dedicated an altar for administering sealing ordinances. The first sealings are administered in the temple.

• January 20, 1846–The floor in the second story was being laid.

• February 7, 1846–Last day for endowments and baptisms. Individuals who had lent furniture, carpet, pictures, etc. began to remove their belongings.

• February 8, 1846–The Twelve met in the attic to dedicate the temple, as it was thus far completed, leaving the building in the hands of the Lord and asking him to preserve it as a monument to Joseph Smith. They also asked Him to enable them to someday finish the lower part of the building (*HC* 7:580).

• February 9, 1846–The roof caught fire at 3 a.m. and burned for a half an hour, damaging the roof and charring the attic.

• February 17, 1846–Workmen re-laid the burnt part of the roof.

• February 22, 1846–During a Sunday meeting of the Saints in the first floor, the floor settled (possibly cracked) causing panic and confusion. Some people jumped out of the windows to escape (*HC* 7:594). Some were badly hurt.

• March 9, 1846–Orson Hyde is appointed from the Twelve to remain in Nauvoo and to see the building is dedicated if others of the Twelve cannot return to do it.

• March to April 1846–Laborers worked on a herringbone patterned brick floor in the basement.

• April 27, 1846–Orson Hyde wrote Brigham Young that the temple would not be ready to dedicate on the Church's sixteenth anniversary April 6, 1846.

• April 13, 1846–Wilford Woodruff returned to Nauvoo from his mission to England.

• April 22, 1846–Carpenters are finished; painters still working.

• April 26, 1846–Brigham Young received a letter from Orson Hyde indicating that an offer to purchase the temple for $200,000 had been received from a wealthy Catholic benefactor.

• April 30, 1846–Joseph Young, Wilford Woodruff, and Orson Hyde with about twenty-five other men who had remained behind to finish the temple, gathered in the first floor hall for a private dedication.

• May 1-3, 1846–Public dedication of the temple by Orson Hyde and Wilford Woodruff. "The Temple was dedicated in the presence of strangers and all who would pay one dollar for admittance" (*Wilford Woodruff Journal*, April 30, 1846).

• May 15, 1846–The temple trustees advertise the temple for sale in newspapers through the remainder of the year without success.

• September 16-17, 1846–Following the "Battle of Nauvoo", anti-Mormon mobs occupied the city, desecrated the temple and began the forcible removal of the remaining Mormons. The following month, the mobs largely left the city, returning to their homes.

<u>1847</u>
• 1847–The Temple Trustees continued their efforts to sell the temple on behalf of the Church. A potential sale to the Catholic Church failed due to a title defect in August.

<u>1848</u>
• March 11, 1848–The Trustees sell the temple to David T. LeBaron, brother-in-law of Church Trustee, Almon Babbitt, for $5,000. He opens the temple to touring visitors. In July of that same year, Wilford Woodruff stopped in Nauvoo on his way East and toured the temple finding it in a better state than he had expected.

• October 9, 1848–Temple burned at the hand of an unknown arsonist. The Keoukuk Register reported that "Great volumes of smoke and flames burst from the windows, and the crash of falling timbers was distinctly heard on the opposite side of the [Mississippi] river. The interior of the building was like a furnace, the walls of solid masonry were heated throughout and cracked by the intense heat. The melted zinc and lead were dropping from its high block during the day." The Nauvoo Patriot also reported: "Our citizens were awakened by the alarm of fire, which, when first discovered, was bursting out through the spire of the temple, near the small door that opened from the east side to the roof, on the main building. The fire was seen first about three o'clock in the morning, and not until it had taken such hold of the timbers and roof as to make useless any effort to extinguish it. The material of the inside were so dry, and the fire spread so rapidly, that a few minutes were sufficient to wrap this famed edifice in a sheet of flame. It was a sight too full of mournful sublimity. . . . Although the morning was tolerably dark, still, when the flames shot upwards, the spire, the streets and houses for nearly a mile distant were lighted up, so as to render even the smallest objects discernible. The glare of the vast torch, pointing skyward, indescribably contrasted with the universal gloom and darkness around it; and men looked on with faces sad as if the crumbling ruins below were consuming all their hopes." The next morning the walls were still too hot to touch. The building was gutted, only the four walls were left standing (Harrington and Harrington, *Rediscovery of the Nauvoo Temple*, 5).

1849

• 1849 The Icarians begin to repair and refurbish the temple for their own use.

1850

• May 27, 1850–A tornado arose toppling the north wall and leaving the east and south walls so damaged that officials declared they would "soon fall down" and concluding they needed to be destroyed. Icarian workers at the site on this day "barely escaped with their lives, scrambling out of the ruins in stinging hail, pouring rain, thunder and lightening, all accompanied by violent winds" (*St. Joseph Adventure*, June 28, 1850, as cited in Harrington and Harrington, *Rediscovery of the Nauvoo Temple*, 6).

244. Two of Joseph Smith's sons, Joseph Smith III and Alexander left affidavits later in their lives stating that the interior of the Nauvoo Temple was never finished and that changes were made in the designs and plans for it after the deaths of Joseph and Hyrum. Alexander stated: "The auditorium or main meeting room was temporarily finished; the seats and pulpit were only temporary. The upper auditorium; the plastering was not done, the floor was only the rough boards, intended only for the lining, was laid, and this floor upwards the stairs, except in the tower, or circular main stairs, were also temporary; the upper floor which was to be divided into numerous rooms was laid, and partitioned off with cotton factory cloth, and used for some purposes before the saints were driven away. I was told that the cloth of those partitions was subsequently used for wagon covers, by the saints on their journey across the plains. To my knowledge the temple never was finished and those who have been led to believe it was have been deceived. I make this statement freely for the benefit of the present and future generations" (Alexander H. Smith, Audubon, Minnesota, July 2, 1897, in *Journal of History Volume 2*, January 1, 1909, Board of Publication of the Reorganized Church of Jesus Christ of Latter Day Saints, 161-162).

While their testimonies may be questioned by Latter-day Saints today, even LDS Church leaders, Brigham Young and Joseph Fielding Smith acknowledged that the temple was not completely finished. Brigham stated: "We build one [a temple] in Nauvoo. I could pick out several before me now that were there when it was built, and know just how much was finished and what was done. It is true we left brethren there with instructions to finish it, and they got it nearly completed before it was burned; but the saints did not enjoy it." (*JD* 18:304; emphasis added) Joseph Fielding Smith acknowledges this as fact but then explains his view of why it did not matter: "I now reaffirm what has previously been said; that it made no difference, so far as the Church and its authority is concerned, even if the Temple had not been completed, or finished, in the technical sense of that word. Some of the embellishments, the ornamentations and fixtures, may not have been placed in the building according to the original intention, and in that technical sense the building may not have been "finished completely." But if so, what difference would it make? The Lord, thank heaven, is not as technical and peevish as men are, or woe be unto all of us. The revelation does not say that the Church would be rejected with its dead if every identical board and plank or fixture was not in the building according to the original design. The thing the revelation does require is that a place be prepared, or built, where the Lord could reveal the Priesthood and its ordinances which had been taken away or that had not been restored (Joseph Fielding Smith, Origin of the "Reorganized" Church and Question of Succession, *Deseret News*, 1913, 47, as cited in *Nauvoo Temple: A Story of Faith*, 223-224).

245. Kenney, *Wilford Woodruff's Journal*, 3: 43. Orson Hyde explained: "If we moved forward and finished this house we should be received and accepted as a Church with our dead, but if not we should be rejected with our dead. These things have inspired and stimulated us to action in the finishing of it which through the blessing of God we have been enabled to accomplish and prepared it for dedication. In doing this we have only been saved as it were by the skin of our teeth." Wilford Woodruff likewise concluded that, "The Saints had labored faithfully and finished the temple and were now received as a Church with our dead. This is glory enough for building the temple and thousands of the Saints have received their endowment in it. And the light will not go out" (*Wilford Woodruff, Journal*, May 8, 1846).

246. Henry Horner, *Illinois, A Descriptive and Historical Guide* (Chicago: Federal Writer's Project of the Work Projects Administration for the State of Illinois, 1939), 352.

247. David J. Howlett, *Kirtland Temple: The Biography of a Shared Mormon Sacred Space* (University of Illinois Press, 2014), 39.

248. *WJS*, 120, emphasis added, (26 May 1842 *Nauvoo Relief Society Minutes*).

249. Ibid.

250. John W. Welch, *The Sermon at the Temple and the Sermon on the Mount: A Latter-Day Saint Approach* (Salt Lake City: Deseret Book, 1990).

251. *TPJS*, 325, emphasis added. See also Hebrews 12:22-24.

252. One evidence of this fact is his statement "The sound saluted my ears—"Ye [you] are come unto Mount Zion, and unto the city of the living God, the heavenly Jerusalem, and to an innumerable company of angels, to the general assembly and Church of the firstborn" (*TPJS*, 320, emphasis added).

253. *TPJS*, 320.

254. *TPJS*, 159, emphasis added.

255. One may also wonder if the events at Nauvoo were not the beginning of the fulfillment of a prophecy Christ left with the Nephites concerning us in the latter days as described in 3 Nephi 16:10.

256. There is some evidence that, at the time of the martyrdom, the plans for the interior had not been completely finalized. The Lord had promised to reveal to Joseph "all things pertaining to this house" (D&C 124:42). If Joseph knew everything concerning the designs and use of the temple's interior space, that knowledge apparently did not survive his death.

257. When the Nauvoo Temple was reconstructed by the Church in 2002, the exterior was replicated almost identically but the interior of the temple was a different story. It was redesigned as a modern temple (Don L. Searle, "Nauvoo: A Temple Reborn", *Ensign*, July 2002). "The first floor Assembly Room, featuring ten chandeliers, was duplicated on a smaller scale allowing enough area for planned administrative offices. The second floor has dressing rooms, and the upper floors house the six sealing rooms and endowment rooms, which were arranged in progressive style to include a Creation Room, Garden Room, World Room, Terrestrial Room, and Celestial Room" (ldsChurchtemples.org/nauvoo/).

258. *HC* 2:197.

259. *TPJS*, 150.

260. *TPJS*, 168. The original reads: "therefore he set the ordinances to be the same for Ever and ever and set Adam to watch over them to reveal them from heaven to man or to send Angels to reveal them Heb 1 Chap. 16 [14] verse. ["]Are they not all ministring spirits sent forth to minister to those who shall be heirs of salvation." These angels are under the direction of Michael or Adam who acts under the direction of Christ" from "Instruction on Priesthood, 5 October 1840," p. 2, *The Joseph Smith Papers*, www.josephsmithpapers.org/paper-summary/instruction-on-priesthood-5-october-1840/3.

261. The 1931 version of the endowment from Temple Mormonism: Its Evolution, Ritual and Meaning (New York: A. J. Montgomery, 1931) as cited at www.ldsendowment.org/1931.html.

262. *TPJS*, 325, emphasis added.

263. Joseph Smith taught "salvation cannot come without revelation, it is in vain for anyone to minister without it." *WJS*, 10, Sermon dated Before 8 August 1839.

264. Ibid.

LIAHONA

CHILDREN'S FOUNDATION

The Liahona Children's Nutrition and Education Foundation (LCF) was started in 2008 by Brad Walker, a physician and public health specialist; Polly Sheffield, a pediatrician and public health specialist; Bob Rees, a Humanities professor from California; and Sara Walker, an international public health specialist. Deeply concerned about the problem of malnutrition among children living in resource poor countries and the effects this problem has on children's growth and development, they established the Foundation in order to address this problem. Linked by their common faith as members of The Church of Jesus Christ of Latter-Day Saints (LDS) they developed a method to meet the needs of the children based on the best scientific and medical information for addressing malnutrition. Although the Foundation focuses on the needs of Latter-day Saint children, it does invite other children to participate. None are turned away.

Since its inception, the Liahona Children's Foundation has expanded to 17 countries and 185 different Stake projects. We are involved with children in Africa, Latin America, Brazil, the South Pacific, the Philippines, and Asia. The LCF will continue to expand as available funding permits to meet the nutritional and educational needs of children throughout the world. For more information, or to make a donation, visit liahonachildren.org. All of the author's proceeds from this book are being donated to Liahona and other similar charitable organizations working to serve those in need.

CPSIA information can be obtained
at www.ICGtesting.com
Printed in the USA
LVHW012228240122
709211LV00005B/146